D0049165

"*The Mind of the Leader* captures the essence of truly human leadership in the digital age—people deeply engaging people on what matters most in the moment. Imagine how transformative you will be when you deliberately give your full focus, attention, and energy to your passions."

—**NATHAN BOAZ,** Senior Managing Director, Talent Strategy
and Leadership Development, Accenture

"*The Mind of the Leader* provides simple yet powerful strategies to help us be more focused, calm, and clear-minded in the face of today's business realities. It is an essential read for any leader who wants to enhance engagement and performance at the same time."

—**HELENA GOTTSCHLING,** Chief Human Resources Officer,
Royal Bank of Canada

"If you aspire to be a more effective leader, you really should read this book. Do the book's exercises too. You'll learn how to be more mindful, selfless, and compassionate. Not only will you improve as a leader, you'll be become happier, kinder, and more fulfilled."

—**MARK R. TERCEK,** President and CEO, the Nature Conservancy, and author
of *Nature's Fortune: How Business and Society Thrive by Investing in Nature*

"*The Mind of the Leader* provides clear guidance on becoming a mindful leader, but also takes it a step further and introduces the practices of selflessness and compassion for leaders. In this way, the book describes the leadership of the future and how leaders enable true engagement, following, and passion."

—**SCOTT SHUTE,** VP of Global Customer Operations and Head of
Mindfulness Programs, LinkedIn

"*The Mind of the Leader* provides a great roadmap for any leader to create real engagement and a sense of purpose for the people they lead. It goes to the heart of what it means to be a people-centric leader who shows up present, selfless, and with care for self and others. In a very disrupting world, it also lays out how to create great organizational cultures with strong trust and social cohesion."

—**TONY STUART,** CEO, UNICEF Australia

"In this beautifully constructed and deeply relatable book, Hougaard and Carter remind us of a deep and profound truth to unlock performance in organizations: the power of a leader's ability to bring presence and fulfill our most basic human needs for connection, meaning, and purpose in an increasingly busy and disconnected world."

—PATRICIA WALLACE, Director, Leadership, Talent & Organization Development, Disney University

"I was first exposed to methods of training the mind in a community setting and immediately saw benefits for me personally. Hougaard and Carter helped me and my organization see how these ancient mind-training tools were equally relevant in day-to-day work. In *The Mind of the Leader*, they have gone one step further and provide strategic guidance on how we as leaders can better lead ourselves, our people, and our organizations."

—ASHWANI DAHIYA, Regional Vice President, Wells Fargo

"*The Mind of the Leader* is a deep well of knowledge and insights about the essence of modern leadership. Leaders need to understand that employees do not want to be viewed as head count but want to be seen and treated as whole people. In this context, the qualities of mindfulness, selflessness, and compassion are essential traits in leadership."

—PÄR STENMARK, Chief Regulatory Affairs Officer, IKEA Range & Supply

"In this groundbreaking book, Hougaard and Carter turn traditional assumptions about leadership on their head and offer a fresh, inspiring, and deeply human vision for leadership— a vision that this world dearly needs."

—ANDY LEE, Chief Mindfulness Officer, Aetna

"*The Mind of the Leader* challenges us to redefine our view of what makes a good leader. Drawing on their extensive experience in bringing mindfulness to organizations, Hougaard and Carter have skillfully laid out a well-structured leadership journey that starts with understanding our mind and training it to be more focused, service-oriented, and compassionate so we can help ourselves and our organizations realize more of their potential. If you want to apply mindfulness to yourself and/or your organization this is a must (and fun) read."

—PETER BOSTELMANN, Director, SAP Global Mindfulness Practice

"In *The Mind of the Leader*, Hougaard and Carter draw from their extensive personal and professional experience to offer practical guidance to bring about positive transformation in the lives of leaders, their professional colleagues, and the workplace. Proper leadership can play an enormous role in alleviating suffering, enriching humanity, and preserving the environment for generations to come."

> —**B. ALAN WALLACE,** President, Santa Barbara Institute for
> Consciousness Studies

"Bringing greater mindfulness and empathetic understanding should really be at the heart of leadership at all levels. This book offers tested methods for how to do this. Anyone who is keen to develop a new way of leading, rooted in greater self-awareness, focus, and compassion, will benefit greatly from this remarkable book."

> —**THUPTEN JINPA,** PhD, founder of Compassion Institute, and author of
> *A Fearless Heart: How the Courage to be Compassionate Can Transform
> Our Lives*

"*The Mind of the Leader* navigates the reader through much of what science has taught us about how our minds work, the dangers of being overly ego- and threat-focused, and how to cultivate minds for creating happiness, meaning, and courage and to live by our principles. Anyone who follows the insights and practices of this outstanding book will give themselves, their colleagues, employees, organizations, and even the world around them ways to live and lead intelligently, effectively, ethically, creatively, and compassionately."

> —**PAUL GILBERT,** PhD, author of *The Compassionate Mind* and
> *Overcoming Depression*

"The art of managing people starts with managing oneself. In *The Mind of the Leader*, Hougaard and Carter provides a clear roadmap for both. When leaders are good human beings, doing good for their people, their organizations will thrive."

> —**ALBERTO RIBERA,** Senior Lecturer of Managing People
> in Organizations, IESE Business School

"We all know that leaders must continue to learn throughout their career. To do so, they must understand the way they currently function and the impact they have on others. *The Mind of the Leader* compellingly shows how improving organizations starts with improving self, which starts with understanding self."

JEAN FRANÇOIS MANZONI, President and Nestlé Professor,
IMD Business School

"*The Mind of the Leader* teaches us how to be a human before being a leader, and to show up authentically, with an intention of benefiting the people we lead and our clients. I have seen, time and again, that these principles are foundational for great leadership."

—JACQUELINE GILLESPIE, Managing Director Leadership & Talent
Consulting, Korn Ferry International

"*The Mind of the Leader* is a roadmap for leaders to navigate the complex disciplines of leading self, people, and organizations. Hougaard and Carter clearly show how being a human before being a leader is foundational for creating people-centered organizations with strong engagement and productivity."

—ÉDOUARD-MALO HENRY, CHCO, Société Générale Bank

"*The Mind of the Leader* serves as a blueprint for how leaders can better foster employees' professional growth, inspiring them to do the best work of their lives."

—ERIC MOSLEY, founder and CEO, Globoforce

"*The Mind of the Leader* provides tools for leaders to put people first. It provides a logical journey, starting with understanding the mind and then cultivating qualities to enhance presence, engagement, collaboration, and performance."

—GISELA A. PAULSEN, Global Head, Product Development and Global
Product Strategy Finance, Genentech

"*The Mind of the Leader* lays out the management paradigm for the coming years. In the same way that our customers' behavior is changing, our employees' values and expectations are also changing. Traditional hierarchical, top-down leadership will not work anymore. To engage top performers, employees, and teams, we need to provide them with an environment that allows more self-management, generates more personal fulfillment, and shares a meaningful purpose. This book helps you develop into the leader whom successful organizations are already requiring.

—**DAVID CAMPOS,** CHRO Volkswagen Group Retail Spain

"At BMS France, we have successfully introduced the personnel practice of mindfulness. This has already deeply benefited our organization. *The Mind of the Leader* will take us further by equipping us with the tools and the compass to become the mindful leaders we aspire to be."

—**JEAN-CHRISTOPHE BARLAND,** Managing Director, BMS France, and President, UPSA Worldwide

"As individuals and as leaders, we are challenged to maintain our own well-being and clarity of mind so that we can also enable others to flourish. In this book, we find theories and practical advice that are enormously insightful in enabling us to look inside to support and lead ourselves effectively, so that we can then be most of service to our colleagues and the organizations we lead."

—**MARIA FARROW,** HRO, LVMH Perfumes and Cosmetics

"In this wonderful book, Hougaard and Carter describe how they have created a system, tested and refined on thousands of leaders, that teaches self-management. They show how this improves leadership effectiveness and organizations' performance. It is a must for anyone who wants to be a better leader."

—**PAUL J. ZAK,** PhD, author of *Trust Factor: The Science of High-Performance Companies*

"*The Mind of the Leader* humanizes the workplace again, reminding us of the all-important intrinsic motivation of people and charting a clear road for leaders to step up and do better, be better."

—**PHIL COX,** Head of EMEA and President of UK, Silicon Valley Bank

"In *The Mind of the Leader,* Hougaard and Carter outline the type of leadership and culture that creates a great employee experience and thereby greater productivity. I recommend it to anyone with the great privilege of leading others."

—**BRECKON JONES,** speaker, adviser, former Director, Total Reward, Australia and New Zealand, American Express, and Director, Employee Engagement, Unilever

"*The Mind of the Leader* is for all leaders—past, present, and future—who now need to have the courage to adopt MSC leadership. An inspirational read that reinforces the great traits I have long believed deliver world-class teams and sustainable business success. This superbly researched book will inspire our next generation of MSC leaders."

—**TRACEY L. REDDINGS,** Head of UK & Ireland, Julius Baer International Ltd.

"In *The Mind of a Leader,* Hougaard and Carter describe the kind of leadership that helps companies, societies, and civilization advance and describes how organizations can train and develop effective leaders. The book is thoroughly researched and theoretically grounded, but never dry or daunting. The result is a compelling, accessible, and practical roadmap for developing a leadership style that motivates people and enhances organizational performance."

—**FRANCESC XAVIER COLL ESCURSEL,** Chief Human Resources and Organisation Officer, CaixaBank

"Hougaard and Carter have completed a diagnosis of the 'dis-ease' that faces leaders today and have created a comprehensive, easy to follow, treatment plan. As a physician, I value the fact that the book is heavily data driven, backed by science, and yet written in a way that is accessible and immediately applicable. *The Mind of the Leader* provides invaluable tools and resources that enable leaders to bring more of their best selves to work and work to create a more mindful and compassionate organizational culture."

—**RACHEL ROBERTS,** MD, Medical Director, UHA Stanford Health Care

"*The Mind of the Leader* brings leadership back to being about humans. We all want to be happy, lead a meaningful life, grow in our thought processes, and remain connected with other people. This book is a blueprint for creating truly human leadership that enables engagement, flourishing, and productivity."

—**RITU ANAND,** Senior Vice President, HR, Tata Consultancy Services

The Mind of the Leader

The Mind of the Leader

How to Lead Yourself, Your People, and Your Organization for Extraordinary Results

RASMUS HOUGAARD

JACQUELINE CARTER

HARVARD BUSINESS REVIEW PRESS

Boston, Massachusetts

HBR Press Quantity Sales Discounts

Harvard Business Review Press titles are available at significant quantity discounts when purchased in bulk for client gifts, sales promotions, and premiums. Special editions, including books with corporate logos, customized covers, and letters from the company or CEO printed in the front matter, as well as excerpts of existing books, can also be created in large quantities for special needs.

For details and discount information for both print and ebook formats, contact booksales@harvardbusiness.org, tel. 800-988-0886, or www.hbr.org/bulksales.

Copyright 2018 Rasmus Hougaard and Jacqueline Carter
All rights reserved
Printed in the United States of America

11 2022

No part of this publication may be reproduced, stored in or introduced into a retrieval system, or transmitted, in any form, or by any means (electronic, mechanical, photocopying, recording, or otherwise), without the prior permission of the publisher. Requests for permission should be directed to permissions@hbsp.harvard.edu, or mailed to Permissions, Harvard Business School Publishing, 60 Harvard Way, Boston, Massachusetts 02163.

The web addresses referenced in this book were live and correct at the time of the book's publication but may be subject to change.

Library of Congress Cataloging-in-Publication Data

Names: Hougaard, Rasmus, author. | Carter, Jacqueline (Consultant), author.
Title: The mind of the leader : how to lead yourself, your people, and your organization for extraordinary results / by Rasmus Hougaard and Jacqueline Carter.
Description: Boston, Massachusetts : Harvard Business Review Press, [2018]
Identifiers: LCCN 2017044298 | ISBN 9781633693425 (hardcover : alk. paper)
Subjects: LCSH: Leadership–Psychological aspects. | Mindfulness (Psychology) | Selflessness (Psychology) | Compassion.
Classification: LCC HD57.7 .H6795 2018 | DDC 658.4/092–dc23 LC record available at https://lccn.loc.gov/2017044298

The paper used in this publication meets the requirements of the American National Standard for Permanence of Paper for Publications and Documents in Libraries and Archives Z39.48-1992.

Contents

PART THREE

Understand and Lead Your Organization

Foreword

Marriott was started in 1927 as a nine-stool root beer stand in Washington, DC, which added hot food to the menu when winter came. Later the business grew to a single hotel and subsequently the world's largest hotel chain. A few years after J. W. and Alice Marriott founded their enterprise, the Great Depression hit, putting all American businesses and employees under pressure. How did J. W. and Alice respond? They put a doctor on staff to make sure their people had health care. Why? Well, they cared about them, of course. But they also wanted a reliable, healthy, well-cared-for workforce. They believed that if their employees had access to good medical care, they would be better able to provide the level of service they wanted for their customers.

Putting people first has always been the cornerstone of our success. We believe that if we take care of our people, they take care of our customers, and business will take care of itself. Even after the 9/11 terror attacks in New York, where we went from an occupancy rate of 75 to 5 percent overnight—where our hotels stood empty of guests but full of staff—putting people first was our priority. Rather than undergoing massive layoffs, we set in place education programs, maintained health benefits, and did all we could to come through the crisis with minimal negative impact on our people.

In a business like ours, and I believe any other industry, we simply cannot succeed unless people are truly engaged and happy in their work. It is our commitment to create an environment where the unique contributions of our people are valued. Marriott being consistently regarded an employer of choice is, I believe, a result of these efforts.

Fostering a "people first" culture starts with leadership. Leaders must model the way. They must act, interact with, and engage with the people they lead in a way that makes people feel seen, heard, and valued.

In *The Mind of the Leader*, Rasmus Hougaard and Jacqueline Carter are providing a clear pathway for creating "people first" organizations. It calls for leaders to be humans first: to be mindful, selfless, and compassionate and in doing so, to develop the qualities that enable engagement, fulfillment, and meaning—which lead to greater business success.

If we as leaders are mindful, we will better know what really matters to our people. We are more present, attentive, and curious. It is not always easy, but I know the difference between being present with my people and when I am not. I only have impact when I am.

If we as leaders are selfless, taking the bigger picture into account rather than our own egoistic needs, we model cultures of growth and learning. Bill Marriott, our executive chairman, even now in his eighties, always has his ears open. He is always looking for the perspective of others, rather than blindly following his own beliefs and ideas.

If we as leaders are compassionate, our people will know we have their back. As this book clearly describes, compassion is not soft and sentimental. It is concrete and practical. It's about doing the right thing, like putting a doctor on staff during the Depression. Again, if we truly care for our people, they will truly care for our customers, and business will take care of itself.

In many ways, the principles of this book go against the grain of how many businesses are run. It inspires me and provides insights to further evolve our culture and put people first. And I believe all leaders and other organizations will benefit strongly from its messages.

—**ARNE SORENSON,** *President and Chief Executive Officer,*
Marriott International

Introduction

During the summer of 2015, Pierre Nanterme, Accenture's CEO, announced that the global professional services company would reimagine its performance management system. The company found that after decades of serving its purpose, the system had become massively demotivating. Accenture's global workforce had changed. Their people—and your people—are not motivated by being a number on a performance rating scale. Rather, today's workforce is increasingly looking for meaning, human connectedness, true happiness, and a desire to contribute positively to the world. Nanterme and his leadership team realized Accenture needed a better way to lead for these foundational human desires and better engage their 425,000-plus employees—to speak to their intrinsic motivation.

Accenture is no outlier. A global movement is taking place in the C-suites of thousands of progressive organizations like Marriott, Starbucks, and LinkedIn. The question the leaders of these organizations ask themselves is, "How can we create more human leadership and people-centered cultures where employees and leaders are more fulfilled and more fully engaged?"

As human beings, we are all driven by basic needs for meaning, happiness, human connectedness, and a desire to contribute positively to society. That's true whether we're at home, out in the world, or at work. But it's one thing to realize this and another to act on it. Speaking to our people's intrinsic motivation calls for leadership and organizations that cater to these desires. It's something that forward-thinking organizations and leaders are increasingly realizing and addressing. As Javier Pladevall, CEO of Audi Volkswagen, Spain, reflected when we spoke with him, "Leadership today is about unlearning management and relearning being human."[1]

The Mind of the Leader provides a way to do this. It outlines how leaders can lead themselves, their people, and their organizations to unlock intrinsic motivation, create real people-centered cultures, and ultimately deliver extraordinary results.

How important is the message of this book? Consider this: In a 2016 McKinsey & Company study of more than fifty-two thousand managers, 77 percent rated themselves as inspiring and good role models.[2] But this stands in stark contrast to how employees perceive their leaders. A 2016 Gallup engagement survey found that 82 percent of employees see their leaders as fundamentally uninspiring. In fact, the same survey found that only 13 percent of the global workforce is engaged, while 24 percent are actively disengaged.[3]

This seeming lack of good leadership is not because of a lack of effort. According to a recent report, organizations around the globe invest approximately $46 billion annually on leadership development programs.[4] That's a lot of money for seemingly little return. What's going wrong?

In part, the system is broken. According to research by Dacher Keltner, professor of psychology at University of California, Berkeley, when many leaders start to feel powerful, their more benevolent qualities start to decline. Leaders are three times more likely than lower-level employees to interrupt coworkers, multitask during meetings, raise their voices, and say insulting things. He also found that leaders are more likely than other people to engage in rude, selfish, and unethical behavior.[5] None of this is going to speak to the intrinsic motivation we all share.

While the $46 billion spent on leadership training might improve leaders' effectiveness—at least in a strictly business sense of focusing on the bottom line—something more is needed: leadership that truly engages employees, is truly human, and addresses basic human needs any employee has.

And it starts in the mind of the leader.

Leadership pioneer Peter Drucker said, "You cannot manage other people unless you manage yourself first."[6] If this is true, the majority of leadership education and training programs have it backward. Most leadership education starts with skills like strategy, people management, and finance. But from Drucker's point of view, this approach starts at the end and misses the beginning. It's like building a house by starting with the roof.

Like Drucker, we argue that leadership starts with yourself. More specifically, it starts in your mind. By understanding how your mind works, you can lead yourself effectively. By understanding and leading yourself effectively, you can understand others and be able to lead them more effectively. And by understanding and leading others more effectively, you can understand and lead your organization more effectively—and by "more effectively," we mean in a way that's going to tap into your own and your people's intrinsic motivations and sense of purpose. If you're able to do that—and we have witnessed that with practice and persistence, anyone can—you'll have a more engaged and productive workforce. And perhaps more importantly, you'll be part of creating more happiness, stronger human connectedness, and better social cohesion within and beyond your organization.

For over a decade, we and our colleagues at Potential Project have trained tens of thousands of leaders in hundreds of companies like Microsoft, the LEGO Group, Danone, and Accenture, utilizing the practice of mindfulness. The outcomes have been thoroughly researched and proven to deliver remarkable results. But with the emerging movement of employees looking for more meaning, happiness, and connectedness, we have asked ourselves what else leaders need for leading themselves, their people, and their organizations for extraordinary results.

As part of this research, we and our research team surveyed and assessed more than thirty thousand leaders from thousands of companies in more than a hundred countries. We have conducted in-depth interviews with hundreds of C-suite executives. And we have reviewed thousands of studies on leadership in the fields of neuroscience, leadership, organizational development, and psychology.

Based on this research, we have conclusively found that three mental qualities stand out as being foundational for leaders today: mindfulness (M), selflessness (S), and compassion (C). Together, we call these foundational skills MSC leadership.

So how do you as a leader achieve MSC leadership, to better engage your people at their intrinsic level and unleash better performance? By applying mindfulness, selflessness, and compassion first to yourself, then to your people, and then to your organization *The Mind of the Leader* takes you step by step through this process.

Since MSC leadership begins inwardly, with your own mind, and then projects outward to your people and your organization, the book is structured to take you on that journey. By understanding yourself—your mind—you can lead yourself effectively. By leading yourself, you'll be able to lead others effectively. And by leading others, you can better lead your organization. This is the overarching structure of the book, as presented in figure I-1. Part 1 is about understanding and leading yourself. Part 2 is about understanding and leading your people. And part 3 is about understanding and leading your organization.

Each part starts with an "understanding" chapter, helping you understand your own mind, your people's minds, and the collective "organizational culture mind." After that, each part moves into more practical chapters on developing and applying each of the three MSC

FIGURE I-1

The three levels of leadership

leadership components—mindfulness, selflessness, and compassion—to your leadership.

We bring this book to you with confidence. In its development, we have been standing on the shoulders of giants: the mind-training masters who have inspired us for decades, the executives who offered their wisdom and the researchers who shared their findings. You are now welcomed into this journey, but you are not alone. Thousands of people have gone through its practices before you and have transformed themselves and the way they lead. You are about to enter a movement, and we are here to support you on your way.

1

The MSC Leader

Traditionally, workplace initiatives designed to increase engagement and productivity are focused on external satisfaction—things like bonuses, raises, funky office environments, free food, flex time, and the like. All of these can be great, but they're short-term solutions. They work for a little while, but the effects wear off as people begin to take the money, titles, foosball tables, and free energy bars for granted. External initiatives and perks never truly motivate people for the long term. Instead, only internal drivers—such as meaningful engagement, connectedness, and feeling valued—can engage employees on the deeper level needed for long-term commitment and productivity.

When we spoke with Steven Worrall, managing director of Microsoft Australia, he put it this way: "In the 1990s, we talked about work–life balance. But with today's 24/7 work reality, we're past that. Today, we talk about engagement and satisfaction. But in the near future, it will be about creating a real sense of purpose and meaning. Successful leaders in the future will be the ones who can facilitate *true happiness* for their people."

If we as leaders want to cultivate truly thriving organizations, we need to understand what really matters to human beings. We all want to be happy. We all want to live meaningful lives and contribute to the well-being of others. This truth also applies to work. People leaving the office every day with a sense of fulfillment will want to come back, focus on tough projects, and work hard. Because of meaningful intrinsic motivation, they will want to continue doing their best day after day, year after year.

So how do you facilitate meaning, connectedness, and true happiness for the people you lead? Or, more specifically, what qualities of mind does a leader need to develop to be better at leading this changing workforce? Based on extensive research—including surveys and assessments of tens of thousands of leaders—we at Potential Project have found that three mental qualities stand out as being critical for increasing engagement, happiness, and productivity: mindfulness (M), selflessness (S), and compassion (C). They are foundational qualities of great leadership that we call *MSC leadership*. Figure 1-1 visually summarizes these three qualities.

All three characteristics are closely linked. In fact, they are mutually enhancing. Mindfulness makes us more selfless, and selflessness makes

FIGURE 1-1

MSC leadership

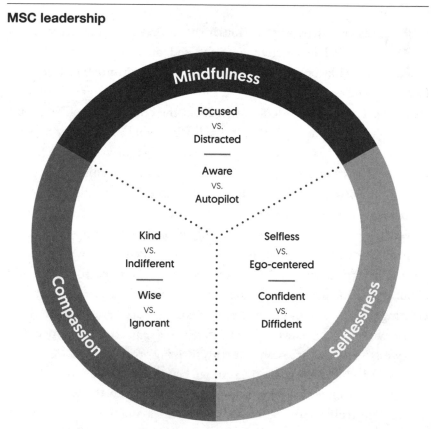

us more compassionate. More compassion in turn, makes us more mind-ful and selfless. While it's true that some leaders have innately developed these characteristics, our experience shows that all three can be learned, practiced, and enhanced.

In the following sections, we'll examine each characteristic in greater detail.

The Anatomy of Mindfulness (M)

Mindfulness refers to both a practice and a state of mind. The more you practice it, the more it becomes your state of mind. Mindfulness is about generating greater mental effectiveness, so that you can realize more of your potential on both a professional and a personal level. Effectiveness in this context is the ability to achieve your goals, objectives, and wishes in life.

Mindfulness training tools and techniques have been around for thou-sands of years. In our work with organizations around the world, we keep the practice and definition of mindfulness simple and close to its ancient roots: paying attention, in the present moment, with a calm, focused, and clear mind.

At the center of the practice of mindfulness is learning to manage your attention. When you learn how to manage your attention, you learn how to manage your thoughts. You learn to hold your focus on what you choose, whether it's this page, an email, a meeting, or the people you are with. In other words, you train yourself to be more present in the here and now.

Recently, research has backed up the claims that mindfulness practi-tioners have been making for years. Mindfulness has a positive impact on our physiology, psychology, and work performance.[1] At the physiological level, researchers have demonstrated that mindfulness training results in a stronger immune system, lower blood pressure, and a lower heart rate.[2] In addition, people who practice mindfulness sleep better and feel less stressed.[3]

Mindfulness training increases the density of grey cells in our cerebral cortex, the part of the brain that thinks rationally and solves problems.[4] Because of this increase, cognitive function improves, resulting in better memory, increased concentration, reduced cognitive rigidity, and faster reaction times.[5] With all these benefits, research has found people who practice mindfulness techniques report an overall increased quality of life.[6]

The benefits of mindfulness have also been demonstrated in an organizational context. For example, Jochen Reb, a researcher from Singapore Management University evaluated the effectiveness of some of our mindful leadership programs at Carlsberg Group and If Insurance, a large Scandinavian insurance company. He found significant improvements in focus, awareness, memory, job performance, and overall job satisfaction after only nine weeks of training for ten minutes each day. Attendees also reported reduced stress and improved perceptions of work–life balance.[7] Other researchers have found similar benefits from mindfulness training in corporate contexts, including increased creativity and innovation, improved employer–employee relations, reduced absenteeism, and improved ethical decision making.[8]

But mindfulness does something far more powerful than all of the above—it constructively alters our perception of reality. Through repeated practice, mindfulness triggers a shift in cognitive control to frontal brain regions (figure 1-2). This enables us to perceive our world, our

FIGURE 1-2

Prefrontal takeover

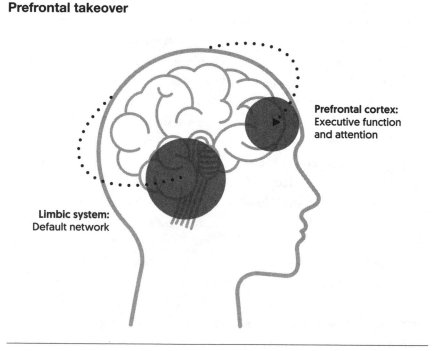

emotions, and other people without fight-or-flight, knee-jerk reactions and have better emotional resilience.[9]

This change in neurological wiring helps us perceive situations and make decisions more from our conscious mind, avoiding some of the traps of our unconscious biases. Operating more from our prefrontal cortex also enhances our executive function, the control center for our thoughts, words, and actions.[10] A well-developed executive function allows us to better lead ourselves and others toward shared goals. With stronger prefrontal activity, we deactivate our tendency to be distracted and we become more present, focused, and attentive. Not coincidentally, mindfulness also makes us happier. The more present and attentive we are, regardless of what we do, the happier we become.[11]

There are two key qualities of mindfulness—*focus* and *awareness*. Focus is the ability to concentrate on a task at hand for an extended period of time with ease. Awareness is the ability to make wise choices about where to focus your attention. Optimal effectiveness is achieved when you're simultaneously focused and aware.

Focus and awareness are complementary. Focus enables more stable awareness, and awareness enables focus to return to what we're doing. They work in tandem. The more focused we become, the more we will also be aware—and the other way around. In mindfulness practice, you enhance focus and awareness together.

Mindfulness can be presented in a two-by-two matrix, as shown in figure 1-3.

In the lower left quadrant, you're neither focused nor aware. There is really not much good to say about this state of mind. Most of the mistakes we make arise from this mind state. And in leadership, as elsewhere, this can be harmful. If we are distracted and on autopilot, we are not present with our people. We can't expect team members to be engaged and feel supported if we ourselves are not fully present.

In the lower right quadrant, you're aware but easily distracted. Great ideas may arise from this state. But if your mind is too distracted, you'll have difficulty retaining them and turning them into actions. Good ideas only become innovative solutions when you have the focus to retain and execute them by bringing them into the upper right quadrant.

Looking at the upper left quadrant, when you're focused but on autopilot, your state of mind can be described as being in "flow." It can be useful for routine tasks or when exercising. But the problem with this state is

FIGURE 1-3

The mindfulness matrix

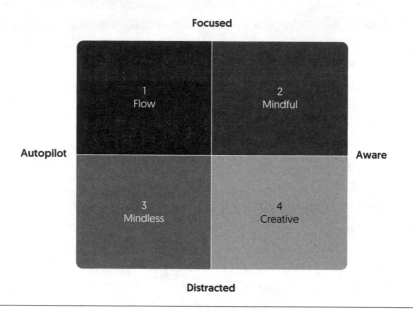

that we are not very aware and therefore are at risk of missing out on valuable information. Without awareness, we may not notice the expressions of the people we are meeting with, and hence we may exercise poor judgment. Also, without awareness, we are not able to see or understand our unconscious biases and may make bad decisions.

In the upper right quadrant—"mindful"—we are focused and aware. We are focused on the people we are with and the tasks we do. And at the same time, we have awareness and the ability to see our unconscious bias and regulate accordingly. In today's always-on and distracted office environments, these two key qualities help us be mentally agile and effective.

In mindfulness practice, we train both our focus and our awareness. When we're mindful, we're able to overcome our minds natural tendency to wander. We can maintain focus on an object of our choice, notice when we get distracted, and then make decisions about where to place our attention. When we're mindful, we also have a greater awareness of what we're experiencing internally and externally. We can observe our thoughts as they arise and make best judgments what to focus on and what to let go.

Over the years, we, along with our colleagues, have been teaching and training mindfulness to leaders and employees in hundreds of organizations all over the world. Our approach has been developed and refined in collaboration with researchers, mindfulness experts, and business leaders. This practice is fundamental to your success in mastering mindful leadership. In chapter 3, you'll find clear instructions for getting started with a daily mindfulness practice. In appendix A, you'll find information on how to access an app that will take you through a comprehensive, individualized training program.

Once you begin applying mindfulness to your leadership, you'll see that as your mindfulness increases, your perception of "self" starts to change. More specifically, a stronger sense of selfless confidence arises, helping you develop the second quality of MSC leadership.

The Anatomy of Selflessness (S)

Selflessness is the wisdom of getting out of your own way, the way of your people, and the way of your organization to unleash the natural flow of energy that people bring to work. Selflessness combines strong self-confidence with a humble intention to be of service. With selflessness, trust increases because we have no secret agendas and followership strengthens because our selflessness sets free our people to be their best selves. Selflessness in leadership manifests itself as humility and service.

In *Good to Great*, Jim Collins showed that humility combined with strong will is a key trait of successful leaders. Humility, his research found, is when leaders are able to keep their egos in check and always put the organization's goals before their own.[12] Humility is a trait of selflessness where we're not attached to an inflated, important sense of self: we have a very real view on how little we actually matter. In the bigger scheme of things, even the best CEO is only one out of hundreds or thousands of individuals contributing to a company's success. In addition, the company's success is heavily determined by market trends and large-scale global forces. Any company is merely the result of an interconnected, global field of events, actions, and intentions. There's no one person who can create this singlehandedly—not even the greatest leader. Understanding this awakens a healthy sense of humility.

Humility allows leaders to understand the value of providing service—a legacy, if you will—to the organization. That is what creates a healthy culture and what creates an organization that can continue from generation to generation. Arne Sorenson, CEO of the hotel chain Marriott, described his role as being a function of service to the company's 400,000 employees. The driving business philosophy of Marriott is to take care of their employees, so that their employees take care of their guests. That way, business takes care of itself. Arne's role is not one of power but one of service.

But what about the ego? What's the role of the ego in selfless leadership? It's small. We all have an ego that longs for attention and recognition. But great leaders are the ones who've tamed their ego so that it doesn't hinder the larger interests of the people and the company they lead.

Indeed, corporate history is full of great examples of the danger of self-centeredness. Consider Nokia's fall from industry leadership in cell phones. Nokia was the global market leader in cell phones when Apple introduced the iPhone, a much more sophisticated, yet simple and compelling product. However, the then-CEO of Nokia announced to his entire organization that the iPhone would never be anything but a niche product, and that Nokia would keep producing the phones with which they had gained their success. A few years later, Nokia had fallen into market insignificance, and Apple was the leader.

It wasn't because Nokia engineers and developers didn't have good ideas or recognize the shifts in consumer demands. The problem came down to leadership and, specifically, the former CEO's emotional and ego attachment to what had made him and the company successful. He and his leadership team had fallen in love with Nokia's past success and created a self-image of success based on that. Because they were not able to let go of this image, they lost major market share almost overnight.

Many of the leaders we've talked to worry that selflessness will make them pushovers. But it's not that simple. A leader's selflessness has to be combined with self-confidence. If you have selflessness without self-confidence, you will indeed be a pushover. Therefore, selflessness cannot stand on its own. It must be paired with self-confidence. Figure 1-4 illustrates this relationship.

FIGURE 1-4

The selflessness matrix

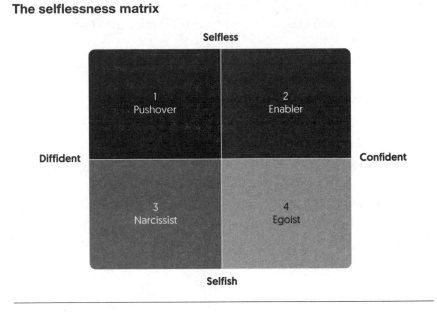

In the lower left quadrant, you lack self-confidence, yet you're very concerned about your own interests. There are strong *narcissist* traits in this quadrant. It's all about you. Few people in this space become a leader of anything but their own desires. There are exceptions, but these individuals tend to generate poor results and, as a result, don't last long in their leadership roles.

In the lower right quadrant, you have a strong sense of self-confidence, but you're driven by selfish goals and desires. The strength of your self-confidence is used to achieve personal gains. Leaders in this quadrant would be considered *egotistical*, with the needs of others rarely recognized or acknowledged. Think of a determined, forceful sales leader, pushing people to sell more and more to make themselves look good. This approach can have some benefits: a strong self-confidence combined with selfishness can create a powerful drive for achieving big results. But this type of approach generally works only in the short term.

This trait can be quite destructive, both personally and for the organizations these leaders lead. As people become leaders, there is a risk of their ethics eroding due to the influence of power. Power can corrupt us and make us more selfish.[13] Also, the desire for fatter paychecks and bigger bonuses can be like drinking salt water—gulping it just makes us thirstier. As many news stories attest, too often leaders at the very top let greed get the better of their ethical judgments, serving their own interests at the expense of others.

In the upper left quadrant, you're a *pushover*. You're not looking out for your own well-being and interest. You have high risk of burning out or being taken advantage of. Not an ideal place to be.

In the upper right quadrant, you have the powerful combination of selflessness and self-confidence. This is the sweet spot. You're not worried about being taken advantage of, because you have the confidence to speak up for yourself if needed. At the same time, you're not driven by your own interests. You have a strong focus on the well-being of your people and your organization. In this quadrant, you're an *enabler*. Your focus is to enable others to perform and shine. You lead for the long run. You don't worry about receiving praise—you have self-confidence—so you pass along the credit for achievements to others. It's not about you. Therefore, you provide inspiration and cultivate a sense of inclusion. In this quadrant, you offer service rather than expect others to be of service to you. Your mission is to contribute to the greater good.

As we let go of our sense of self-importance, we naturally begin attending more to other people: we show more interest in them and offer more care. In this way, compassion arises as a natural outgrowth of selflessness.

The Anatomy of Compassion (C)

Compassion is the quality of having positive intentions for others. It's the intention of being of service to other people's happiness and the desire to help alleviate their problems. It's the ability to understand others' perspectives and use that as a catalyst for supportive action.[14]

Compassion is different from empathy. Jeff Weiner, the CEO of LinkedIn, describes empathy as being when you take on the suffering of others and you both lose. With compassion, you are empowered to skillful action.[15] The difference between compassion and empathy becomes clear through the following example. Imagine that you meet one of your colleagues at the office. He looks stressed and under tremendous pressure, on the edge of panic. If you reacted with empathy, you would feel sad for him, sit down with him and feel the stress and pressure together with him. In contrast, the compassionate response would be to put yourself in his shoes for a moment, notice his pain, and then see if you can help him address the challenges he is facing.

Empathy and compassion are also different from a neurological perspective.[16] Compassion allows us to be rational, see the bigger picture, and make better decisions for other people—all for the greater good, as opposed to empathy, which narrows our field of vision to single individuals or causes.

Compassion is often mistaken for softness, but nothing could be less true. Compassion is not about giving in to other people. Compassion requires courage and strength to sometimes have difficult conversations or make tough decisions. Let's clarify a few misconceptions about compassion.

First, compassion is not soft, warm, or fuzzy. It's hard. Compassion means giving an employee tough but appropriate feedback. Compassion means making difficult decisions for the good of the organization, even when it negatively impacts individuals.

Second, compassion is an intention that does not necessarily change your actions but changes the way you conduct your actions. For example, there is a big difference between giving feedback out of compassion as opposed to giving it out of frustration.

Chris Schmidt, CEO of the US accounting firm Moss Adams, finds compassion to be the most powerful quality to have when laying off people. "I think being compassionate is part of maturing as a leader," Chris explained. "I always look for the best in people. But when you have to lay off a person, that's always difficult. I give them many, many opportunities to demonstrate their value. And then, if and when the time comes, I balance the human side with the factual, business-case side. I make it clear that I do feel for that individual, but I keep it within the context of the business decision." This balanced approach helps him and the other person maintain mutual respect and move on in the best possible way.

Compassion, in more traditional business paradigms, makes you seem weak and emotional. But times are changing. Of the more than a thousand leaders we surveyed, nearly 92 percent stated that compassion is "important" or "extremely important" for effective leadership. Similarly, 80 percent of surveyed leaders stated that it would be "valuable" or "extremely valuable" to enhance their compassion—but that they didn't know how.

Shimul Melwani, a professor of organizational behavior and leading researcher on the topic, from the University of North Carolina Business School, has found that compassionate leaders are perceived as better and stronger leaders.[17] In addition, compassion fosters true following, trust, and engagement. When you have compassion, the people you lead will better trust in your actions and judgments, because they know you have positive intentions.

Organizations with more compassionate cultures and leaders have stronger connections among people, better collaboration, more trust, enhanced commitment, and lower turnover.[18] Also, compassion in organizations makes people feel more valued, feel an increased sense of dignity, and have greater pride in the collective culture. This all leads to more positive emotions, less anxiety, and quicker recovery from illness. Finally, compassionate company cultures make people act more for the common good within the organization—and beyond corporate walls.[19]

The trick is, of course, to determine how to appropriately harness compassion in a way that best serves you, your people, and your organization. Jeff Weiner, who has made compassion his core leadership principle, paraphrases Fred Kofman, the author of *Conscious Business*, by saying: "Wisdom without compassion is ruthlessness, compassion without wisdom is folly."[20] Combining compassion with wisdom helps create a framework that effectively informs tough decisions and helps keep the bigger picture in sight. Figure 1-5 depicts this framework.

The lower left quadrant represents a lack of both compassion and wisdom. Without compassion, we're indifferent; without wisdom, we are ignorant. Nothing good comes from this space, and a leader operating from this mindset is utterly incompetent.

In the upper left quadrant, we have compassion but lack the wise discernment to judge the impact of our actions. The result is that we risk damaging the cause we intended to support. People and organizations that are single-mindedly focused on compassion risk creating an atmosphere of naïveté and well-intended mistakes. If our organization is about to go bankrupt and we have compassion but no wisdom, we may not lay off the few people that could save the jobs of the majority.

FIGURE 1-5

The compassion matrix

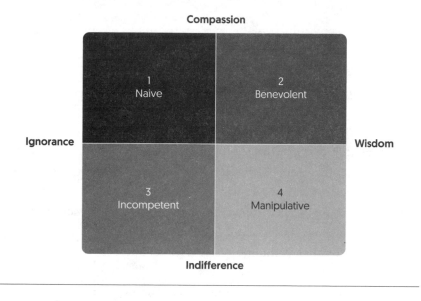

Compassion

| 1 Naive | 2 Benevolent |
| 3 Incompetent | 4 Manipulative |

Ignorance · Wisdom

Indifference

The lower right quadrant characterizes a mind in which skills and expertise exist, but a wholesome intention is missing. This is a dangerous place. The 2008 financial crash came as a result of too many leaders and companies operating in this quadrant. Often manipulative leaders operating in this space can effectively deliver short-term results. In the long term, however, people will not follow their lead.

The upper right quadrant denotes the successful combination of compassion and wisdom creating benevolent leadership. We act compassionately while closely observing the impact of our actions. Wisdom is the thoughtful, measured, and discerning judgment that allows us to keep professional measures and strategic objectives in mind while acting to bring the most benefit and happiness to the people involved. Organizations like Patagonia, Whole Foods, LinkedIn, and Eileen Fisher are operating in this space, balancing compassion with a wise focus on the bottom line and strategic goals.

Take a moment to consider where in the matrix you would place yourself. Also consider where you would place the leaders in your organization that are closest to you.

MSC Leadership—Start with Yourself

Leading with mindfulness, selflessness, and compassion makes you more human and less leader. It makes you more you and less your title. It peels off the layers of status that separate you from the people you lead. Mindfulness, selflessness, and compassion make you truly human and enable you to create a more people-centered culture where your people see themselves and one another as humans rather than headcounts.

Michael Rennie, global leader of Organisation Practice for McKinsey & Company, having spent forty years making organizations and leaders more effective, concluded: "A good leader must understand what makes a good life and how to help people find that. A leader's job is not to provide a paycheck and benefits: It's about helping people be truly happy and find meaning in their work and life. When a leader succeeds with this, it unlocks real performance."

MSC leadership enables this. Mindfulness allows you to be present and attentive to what really motivates the people you lead. Selflessness helps you get out of the way and provide the space and support they need to thrive. And compassion makes you connect on a truly human level and allows your people to trust that you have their best interests in mind. When leaders model mindfulness, selflessness, and compassion, they speak to employees' intrinsic motivations. They enable a stronger sense of meaning, real happiness, connectedness, and contribution.

MSC leadership is simple in theory, but it requires courage and hard work to develop. And it requires that we take an unflinching look at ourselves, at how we interact with our people, and at how our organizations operate. It will radically transform your own performance, the performance of your people, and that of your organization. And along the way, you all benefit by becoming happier as you experience better human connections with a stronger sense of meaning and shared purpose.

And it all starts with you.

PART ONE

Understand and Lead Yourself

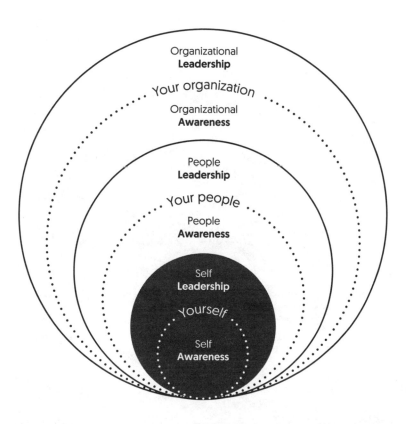

Imagine this scenario: A researcher brings you into a room with a chair. There are no windows. No pictures. No TV. Just you and the chair. You're asked to sit down and think. For a time ranging from six to fifteen minutes, you'll be on your own. Could you sit and be by yourself, or might you prefer painful electric shocks as a distraction?

Astonishingly, this experiment, published in the journal *Science*, reported that 67 percent of men and 25 percent of women found being alone with themselves so unpleasant that they ended up self-inducing electric shocks.[1] One man even shocked himself 190 times. People are so uncomfortable with their own thoughts that they'd rather have any distraction—even a physically painful one—than spend a few minutes being on their own. On the flip side, that's how few of us have the focus, discipline, and restraint that define self-leadership. When we truly lead ourselves, it manifests itself as strength, determination, control, and balance.

Simply put, self-leadership is the ability to manage your own thoughts, behaviors, and actions. Self-leadership is the foundation for effectiveness and productivity, and for living a life according to our values and aspirations. It's about having the mental strength to delay gratification and instead work toward long-term solutions. Self-leadership is about managing ourselves, so we can better lead our people, creating more meaning, connectedness, and a more people-centered culture.

Self-leadership starts in the mind. As an ancient Chinese proverb says, "Observe your thoughts as they become actions. Observe your actions as they become habits. And observe your habits as they shape your life." Our minds shape our thoughts, and our thoughts shape our lives and the lives of those we lead. If we're unable to lead our minds, then to a large degree we're unable to lead our lives—let alone lead others.

To lay the necessary foundation for self-leadership, part 1 opens with a chapter on self-awareness. Self-awareness is the ability to monitor the mind so we can lead it better. Self-awareness is the foundation for self-leadership. We must understand our mind before we can lead it. This includes understanding how our mind works, the importance of values, and what truly makes us happy.

Chapters 3, 4, and 5 then focus on three core elements of self-leadership: mindfulness, selflessness, and compassion. Self-leadership requires focus (mindfulness), humility (selflessness), and the discipline of self-care (compassion). These three qualities—that is, MSC leadership—combine to provide a basis for effectively leading yourself—and in turn, your people—for stronger connectedness, increased happiness, and ultimately, increased productivity.

2

Understand Yourself

Vincent Siciliano, CEO of California-based New Resource Bank, shared with us the story of how he started with the bank. He was brought in to turn the bank around and restore it to its founding mission. When he showed up, all the other members of the executive team resigned, giving him the opportunity to rebuild with people of his own choice. Within a few years, under Vince's leadership, the bank was back on track in terms of profitability and mission alignment.

The leadership team decided to take the pulse of the organization and launched the bank's first employee survey. The results revealed low levels of engagement and criticism of senior leaders. Vince assumed this was left over from the many changes the organization had gone through and chose not to take any action.

A year later, the bank sent out another employee survey. This time, the results were more specific: morale was a significant issue and the majority of people, including members of the senior leadership team, identified Vince as the root cause.

Vince was crushed. His mind oscillated between anger, indignation, defensiveness, and blame. He wondered, "How could they say these things about me? Don't they understand how far we've come under my leadership?" He could have stayed in this negative mindset, wallowing in self-pity and searching for excuses. Instead, he decided it was time to take a hard look at himself. Despite being a high achiever and successful throughout his career, Vince came face to face with an uncomfortable truth: he wasn't the great leader he thought he was. He was leading by the book and trampling over the concerns of others who were not ready to move so fast or didn't understand reasons for changes.

In our conversation with Vince, he said: "There was a gap between my internal reality and my external behavior. My ego had run amok. I was leading from my head and not from my heart." He realized that despite all the skills he had developed through his years of management education and professional development, he'd never been directed to take a long look in the mirror and ask questions about who he was, what he valued, and what it really meant to be a leader.

Bill George, a Harvard leadership professor, former CEO of Medtronic, and author of *True North*, says that self-awareness is the starting point of leadership.[1] Self-awareness is the skill of being aware of our thoughts, emotions, and values, moment to moment. Through self-awareness we can lead ourselves with authenticity and integrity.

Vince's experience is not unique. Self-awareness is not standard curriculum in most management education programs. The majority of MBA degrees focus on strategy and profitability—the things Vince excelled at. But this focus blinded him to what was actually happening in his organization.

Approximately 40 percent of CEOs are MBAs.[2] Many large-scale studies have found that leadership based solely on MBA-trained logic is not enough for delivering long-term sustainable financial and cultural results, and that it often is detrimental to an organization's productivity. In one study, researchers compared the organizational performance of 440 CEOs who had been celebrated on the covers of magazines like *BusinessWeek*, *Fortune*, and *Forbes*. The researchers split the CEOs into two groups—those with an MBA and those without an MBA—and then monitored their performance for seven years. Surprisingly, the performance of those with an MBA was significantly worse.[3] Another study published in the *Journal of Business Ethics* looked at the results of more than five thousand CEOs and came to a similar conclusion.[4]

To be clear, we're not saying MBAs are not useful in leading an organization. But if the linear MBA-trained logic becomes the sole focus—at the cost of other skills, like self-awareness—the leadership approach is out of balance.

That was the case for Vince. He had all the numbers right. His strategy was clear. But people didn't like working with him and were increasingly unhappy. He was managing based on prevailing business theories, but he didn't know or understand himself. Because he lacked self-awareness, people found Vince inauthentic. Subsequently, they weren't keen to follow him or support his leadership. Luckily for Vince, he was open to change and through a journey of mindfulness and coaching toward developing self-awareness, he was able to become more of the leader he wanted to be.

Self-awareness is where leadership starts. We must have awareness of ourselves to lead ourselves. In this chapter, we start by exploring self-awareness, examining how our mind works, and introducing how you can gain better self-awareness through mindfulness. Then we explore the importance of values, followed by a look at what it means to truly be happy. Finally, the chapter ends with practical tips for increasing your self-awareness.

Self-Assessment versus Self-Awareness

Many leadership development programs start with some form of self-assessment. But what do you actually learn from these assessments? In truth, most assessments just scratch the surface of who you are. Sure, they might provide you with insights into dominant traits and behaviors. But is that the real you?

Take a moment to consider the last assessment you did. What did you learn? Perhaps you discovered that you are a visionary thinker and it's hard for others to keep up with your innovative strategies. Perhaps you learned that people find you unapproachable and you need to work on engagement.

These types of insights can be valuable; they can help you understand yourself and how you work with others. But they don't necessarily provide you with the tools needed to solve difficult or complex leadership challenges. To do that, you need real self-awareness.

Take Maura McCaffrey, CEO of Health New England, a US health insurer. Like many CEOs, she's passionate about her work and driven to get results. In her early years as a leader, this passion could occasionally create challenges. As she described it, "I would enter a meeting with a clear strategic plan and, without taking the time to engage others, move forward. I felt so strongly about it, no one could stop me." Call it passion-bias. Her drive for results would lead her to steamroll the group into following her plan, regardless of objections or suggestions.

A 360-degree assessment illuminated this issue. The assessment was clear, but how to move forward was not. The assessment itself didn't provide the tools to fix the problem. Instead, self-awareness did. With the help of mindfulness, Maura gained a new level of self-awareness and started to understand the downsides of her passion-bias. She began to understand how this drive was not always beneficial for her relationships, team engagement, or alignment with her values or organizational objectives.

Self-awareness is what enables you to translate the insights from an assessment into action. Self-awareness is getting to know yourself, moment by moment. Self-awareness is knowing what you are thinking while you think it and what you are feeling when you feel it. It's the ability to keep your values in mind at all times. Self-awareness is the ability to monitor yourself so you can manage yourself accordingly.

In Maura's case, self-awareness was what enabled her to monitor her behavior and change it in the moment. Self-awareness allowed her to notice when her passion-bias was about to manifest itself and take a pause. She learned to become more inclusive in her ways and engage others at their pace. Yes, it could sometimes take longer to put strategies into action. But in the end, those strategies showed much better results, because the people on her team were more engaged and better able to follow through on a vision they helped create.

A general lack of self-awareness, like Vince and Maura experienced in their early leadership years, is one of the key factors in many of today's leadership issues and leadership failures. But to have better self-awareness, we must first understand how our mind works.

Welcome to Your Mind

Who manages your mind? The answer may not be what you think—or hope—it is. Here are a few facts all leaders should know about their mind:

- You do not control your mind.

- You are not rational.

- Your mind creates your reality.

- You are not your thoughts.

The first point: *You probably don't control your mind as much as you think.* To test whether that's true for you, focus on any word in this sentence for a full minute. Don't think about anything else. Don't get distracted. Just focus on one word for a full sixty seconds. No cheating. Okay, go ahead.

How did it go? Were you able to maintain complete focus for a minute? Or did you question the purpose of the exercise? Did you debate which word to focus on? Did the word catalyze new thoughts, leading you to think of other things? The point is that if you strayed from complete focus on that one word, you failed in leading your own mind, even just for a minute.

If you failed, don't worry. You're normal. Most people fail this test. Why? Researchers have found that on average, our mind involuntarily wanders nearly half our waking hours.[5] While you think you're managing your mind, you're not. Think for a moment about the implications of your mind being distracted from what you're doing nearly half of the time. How might it impact your effectiveness? How could it affect your ability to be present with others? How might it impact your well-being?

The second point: *You are not rational.* Sure, we like to think we're rational beings. But in truth, we make choices based on emotions and rationalize them afterward. For example, numerous studies confirm that our decisions are influenced by how options are framed. In one study, faced with making a medical decision, subjects chose the riskless option when outcomes were positively framed in terms of gains, and the risky option when outcomes were phrased negatively in terms of losses.[6]

The third point: *Your mind creates your reality.* Consider the last time you believed you led a meeting where everyone was perfectly aligned, only to later find out that some participants perceived it differently. This type of situation happens all the time. We all have unconscious biases that influence and filter everything we experience. Put more succinctly: we don't perceive things as they are, but as we are. Literally, our mind creates our reality.[7]

The fourth, and final, point: *You are not your thoughts.* In the vast majority of cases, thoughts arise randomly in the mind.[8] But they're not you. Instead, they're just events playing out in your mind, as if your mind is arbitrarily flipping through TV stations. We often identify with our thoughts, believing they are true and believing they define who we are. And that's a problem, since we have thousands of random, repetitive, and compulsive thoughts every day. They're random because they often come out of nowhere, and for no reason, such as thinking about a meeting you attended earlier in the day while you're trying to be present with your family. They're repetitive because we often repeat the same thoughts again and again, like a childhood memory that comes to mind thousands of times throughout life. And they're compulsive because they just keep coming, flowing like a waterfall, even if we try to stop them.

Think about it this way. Have you ever had a bad thought? Does that make you a bad person? Of course not. But when you identify with your thoughts, you become their victim. This is especially true if you tend to be critical of yourself. Then every mistake means you're "stupid," "lazy," "incompetent," or a "failure." To avoid being victimized, don't believe all your thoughts.

These mind facts should be concerning, especially for leaders. If we as leaders don't manage ourselves, how can we lead others effectively, and, ultimately, lead our organizations? This challenge is best faced by first understanding more about the mind, how it works, and how it can be trained.

The mind and the brain are not the same thing. Your brain is the 85 billion neurons, between your ears, as well as the 40 million neurons around your heart and 100 million neurons in your gut.[9] In contrast, your mind is the totality of your experience of being you—cognitively, emotionally, physically, and spiritually. When we speak about the brain, we refer to the physical collection of neurons in our heads and bodies. When we speak about the mind, we refer to the bigger perspective of being ourselves.

Neuroscientists have found that by training our mind, we can change our brain.[10] Physiologically, we can change the structure of our brain by training our mind. When this happens, we can become more focused, kinder, more patient, or any other qualities that we train for. Simply put, what we do is what the brain becomes. Focus for ten minutes every day for two weeks, and our prefrontal cortex—a part of our brain that contributes to focused attention—is strengthened.[11] The brain is taking shape according to how we use it. Scientists and researchers call this *neuroplasticity.*[12]

Neuroplasticity is great news for all of us. It means that we're not limited by the faculties and aptitudes we've already developed. On the contrary, we can keep learning and growing and can effectively rewire our brain throughout our entire lives. And as leaders, we can learn to better manage our mind.

But here is an important caveat for neuroplasticity. Just because our brain is constantly changing doesn't mean that it's automatically changing in ways that are helpful to us. In fact, in our distracted work environments, we tend to rewire our brain to be more distracted. If those sentences make you think about your smartphone or meeting schedule, you're on to something. If we're constantly asking our brain to shift from one task to another, our brain's ability to focus on a single task will diminish. And if we allow ourselves to be constantly impatient and not particularly kind to others, these two characteristics can become the default operations of our brain. In this sense, we get the brain we get based on how we use it. Which means we should all place greater value on creating and managing our mind in ways that are beneficial to us as leaders and the people we lead.

But make no mistake: this process is not easy. It requires training. It requires effort. It also requires a deep understanding of yourself, your values, and your behaviors. But how do you begin to know yourself more deeply and gain this type of self-awareness?

A Mindful Path to Self-Awareness

The starting point for self-awareness is mindfulness. In a busy, distracted work life, focus and awareness—the two central characteristics of mindfulness—are the key qualities for effective mental performance and self-management. As we become more aware of our thoughts and feelings, we can manage ourselves better and act in ways that are more aligned with our values and goals.

Focus is the ability to be single-mindedly directed in what you do. Focus is what allows you to finish a project, meet your goals, and maintain a strategy. When you're involved in an important conversation, focus is what enables you to stay present and not mentally wander off.

Awareness is the ability to notice what is happening around you as well as inside your own mind. When you take part in a conversation, self-awareness allows you to know what you're thinking, recognize how you're feeling, and understand the dynamics of the conversation. Awareness is also the quality that informs you when your focus goes astray and helps you redirect it back on track.

Our previous book, *One Second Ahead*, is an extensive manual for developing mindfulness at work and being in the upper right quadrant of the mindfulness matrix presented in chapter 1.[13] The book provides practical tips on how to enhance effectiveness and well-being in daily work life by bringing mindfulness to tasks like email, meetings, prioritization, and goal setting. We won't repeat all the directions for developing and maintaining a mindful practice here; instead, in this chapter, we'll look at the mindful characteristic of awareness and how you can cultivate self-awareness as part of your own leadership practice. Chapter 3 will look at how mindful focus enables more effective self-leadership skills.

Shut Off the Autopilot

We all have the powerful illusion that we're consciously in charge of our actions and behavior at all times. But in fact, scientists estimate that 45 percent of our everyday behaviors are driven by reactions below the surface of our conscious awareness.[14] This may sound like bad news, but it's necessary and extremely valuable. Imagine trying to drive a car if you consciously had to remind yourself to push the pedal to speed up or ask your hands to move when you needed to turn the wheel. You'd be overwhelmed—and you probably wouldn't get very far. In certain circumstances, these autopilot actions, reactions, and behaviors are vital. These unconscious processes allow you to perform tasks without having to think about them. But not all your autopilot actions and behaviors are useful in leading yourself or others.

As leaders, we impact the people we lead. They pick up on every subtle cue we send, whether we send it consciously or unconsciously. And many of the cues we send can be discouraging, distancing, or confusing. This is not necessarily due to bad intentions, but rather because the behaviors, actions, or reactions happen while we're operating on autopilot. Therefore, gaining greater awareness of our subtle actions and behaviors, and eliminating autopilot behaviors that are detrimental can be highly beneficial.

Mindfulness training enables us to expand our awareness of what's happening in the landscape of our mind from moment to moment. It also helps us pause in the moment, so we can make more conscious choices and take more deliberate actions. These are powerful skills to have as a leader.

Fortunately for all of us, awareness can be enhanced. We can change the ratio of our conscious to unconsciousness behaviors, which can make the difference between making good or bad decisions. But what is awareness really? Do you know what awareness feels like? Take a moment to experience it:

1. Let go of this book. For one minute, sit still.

2. Whatever comes into your mind, be aware of it. Simply notice it.

3. Let go of any inner commentary of why you are doing this exercise.

4. No analyzing, no judging, no thinking.

5. Simply be aware.

6. Just be.

That is awareness. A direct experience of what is happening for you, right now. And paying attention to it helps us understand ourselves. Did you become aware of anything about yourself that you were not aware of before the exercise? Did you find that maybe you're tired? That you perhaps felt tension or stress somewhere in your body? Or that you have a lot on your mind? What did you discover?

If you didn't actually do the one-minute exercise, go back and actually try it.

If you found the exercise difficult, you're not alone. In our busy lives filled with constant distractions, our mind is often racing. The flood of activity can feel like a waterfall pouring down on us with a million bits of information. As a result, we're less aware than we should be. Simply because our mind is too full to be aware. Mindfulness can address that. At the end of this chapter, you'll find simple tips and reflections for mindful awareness training. This training empowers you with greater awareness throughout your day. How? By helping you get one second ahead of your autopilot reactions and behaviors.

Jacob Larsen, vice president of The Finance Group, explained the power of getting one second ahead in a clear way. After he completed one of our ten-session mindfulness programs, we asked him what he had gained. His answer: "One second." He explained that mindfulness gave him a one-second gap between his thoughts and his actions, between his impulses and his reactions. And this gave him greater control over his decisions and his responses. In any given situation, he said, he could better manage himself—all because of a single second. In this way, mindfulness can provide the moment-to-moment awareness needed to make better choices and take more productive action, as figure 2-1 illustrates.

One second can be the difference between making a good or bad decision. It's the difference between saying the words that motivate an employee and the words that disengage him or her. A second is the difference between lashing out at someone for an error or turning an unintentional mistake into a learning moment. A second matters. Especially for you as a leader.

Mindfulness training—and utilizing this one-second mental pause— is what helped Maura McCaffrey, whom we met earlier in this chapter,

FIGURE 2-1

The one-second mental gap

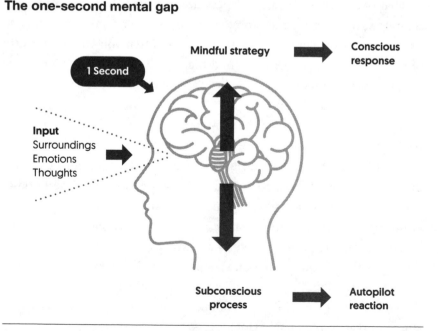

control her passion-bias. Through mindfulness training, she was able to become aware of the initial signs of her passion-bias and pause before reacting. With this pause, Maura began replacing her passion-bias with inclusiveness. After a little practice, it became natural for her to get buy-in from the group instead of forcing her own agenda.

Our survey results found that leaders at the highest levels tend to have better self-awareness than leaders further down the hierarchy. This could be because stronger self-awareness accelerates the promotion process or because, like Maura, we're nudged toward enhancing our self-awareness as our leadership responsibility increases.

Take a moment to consider which automatic behaviors you have that sometimes hinder your leadership. What interferes with your team member's feelings of engagement? What decreases the willingness of others to take your lead? What makes people feel insecure or disregarded? Ask yourself these questions from time to time to gradually increase your self-awareness and spur changes in your automatic reactions and responses. Doing so will not only make you a more effective leader, it will also help you better understand, align with, and act on your own personal values.

Calibrate Your Value Compass

In competitive business environments, it can be tempting to compromise our core values. The history of business is littered with leaders who have caused scandals, destroyed companies, wrecked economies, or ruined the lives of thousands of people because they strayed from a strong moral basis. Just think of companies like Enron, WorldCom, or Tyco. Or consider the 2008 financial crisis, BP's *Deepwater Horizon* oil spill, and Volkswagen's emissions fraud. These are just a few more recent examples of a broader trend. A national business ethics survey done by the Ethics Resource Center found that of the US workforce, 41 percent of workers have observed unethical leadership behavior in the previous twelve months, and 10 percent felt organizational pressure to compromise ethical standards.[15]

It's easy to look at these cases, feel righteous indignation, and label the responsible leaders as evil. But it's not that straightforward. Few people truly want to hurt others. According to extensive neurological and social science research, we're genuinely good beings with positive intentions. We all want to contribute to the well-being of others.[16] Some studies find that one of the only consistent neurological traits across cultures and races is that we are predisposed to kindness and altruism.[17] Other studies indicate the general human impulse is to help and support others in need.[18] We are truly good beings.

But if we are genuinely good beings with good intensions, why do we witness corporate leadership scandals one after another? Because intense pressure to increase revenue or make the quarterly numbers can erode our sense of self-awareness, which can lead to letting our values slip.

The rise of technology has also contributed to the weakening of our value compasses. With the rise in distractions, it has become increasingly difficult to keep our values in mind, simply because our mind is so busy with ever-increasing flow of information. With a heightened level of self-awareness, however, we're better able to identify, acknowledge, and communicate our values. These values can help us navigate ourselves, our people, and our organizations in a more ethical manner and align our actions with what we want to offer to the world. In this way, awareness of our values becomes a compass, indicating instances when our choices don't align with our ethical and moral standards. This, in turn, keeps us from cutting corners and helps us sleep better at night.

Thomas, an IT director we worked with at a global pharmaceutical company, shared a story with us about how he once found himself in an ethical dilemma. Two vendors were bidding on a major contract he was overseeing. One offer was slightly better than the other, but the vendor of the lesser offer had subtly offered a kickback to sweeten the deal. Pressured by a tight timeline, Thomas struggled with his decision for most of a day, constantly changing his mind.

To clear his head, he decided to do a few minutes of mindfulness practice, hoping to find clarity. As his mind calmed and he gained an increased level of awareness, his value compass clicked into action, pointing him in the right direction. While the kickback was attractive, he knew it was wrong to take it. He chose the other offer instead.

Reflecting on the dilemma, Thomas acknowledged that if this had been presented as a classroom ethics simulation, he never would have considered the offer with the kickback. But, as he explained, "With the complexity of the deal and the intense pressure to make a decision, it was hard to focus on the idea of right and wrong. Sometimes in business, with all the pressure, decisions don't seem so clear-cut."

Thomas's experience is not unusual. Research has found that mindfulness practice enhances our ethical decision making.[19] But if we lack the self-awareness necessary to have a strong value compass, we have a much greater chance of making the wrong choice or doing the wrong thing. This is especially true in morally ambiguous circumstances or high-stakes situations. And in the end—regardless of money or success, regardless of stature or fame—making unjust decisions or taking unethical actions will have a detrimental impact on our sense of self. And ultimately, it will negatively impact our happiness.

True Happiness—It's Not What You Think

Self-awareness helps us answer one of life's big questions, one that is foundational for leading our people: What makes us truly happy? This question should be front and center for any leader. Being self-aware of what constitutes true happiness helps in better leading people and tapping into what really drives them. True happiness bolsters feelings of fulfillment, engagement, and commitment. Because of this, it's time for the practice and science of true happiness to enter basic leadership knowledge.

Take a moment to consider the following question: How often do you wake up in the morning *wishing* for a stressful day?

Now ask yourself another question: How often do you have a stressful day?

The point is, we humans do a great job of messing things up for ourselves. We hope to have great lives. We desire lives with few worries, with harmonious relationships, with balance and joy. Lives with fun and meaning. And in our developed world, we have the means to make this happen. We have advanced systems of education. We have state-of-the-art health care. We have enormous financial means. We have plentiful food. We have safe environments. We have resources and amenities that our ancestors could only dream of. Yet we manage to fall short of creating deeply meaningful, satisfying, and joyful lives.

What's wrong with us?

We'll get to the answer in a moment. First, on a scale from 1 to 10, how important is it for you to be happy, fulfilled, and satisfied with your life? Close your eyes and take a moment to consider the question. Don't feel a need to come up with an answer. That's not the point. Instead this should be a question you occasionally reflect on throughout your life. Now consider: Is your happiness more important than your professional achievements? Is your happiness more important than your wealth? Again, don't feel a need to come up with rushed answers. These are questions for thoughtful reflection.

Frankly, we as humans have one go at a good life—and it's a short one. Our childhood sometimes feels like yesterday. In thirty or fifty years, we may look back on today as yesterday, and our lives will almost be over. Life passes quickly. Think about how many people around the world went to bed last night, just like yourself, expecting to wake up this morning to another day in their lives—to another go at being happy. But instead, they didn't wake up. They passed away in their sleep. Their chance at a day of happiness was lost forever. The difference between being alive or not exists in a flash, in a brief moment of transition. And we never know when that moment will arrive.

Having a happy life should be important. If we exit life without having tasted true happiness, without having experienced meaning and fulfillment, then what did we do? We missed the one chance we had.

We Don't Know How to Be Happy

Now the answer to the earlier question: What's wrong with us? Why do we fall short of being happy when we have so much? Quite simply, because we don't know how to be happy.

From a leader's perspective, understanding happiness and its roots permits us to create more meaning, purpose, and fulfillment for our people. This in turn can unlock great productivity. But as leaders—and as humans—we're generally mistaken about happiness. It's like we're chasing it blindfolded. The things we generally look to for happiness don't actually provide it. Research conducted at places like the London School of Economics and Political Science, Harvard Business School, and leading neuroresearch centers around the world and brought together by the United Nations in its annual World Happiness Report shows us our biases about happiness. We're generally mistaken about happiness in two ways: (1) We believe happiness comes from the outside, and (2) We mistake pleasure for happiness.[20]

You Can't Buy Happiness

Major research studies show conclusively that true happiness doesn't come from external sources. This is particularly true of external factors like money (see figure 2-2). For more than fifty years, researchers have looked at the correlation between happiness and wealth in the United States and other countries. Wealth has more than doubled, but the happiness level has decreased.

A separate study found that winning the lottery increased participants' mood significantly, but after a while they returned to their normal baseline of happiness. Another study showed that while experiencing difficult situations, such as a job loss or major illness, participants' happiness decreased significantly. But eventually, they also returned to their original baseline.[21] In each of these instances, outside events—gaining wealth, winning the lottery, or losing a job—had a short-term effect

FIGURE 2-2

Income and happiness

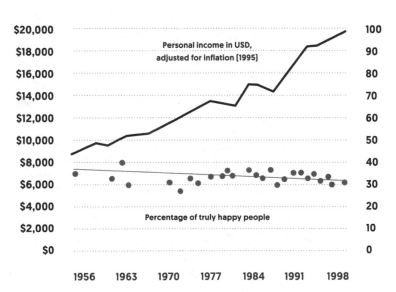

on happiness but didn't influence people's long-term sense of happiness (see figure 2-3).

The message? External events and experiences do not create true happiness. Nor do difficult events and experiences create lasting unhappiness. This should be considered great news. It means that we as individuals can be in control of our own happiness. We may not get the desired promotion, the fancy car, or the magnificent house, but our happiness is not dependent on those types of things. It doesn't depend on our status or wealth.

But our happiness does depend on the wealth of our neighbor. Consider the following two scenarios:

- You live a life in which you earn $50,000 a year while other people get $25,000 a year.

- You live a life in which you earn $100,000 a year while other people get $250,000 a year.

Which of these two scenarios would you prefer?

A joint study by researchers from the University of Miami and the Harvard School of Public Health found that the majority preferred the first option.[22] This illustrates a paradoxical fact: when people become

FIGURE 2-3

Happiness and life events

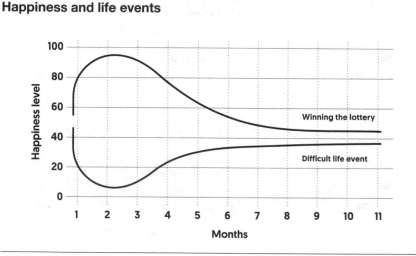

richer compared with other people, they feel happier. But when whole societies become richer, they don't. Our happiness is relative to the wealth of our neighbors. Again, happiness does not come from the outside, but from how we relate to what we have. Happiness is an inner state deeply influenced by how we relate to what others have.

Pleasure Isn't Happiness

We generally equate pleasure with happiness. We think that if we get enough pleasure, we'll be happy. But we're wrong. The two experiences are completely different.

In a way, pleasure is pure chemistry. When we get or do something we like—a promotion, praise, a new car—dopamine is released in our brain, giving us a sense of pleasure. Dopamine is a neurotransmitter that helps control the brain's reward and pleasure centers. It enables us not only to see rewards but also to take action to move toward them. However, dopamine can lead to addiction.[23] The more pleasure we allow ourselves, the more we risk becoming addicted to it. The final result is a constant rat race in which we're continually looking for that next rush of dopamine. Pleasure is a momentary experience that quickly fades as the neurochemicals subside.

True Happiness Is . . .

True happiness, in contrast, can't be so easily located or pinpointed in the brain. It's not in a specific region, and it can't be found in a single hormone, neurotransmitter, or molecule. True happiness is an experience of fulfillment and of lasting well-being. True happiness is a long-term experience of a meaningful, purposeful, and positive life. It's a deeply felt existential experience that can be maintained irrespective of the ups and downs of life, not a fleeting sense of gratification like pleasure.

We're chasing pleasure in new business successes, more praise, and better pay, hoping it will make us happy. But it doesn't. It just puts us on the treadmill of wanting more and more. This is not to say pleasure is wrong. Pleasure is great. It adds flavor to life. But pleasure is like eating honey from the blade of a knife. It tastes great, but if we're not careful, we may hurt ourselves by craving more.

And never mistake it for happiness.

Take a moment to consider how these facts about true happiness might inform your leadership. Are there things you could do differently to help your people be happier and more engaged? Just think about this for a few moments. We'll dive into these questions in more detail throughout the book.

Awareness Training

Mindfulness training helps you increase your self-awareness and thereby become more aware of what makes you truly happy. It helps you avoid your compulsive reactions and replace them with more useful behaviors. And it helps you stay true to your values. These are foundational skills for effective leadership, for being authentic, and for increasing team engagement.

But awareness training does more than that. The more time you spend training your awareness, the more you'll come to fully appreciate that you are not your thoughts. Your thoughts are not you. The training helps you create a healthy and realistic distance from your mental activities. You start to observe your thoughts as fleeting events that have no real substance or importance. They're just like clouds in the sky: they come and go. And they only have an impact on you if you allow them to. So many of our thoughts and feelings spark emotions or action. But really, many of them are random and insubstantial. We don't need to react to them. We can simply let them be.

Bring this insight to how you perceive yourself, and you will be more at ease. Bring this insight to how you perceive others, and you will find it easier to lead them. Bring this insight to how you lead your organization, and you will find that you need to exert much less effort and control. As much as we like to think of ourselves as important because we are leaders, a realistic, self-aware, hard look will show that we are less important than we think. And the most appropriate response to that is to develop a realistic, selfless view of ourselves, as we explore in chapter 4.

The mental strength and freedom you develop through awareness training cannot be overstated. Through it, you come to know yourself in the moment, to know what you think, what you feel, and what is important to you (see "Training for Mindful Awareness").

Training for Mindful Awareness

1. Set a timer for ten minutes.

2. Sit in your chair, comfortably, with a straight back and relaxed neck, shoulders, and arms. Close your eyes and breathe through your nose.

3. For a minute, direct your full attention toward your breathing. Simply observe your breath neutrally. Don't try to control it. Allow your mind to stabilize and settle.

4. Now, let go of your attention on your breath and open your awareness to whatever arises. Whatever arises—a sound, a thought, a physical sensation, or anything else—just be aware of it.

5. Observe it neutrally. Don't think about it. Don't engage it. Don't try to make it stay or go away. Simply observe it.

6. New experiences will arise, change, or fade away. Whatever occurs in your awareness, just be aware of it.

7. If you find it challenging to observe without engaging your experiences, give the experience a label—for example, *thought*, *email*, *task*—and let it go.

8. If you find you get caught up in thinking about and analyzing your experiences, return your focus to your breath. Then open your awareness again.

9. When the timer sounds, let go of the training.

This practice, and the rest of the practices in this book are all recorded in a guided training app designed for this book. See appendix A for information.

Quick Tips and Reflections

- ✓ Commit to practicing ten minutes of mindful awareness training on a regular basis as recommended in the app.

- ✓ Identify one autopilot behavior you would like to change; set an intention to notice when the old behavior arises, pause, and chose a new response.

- ✓ Write down the values that are most important to you in your work life and as a leader; consider when these might be challenged and how you will respond.

- ✓ Consider what the difference between "pleasure" and "happiness" means for you and what insights this might have for how you lead yourself.

- ✓ Commit to one thing you will start, stop, or continue doing to increase genuine happiness.

3

Mindfully Lead Yourself

For today's leaders, mindfulness—training the mind to be more focused and aware—is becoming a survival skill and a cornerstone of self-leadership. The pressure on leaders is increasing, as are the pace of change, the volume of information available, and the scale of complexity. A managing director of a global consulting firm told us that he had exhausted every tool on the market that promised to help him become more effective. He had applied all of the most popular time-management techniques. He had tried all the newest productivity software. He had incorporated the latest collaborative platforms. And yet he was still working as many hours as he possibly could. No additional apps could help, no more techniques could be applied, and no more minutes could be squeezed into the workday. He had run out of possible solutions.

His last resort: *Train his mind.*

With this realization, he became part of the global movement of leaders who are practicing mindfulness to increase awareness and improve focus.

As we discussed in chapter 2, mindful awareness helps us to switch off the autopilot and get in the driver's seat of our mind. Mindful focus, which we explore in this chapter, helps us to be more effective and improve our well-being. In the first few sections of this chapter, we'll examine the faculties of focus and provide strategies for more focused performance. We'll then end the chapter with instructions on how to enhance focus through a guided mindfulness practice.

Survival of the Focused

Leaders—and people at work in general—have a problem. Our ability to focus and manage our minds is deteriorating. Research has found that we're distracted from what we do 47 percent of the time.[1] That's an alarming number. Throughout any given day, we're constantly thinking about things that happened in the past and things we need to do in the future. Meanwhile, we've lost focus on what's happening right now. Although this research is a bit depressing, it also presents a massive potential for improved performance.

In our survey results, we found that 73 percent of leaders feel distracted from their current task either "some" or "most" of the time. We also found that 67 percent of leaders view their minds as cluttered, with lots of thoughts and a lack of clear priorities. As a result, 65 percent find that they fail to complete their most important tasks. When asked about the primary challenges to maintaining focus, the leaders answered that the biggest sources of distractions are the demands of other people (26 percent), competing priorities (25 percent), general distractions (13 percent), and workloads that are too big (12 percent). Not surprisingly, 96 percent of the leaders we surveyed said that enhanced focus would be valuable or extremely valuable.[2]

With the excessive number of distractions we face, attention deficit has become a norm in businesses.[3] Thomas Davenport, author of *The Attention Economy*, wrote: "Understanding and managing attention is now the single most important determinant of business success."[4] The "attention economy" is an apt term for our current organizational environments. In today's business world—with its seemingly endless distractions—our ability to focus is just as important as skills like financial analysis and time management. If there is one secret to effectiveness, said leadership pioneer Peter Drucker, it's concentration.[5] In our age of information overload, this is truer now than ever before.

Imagine a standard ten- to twelve-hour workday, with back-to-back meetings, a nonstop stream of emails, and the need to make good decisions in constantly shifting and complex contexts. The ability to apply calm and clear focus to the right tasks, at the right time, in the right way is what makes a leader exceptional. Even one second of misplaced focus is enough to miss a critical cue from a client during a tough negotiation.

Productivity has traditionally been measured in terms of time and competency: how much time we have for a task and our ability to solve it efficiently. But in an attention economy, focus is now such a scarce leadership resource that it overshadows time and competence. Imagine you spent thirty minutes on a task, occasionally checking your email and dealing with other distractions. The task itself should have only taken ten minutes, but you weren't able to maintain a clear focus. That's a significant loss in productivity. But the problem wasn't mismanaged time—it was mismanaged focus.

In this light, a simple equation for productivity in the attention economy is $Focus \times Time \times Competence = Productivity$. Without focus, you will spend more time on a task and your productivity will be negatively impacted.

There also seems to be a direct correlation between people's level of focus and the advancements they make in their companies. Of the thousands of leaders we've worked with over the years, the vast majority possess an above-average ability to focus. This is not to say that exceptional focus is a sure way to the top. But certainly, without focus, career success will be much more difficult to attain. For aspiring leaders, focus should be a daily mantra.

Through our research and fieldwork, we've come to a clear conclusion: focus must be at the forefront of any—and all—leadership training. The leaders we interviewed for this book all emphasized their need to cultivate and protect their focus amidst the relentless flow of details and distractions that assault their minds.

And yet, in our view, the business world is not focused enough on focus.

Consider these questions. When were you last exposed to focus training during a leadership development program? When did you last consider a calm, clear focus as part of an effective way to use your time? Just in the past week, how often have you experienced unfocused or distracted people in meetings?

Focus is rarely part of a training program or considered critical to effective time management. And many people are distracted during meetings, but they are rarely called out on it. This leads us to a great evolutionary irony: for most of human history, being prone to distraction ensured survival. Our alertness to sounds, smells, and movements that could indicate a threat was vital to our continued existence.

But today, the survival paradigm has reversed. In today's distracted office environments, only the focused survive. And certainly, only the focused excel. All of the C-suite executives we interviewed shared stories of the importance of focus to survive and more importantly, to thrive. It was one of the qualities they considered as key to their success and valued for their people and their organization.

But it's not easy to maintain focus. From a neurological perspective, we are wired for distractions. Part of our brain is devoted to constantly scanning our surroundings and reporting any new information of importance that may require our attention.[6] The tendency to be distracted is deeply ingrained in older parts of the brain like the temporal cortex and the posterior cingulate cortex. Test it for yourself. Stop reading and pay attention to your surroundings. Is your attention naturally directing itself toward movements and sounds?

Distraction is the default setting of the human brain. Focus occurs mainly in the prefrontal cortex, the newest part of our brain, as illustrated in figure 3-1.

The prefrontal cortex is also the home of executive function, which is our ability to deliberately choose our actions and behavior.[7] When we are

FIGURE 3-1

Where distraction and focus are found in the brain

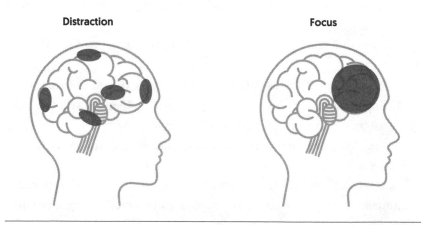

able to operate more out of this part of our brain, we have greater ability to minimize the noise from our wandering mind, are more focused on the task at hand, and can take more deliberate actions when engaging meaningfully with our people.

The Faculties of Focus

We're all genetically predisposed for a certain baseline of focus. But we can improve on this baseline. For every moment we intentionally focus, our focus improves. Understanding the "anatomy" of focus can help us better develop it. Focus has six distinct faculties: control, capacity, speed, agility, clarity, and durability. The stronger each of these faculties is, the more effective our focus will be. Different situations require different faculties (see figure 3-2). And through well-guided mindfulness training, we can enhance them all.

Let's take a close look at each faculty.

Control

Controlled focus enables you to prioritize your attention and actions from moment to moment. It's the opposite of distraction. It's the quality of deliberately being attentive to one object or task. It's the core of attention.

FIGURE 3-2

The six faculties of focus

	Faculties are important for . . .
Control	Moment-to-moment prioritizing, people contact, task processing
Capacity	Reading and learning, dealing with complex issues
Speed	Information processing, decision making, high-stakes interactions
Agility	Creative processes, problem solving, brainstorming
Clarity	Dealing with complex issues, high-stakes work
Durability	Meetings, facing challenges, long days, negotiations

As you're reading this book, are you fully focused on reading? Or do other unrelated thoughts sneak into your mind?

In a study investigating the neurobiology of what happens when we become distracted, researchers found that during controlled focus, the prefrontal cortex becomes active to sustain attention.[8] This neural synchronization is critical for getting things done. Without controlled focus, it's virtually impossible to be effective. Without controlled focus when we're with others, it's difficult to make the connection necessary for meaningful communication. But with controlled, laserlike focus, astonishing accomplishments are possible.

For leaders today, there are more issues to deal with than there is time. Trying to focus on many important issues at the same time is a recipe for disaster. Leaders need to constantly focus and refocus, to give undivided attention on the most important issues moment to moment.

Capacity

Focus capacity enables you to absorb and process large volumes of information and cut through complexity. Focus capacity is the amount of data you can consciously be aware of at any given moment. It's like your internet bandwidth, determining how much data you can download per second.

You can get a sense of your capacity right now: stop reading, close your eyes for a moment, then open them and look in front of you for one second, then close your eyes again. How many details can you recall from what you saw in that one second?

Researchers have been trying to measure focus capacity for years, with varying results. An average mind can comprehend between four and forty bits of conscious information per second.[9] Our research shows that this is significantly *less* than the desired level needed for most leaders, as information overload is perceived as one of the five biggest challenges to their leadership effectiveness.

Loren Shuster, chief people officer at the LEGO Group, shared with us how mindfulness practice helps him absorb and retain many hundreds of pages of briefings before board meetings: "Doing a few moments of mindfulness before reading a briefing or report, calms and clears my mind. It creates the necessary bandwidth to absorb the details I know I'm about to read—and that I know I need to retain." Loren added that by allowing himself a few more moments of mindfulness practice after reading, he is better able to synthesize and store information. "It's been a revelation for me," he told us. "I can recall the facts and figures I need, when I need them most—when the pressure is on."

Speed

Your focus speed is the rate at which you process the flow of your experiences. Focus speed allows you to think on your feet and make fast decisions. Recall the last time you were in some kind of accident. Did time slow down, allowing you to vividly experience every split second? Of course, time didn't actually slow down. It was instead your focus that sped up, providing you a close-up, seemingly slow-motion experience of the event. It's as though a faster data processor kicked in.

Notice your focus speed right now as you read. How quickly are you able to get to the end of the sentence while still understanding the words in it?

Our focus speed varies, depending on how engaged we are, how complex a situation may be, or other environmental factors. During accidents, focus speed can be very high. But when we've imbibed alcohol, when we're tired, or when we're operating on autopilot, our focus speed is limited. Fighter pilots are known to have above-average focus speed. Imagine flying at more than a thousand miles per hour while having to navigate, keep track of your plane, and coordinate a precise flight path. This is daily work for a fighter pilot and calls for high focus speed.

Sue Gilchrist, regional managing partner for Asia and Australia, of the global law firm Herbert Smith Freehills, shared how she reads the underlying dynamics in client meetings. With mindfulness, she told us, her focus speed increases, whereby the speed of conversation seemingly slows down. "This allows me to pick up on more cues and implicit messages," she asserted. "And the ability to see more of what is happening moment-to-moment in highly politicized or otherwise challenging environments is an invaluable asset, no matter what industry you're in."

Agility

Focus agility allows you to mentally switch from one task to another without lingering on the previous activity. This includes shifting from one meeting to the next or from writing an email to joining a conversation.

In a hypercomplex world, focus agility allows you to mentally move efficiently among multiple complex contexts. It allows you to hold multiple opposing perspectives, values, and emotions and make more holistic decisions with less bias.

Focus agility, like the other faculties of focus, is impacted by internal and external factors. Tiredness, alcohol, mental busyness, and rapid task switching can decrease your focus agility and make you slower.

To test your focus agility, try this: As you read this sentence, abruptly shift your focus away from these words to something in your surroundings and focus on that object or image.

Did the switch happen swiftly or was there any mental lag? How quickly were you fully focused on the new object? Did any part of your focus still linger on the words you just read? If you're not sure about your experience, try again; shift from one object to another object. Then observe the agility with which you transition your focus.

Focus agility should not be confused with multitasking. Extensive research has confirmed that humans are incapable of multitasking. We'll explore multitasking in greater detail later in the chapter. For now, just understand that focus agility is the faculty that allows you to shift or switch between tasks—it is not the ability to perform multiple tasks at once.

Consider the following example from the CEO of Heineken, Jean-François van Boxmeer. As we entered the Heineken headquarters in Amsterdam to interview Jean-François, he was discussing the technical details of a complex acquisition with his legal counsel. In less than a second, however, his attention switched to the context of our interview. He was fully present, fully engaged. When we asked him how he switched his focus so quickly, he explained that his role does not allow for a lack of focus. "I can't afford to be distracted. I must be on point. I have trained my focus while at work for fifteen years, moment-to-moment. I feel the brain is like a muscle, and I exercise it all the time. It's about disciplined presence." His day is packed with meetings from early morning until late evening; even meals are mostly organized as working meetings. In these kinds of extreme conditions, there's little room for lingering on past activities. His well-trained mental agility makes this regimen possible.

Clarity

Focus clarity helps you register the details of your current task or object of attention. This means you experience whatever you focus on in high definition and maintain a distinct recollection of what has taken place in past moments.

Right now, how clear is your focus? Are you fully aware of what you've been reading? Or has reading made you a little drowsy? Take a moment to check in with yourself. How many facts can you recall from the last three pages?

Our research found that 90 percent of leaders believe that more reflection time would enhance their mental clarity. One way to visualize this is to think of the mind like a snow globe that gets shaken up throughout the day. Reflection time—as well as mindfulness practice and other activities—lets the snow settle, making everything easier to see and put into perspective.

James Doty, clinical professor of neurosurgery at Stanford University, describes how mindfulness training improves his focus clarity during surgery. This clarity provides him with a serene perception during the act of operating, including observations of the state of the patient, the state of the supporting operating staff, the granular details of the brain he's operating on, and his own mental and physical state.

Durability

Focus durability is the span of time you can maintain a continuous state of focus on any given object or experience. A well-developed focus durability allows you to stay focused for hours without becoming distracted. But in an age of major technology distractions, our durability of focus is deteriorating.

How long do you think you can maintain focus on one object before becoming distracted? Try this quick test: Start a stopwatch or timer, focus on one object, stop when you first get distracted. Are you surprised by the result? If you managed less than ten seconds, don't worry, that is normal. Having trained tens of thousands of people in mindfulness, we can testify that the majority of people last less than ten seconds on their first try.

Researchers have found a direct correlation between the heavy consumption of multiple forms of media—for example, print, television, phone calls, texts, video games—and shrinkage in our prefrontal cortex, the home of executive function.[10] In other words, the more we allow ourselves to be inundated with information and distractions, the less brain capacity we have to maintain focus. But remember, thanks to neuroplasticity, with mindfulness training you can improve your focus durability. Even after as little as eight weeks of daily mindfulness practice, your prefrontal cortex gets thicker as your ability to focus improves.[11]

The next section includes some strategies to help you strengthen the six faculties of focus. After reviewing these strategies, we'll present a mindfulness practice specifically for improving focus.

Strategies for Focused Performance

Based on our research and fieldwork, four strategies are particularly effective for leaders when it comes to focused performance: understanding what impacts focus, avoiding multitasking, thwarting action addiction, and creating focus time.

Understand What Impacts Focus

To maintain a strong focus throughout the day, it's useful to know what impacts it, and how good your general focus is at different times of the day. Is your focus as strong at 8 a.m. as it is at 2 p.m.? How about at 10 p.m.? Consider how your focus is impacted by the time of the day, when you eat, what you eat, your mental state, and how many hours you slept.

For example, judges are trained to be neutral and objective in their legal rulings. From a statistical point of view, they should be making balanced, neutral rulings throughout the day. But studies have found that judges rule more favorably in the morning than in the afternoon. This means that it's possible that a defendant may be sentenced to prison rather than set free if he or she enters the courtroom sometime after lunch.[12]

This pattern correlates directly with our research determining when leaders feel most focused. See the daily focus pattern of leaders in figure 3-3.

FIGURE 3-3

The daily focus pattern

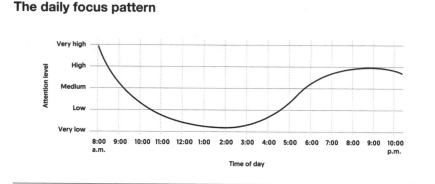

With this pattern in mind, consider which activities you do at various times of the day. Make sure your most important activities are planned around the times when your focus is strongest. And plan to do more practical and active tasks during the hours when your focus is weaker.

Our focus and its six faculties are also impacted by other mental and physical factors, including sleep, emotions, and food. For an overview, see figure 3-4.

Consider the mental factors first. Negative emotions generally decrease most of our faculties. Paul Ekman, a groundbreaking researcher in emotions from the University of California, San Francisco, described how difficult emotions create a refractory period that narrows our focus on the object of our emotion.[13] In contrast, positive emotions generally have the opposite effect, opening up our focus to see the bigger picture.[14]

From a physical perspective, relaxation is a prerequisite for strong focus. Relaxation is the absence of unnecessary effort, of both mind and body. When we relax our body, our mind follows. When we relax our mind, we also relax our body. In this way, mind and body are linked. Also, if we care for our body with quality sleep, nutrition, and exercise, our focus is enhanced. Coffee, contrary to what many of us believe, is not useful for focus. The caffeine enhances wakefulness but scatters focus.[15] And not surprisingly, alcohol is harmful in most aspects as well.

What other activities do you do that impact your focus, whether positively or negatively? You're likely facing competing demands most of the time: people in need of your attention, urgent emails, and high-stakes decisions. The automatic response of the brain is to try to focus on them

FIGURE 3-4

Factors that impact focus

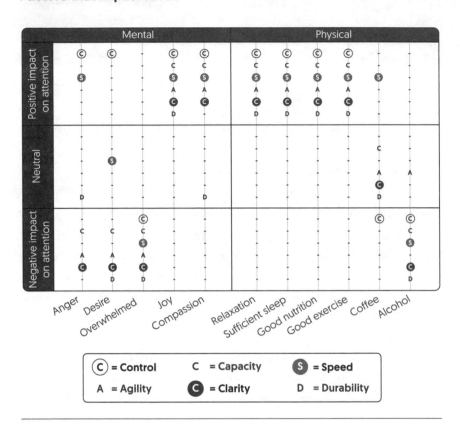

	= Control	C	= Capacity		= Speed
A	= Agility		= Clarity	D	= Durability

all at once. By default, the brain wants you to multitask. But multitasking kills your focus.

Stop Multitasking

Our ability to multitask is a myth. Most of us carry around the powerful illusion that we can pay attention to more than one thing at a time. We think we can drive a car while talking on the phone, participate in a meeting while checking emails, or engage in a conversation while writing a text message. To be clear, we can do many activities without paying attention; that is, without conscious thought. For example, we can walk and talk at the same time. Experienced drivers can handle many of the elements of driving, such as changing gears and turning the steering wheel, on autopilot.

But from a neurological perspective, we're not capable of focusing attention on two things at the same time. Multitasking is really *shift-tasking*: shifting attention rapidly between two or more things. For a second, we're aware of traffic; the next instant, we're attending to the phone. Sometimes we switch so rapidly between tasks we have the illusion we're paying attention to both at the same time, but in reality we're not.

In the context of multitasking at work, researchers have found that when we multitask, we become "masters of everything that is irrelevant, we let ourselves be distracted by anything."[16] Perhaps you've experienced losing track of what you are doing even when you have a simple task and clear intentions. For example, imagine that you're looking at LinkedIn for information about a person you're considering for a job. Then you notice a link to an article that looks interesting. You hit that link and start reading and find a link to an interesting video on YouTube. An hour later, you catch yourself still watching videos and have completely lost track of what you started out to do. Sound familiar?

Studies have shown that multitasking lowers people's job satisfaction, damages personal relationships, adversely affects memory, and negatively impacts health.[17] Many of these studies have demonstrated that multitasking reduces effectiveness because it takes longer to complete tasks and leads to more mistakes. This is because when we switch our focus from one task to another, it takes time to make the shift. Depending on the complexity of the new task, that can take anywhere from a few seconds to several minutes. This phenomenon is called *shift-time*. Shift-time saps our mental energy and taxes our productivity.

In addition, researchers from Harvard Business School discovered that multitasking hinders creativity.[18] After assessing nine thousand employees working on projects that required creative thinking, researchers found a notable drop in creative thinking among employees who multitasked and an increase in creativity among those who focused on one task at a time.

When we don't multitask, when we stay focused on one thing at a time, we benefit. We also benefit from not getting trapped in activity.

Avoid Action Addiction

Action addiction is characterized by an uncontrollable urge to be doing something and a discomfort with being still. It includes behaviors like constantly checking emails, texts, news feeds, or social media. Action addiction keeps us busy and may help us complete many "tasks," but activity is not the same as productivity.

One could argue that when we're action addicts—when we constantly answer email, shoot off texts, or take phone calls—we get a lot done. Sadly, that's not the case. In the 2002 *Harvard Business Review* article "Beware the Busy Manager," researchers shared findings on managers' ability to prioritize. After an in-depth study of leaders in companies like Sony, LG, and Lufthansa, they conclude: "Very few use their time as effectively as they could. They think they're attending to pressing matters, but they're really just spinning their wheels."[19] Another study looked at the priorities of more than 350,000 people and found that they spend an average of 41 percent of their time on low-level priorities.[20] In other words, they're doing lots of things but not getting the right things done.

We are so wired for doing things that a survey found that 83 percent of Americans spent no time relaxing or doing nothing in the past twenty-four hours.[21] When did you last sit without doing anything? Try it out now. Put the book aside and do nothing for three minutes. Observe your reactions to it.

How did it go? Did you feel an urge to check your email, or do something else? If yes, you may be suffering from action addiction.

Action addiction is a very real condition most of us have to some degree, and the cause lies in our brain. When we complete a task, even the smallest insignificant task like sending an email, dopamine is released in the brain. This can make the task addictive. But dopamine is blind and does not distinguish between activity and productivity. This means we get a dopamine hit just for doing something—anything. And this makes us effective at doing a lot of things but not necessarily at doing the right things.

The obvious consequence of action addiction is that we're constantly chasing short-term wins and losing sight of our bigger goals. When this happens, our ability to prioritize suffers and our performance diminishes. Because action addiction is a mental state, we can overcome it through the practice of mindfulness. Mindfulness training improves focus and impulse control. It provides you with the mental strength for observing, reflecting, and doing important things, rather than just doing a lot of things.[22] In addition, we can carve out time for focus.

Create Focus Time

Our propensity to multitask and get caught in action addiction are increased with the continuous rise in and reliance on technology. But we have a choice in how we respond to technology. With a well-trained mind, we have a choice of what to focus on and the ability to avoid multitasking and action addiction. We also have the choice of planning our time and activities in a way that facilitates getting important things done.

Arne Sorenson, CEO of Marriott, plans uninterrupted hours of focused meetings with members of his team with no phone, computers, or other devices in the room. Jean-François van Boxmeer, CEO of Heineken blocks out a percentage of his time specifically for tackling important tasks. Dominic Barton, global managing partner of McKinsey & Company, takes a long run every day to process, reflect, and synthesize. In each case, these exceptionally busy leaders are putting aside specific blocks of time designed to increase their focus. For them, disciplined focus is a mantra for productivity. They understand that if they do not plan time to do focused work, they easily end up doing everything that is urgent and not what's important.

Cal Newport's book *Deep Work* describes the need and techniques for focused work for leaders.[23] When we dedicate our full attention, pointedly and without distraction, to any task, we are more productive. We also experience a greater sense of fulfillment as well as a comforting sense of being in control. This experience carries over into the rest of the day, decreasing stress and increasing focus and calm.

Focus time often conflicts with an always-on organizational culture. Focus time therefore requires some principles, discipline, and preparation. To secure focus time, the following steps can be helpful:

- Block out focus time on your calendar. Rather than prioritize what's on your schedule, schedule your priorities.

- Block out one hour—or more—every work day of the week, the month, and the year. Be disciplined about utilizing this hour for focus work. Schedules can change, but do what you can to avoid having other people claim your focus time for meetings.

- Plan your time during the hours when you are most focused. Save email and other activities for times when your focus is lower.

- Share the importance of focus time with your peers and colleagues. Make your closest associates allies in protecting your (and their) focus time.

- As you start your focus time, define clear goals for how you will use it. Then stick to these goals. Don't open your email (unless that is the goal of your focus time), don't respond to texts, don't participate in any other unfocused activities.

- Eliminate distractions. Close your door or find a space where you will not be interrupted. Put your phone away. Keep your desk clean and free of any distractions.

- The challenge is not only external distractions; internal distractions can be even stronger. Other issues may be pushing their way into your consciousness. Compartmentalize them. Right now, you're doing more important things.

- While you're in your focus time, be disciplined. Be disciplined about staying focused, so that you get the most out of the time. Do not give in to a dopamine craving. As much as you may feel like checking email or messages, refrain from it.

All the above strategies have been demonstrated to be highly effective in enhancing performance and well-being. But as simple as they may sound, without having a well-trained, focused mind, they are challenging to implement. The true foundation of greater focus is a disciplined daily practice of mindfulness.

Mindful Focus Practice

Focus is the core of self-leadership. Without it, your mind is like a boat without a rudder. Training your focus through daily mindfulness practice will enhance your ability to be more focused during daily work. The following are instructions on how to do this (see "Training for Mindful Focus"). The practice has four primary instructions: A for anatomy, B for breath, C for counting, and D for distractions. For ease of practice, download the app that you can find in appendix A.

Training for Mindful Focus

1. Set a timer for ten minutes.

2. **Anatomy:**
   - Sit on your chair, comfortably, with a straight back and relaxed neck, shoulders, and arms. Close your eyes and breathe through your nose.
   - Allow your entire body to relax. Allow your mind to relax.

3. **Breath:**
   - In a relaxed way, direct your focus to your breath and observe the experience of breathing in and breathing out.
   - Focus on your breathing in a neutral way, without controlling it and without trying to make it different. Simply notice your breath as it is.

4. **Counting:**
   - To help you focus on your breath, count at the end of each exhale. Slowly count up to ten, and then backward to one.
   - If you lose track of the count, start at one again.

5. **Distractions:**
   - You will get distracted. In this practice, a distraction is anything that is not your breath or your count. It could be sounds, feelings, thoughts, or bodily sensations. Whatever distraction you encounter, consider it a friend, reminding you to go back to your breath.
   - When you get distracted, be aware of it, and gently return your focus to your breath.

6. When the timer sounds, let go of the training.

In an always-on, distracted world, we shift between tasks constantly. But focus is critical to us as leaders, to improve both our effectiveness and our productivity. With enhanced focus, our self-leadership is strengthened. All the tips and strategies presented in this chapter will help you strengthen your focus—and as a result, improve your outcomes. The next chapter builds on the foundation of focus by examining how selflessness—letting go of ego—is essential in leading yourself effectively.

Quick Tips and Reflections

✓ Commit to practice mindful focus training on a regular basis, as recommended in the app (see appendix A for information).

✓ Take *Harvard Business Review*'s "Mindfulness Assessment" (https://hbr.org/2017/03/assessment-how-mindful-are-you) to assess your level of focus and awareness.

✓ Record what impacts your focus and how it changes throughout the day; make a commitment to change one thing to enhance your daily focus.

✓ Commit to being more intentional about how you spend your time, and whatever you do, do it with a calm, clear, relaxed focus.

✓ Block focus time in your calendar and determine when and how you can mindfully "disconnect" to enhance openness and creativity.

4

Selfless Self-Leadership

S elflessness is the only appropriate response to knowing that our 'self,' our ego, is a mere product of our imagination," said Steven Worrall, managing director of Microsoft Australia. He is spot on. We have no fixed and solid self. This is a neurological, biological, and psychological fact. Instead, all we have is a brain that constantly refers to ourselves, creating the illusion of a fixed and solid self.

Over the past thirty years, psychologists and neuroscientists have searched for the brain's control center—the one place where orders come from, the center of our ego, our "I," our true "self." Despite there being billions of neurons in the brain, no control center has been identified as the essence of an individual or a self.[1]

From a scientific point of view, we appear to be an amazing collection of extremely complex systems and processes. Despite having no control center, we're neurologically disposed toward the illusion of having an inherently existing self. We tend to experience ourselves as clearly defined, fixed entities with specific characteristics and properties. But according to leading researchers, in reality, the ego is a creation of our imagination.[2] The ego is a constantly self-referential voice that creates the impression of a solid, stable, and inherently existing *I* that runs the show.

In truth, though, it's just a transitory self-image that changes through neurotransmitters, hormones, and synaptic reactions.

To explore this idea further, take a moment to reflect on your experience with the awareness training introduced in chapter 2. When you were observing your thoughts, who was doing the observation? If you're not your thoughts, then who exactly are you? Take some time to think about these questions and consider the ramifications.

To be clear: this doesn't mean you don't exist. Rather, it means you don't exist in the way you think you do. If this sounds strange, then test it out for yourself. When you're training open awareness and you notice a sensation somewhere in your body, see if you can pinpoint what part of you is having the sensation. At some point, you'll discover what many people have realized—it's impossible to find exactly what part of you is experiencing the sensation. Instead, you'll find a lot of processes. There will be thoughts, feelings, perceptions, and sounds, but you won't be able to localize the owner of the sensation. The logical conclusion is, you're not as clearly defined as you thought.

This may seem strange, but if there's no specific owner of any experience, then it opens up a world of possibilities. If our ego is not fixed and is just something we've created, we can change it.

Nothing is fixed. Everything is potential.

The insight that everything is potential and that there is no solid, isolated self means we can redefine ourselves. We can break free of our own limited definitions of who we think we are, and, equally important, who we think others are. New possibilities open up in every situation we encounter. We have the choice to define all people and all situations based on our perspectives, however narrow or expansive they may be. When everything is potential, it offers each and every one of us an abundance of positive benefits. From a leadership perspective, it means we can be more of the leader we want to be—without our fears, defense mechanisms, and self-limiting beliefs getting in our way. This includes regulating our sense of ego, minimizing the traps it creates, and remaining grounded in the face of success.

In this chapter, we look at the illusory nature of ego, the problems it creates, and how self-confident selflessness is a sound approach to more effectively leading yourself.

The Problem with *I*

Ego equals problems. This could be the short conclusion based on various studies conducted on the role of the ego. One study from the University of California found that the more people use the pronouns *I, me, my,* and *mine*, the higher the correlation to coronary heart disease incidence and mortality.[3] Another study found that individuals with depression and anxiety have a higher-than-average use of first-person pronouns.[4] A related study looked at poets and suicide and found a staggering result: their increased use of first-person pronouns was strongly correlated with later suicide.[5] In contrast, a study published in *Psychological Science* found that when we actively start to use other pronouns, such as *we, he, she,* and *you,* and make less use of self-referencing pronouns like *I, me,* and *my,* our health improves.[6]

Let's look at this through a leadership lens. A study from the University of Texas found a clear correlation between leadership positions and the use of pronouns. People with higher leadership positions use significantly more first-person plural pronouns like *we,* as well as second-person pronouns like *you* and *your.*[7] In contrast, people with lower or no leadership status overwhelmingly tend to use the first-person singular pronoun *I* when they speak. The study further found that individuals in higher levels of leadership demonstrate a stronger "others-orientation" in their way of talking. In other words, people of higher power status seemed to demonstrate greater concern with the well-being of the group as opposed to their own well-being, whereas lower power status people demonstrated stronger self-orientation.

Another study analyzed the use of pronouns in all forty-three Australian elections since independence from Britain in 1901. The more candidates used *we, you,* and *us,* the more likely they were to win—and win by a larger margin. Victors used more collective pronouns than their unsuccessful opponents in 80 percent of all elections. Across all elections, victors made 61 percent more references to *we* and *us* and used these terms once every 79 words. Losers only used them once every 136 words.[8] The study again suggests that successful leaders are more others-oriented and have better ability to engage with and speak to the collective identity of themselves and the people they address.

So caring about others not only seems to be part of our nature as presented in chapter 2, it appears to enable us to be healthier and more successful as leaders. Yet it isn't easy. Try this experiment. Set a timer for two minutes. When ready, start a monologue describing your day from when you got up until this moment without using *I*, *me*, *my*, or *mine*.

Go ahead, give it a try.

If you found it difficult, that's okay. In addition to being hardwired for kindness, we are also deeply programmed to look out for ourselves and see things from our own perspective.

Ego and Leadership

In our interviews with senior executives, we asked the question: "Are there any benefits of having a big ego in leadership?" The repeated answer was a resounding "No." The leaders we interviewed recognized many of the downsides of a big ego: it makes you vulnerable to criticism; it makes you susceptible to manipulation; it narrows your field of vision; and it corrupts your behavior and causes you to act against your values. Let's explore these downsides of ego one by one.

Ego Makes You Vulnerable to Criticism

Our ego is like buttons we carry with us that contain ideas about who we think we are and what is important to our sense of self. These buttons can be things like "I am an engaging leader," or "I am a strategic thinker," or "I am a team player." In daily work interactions, these buttons can be pushed by others if they say or do something that goes against our idea of self. When that happens, our ego is triggered. In this way, our ego is like a target we carry with us and, like any target, the bigger it is, the more vulnerable it is to being hit.

Roy Harvey, general manager of EA Sports, had just overseen the launch of the latest version of the video football game, *Madden NFL*, one of the most popular video game franchises in the world. The upgrade was a significant investment, costing many millions. As with all software, first versions have a lot of bugs. With so much at stake, Roy had an entire team detect and rectify over 22,000 bugs before launch. One bug slipped through the cracks and Roy found himself in a meeting with angry stakeholders. They wanted to know how this could have happened.

Roy shared with us how in the moment, his ego felt under attack. He wanted to fight back, blame others, and deflect the criticism. His ego wanted to shout how thorough and diligent he and his team had been. But instead, as he explained to us, he told the stakeholders around the table: "We found and fixed something like 22,358 bugs this year. And we missed one. That should provide perspective for all of us. That's the nature of software. And that's why we have patches and updates." He didn't point fingers; he didn't place blame. Instead, his calm statement of the facts settled people down and refocused the conversation.

Fortunately for Roy, he has been a practitioner of mindfulness for many years. He was able to understand the messages coming from his ego and resist the urge of lashing out or getting overly defensive. He knew that if he responded from a place of a wounded ego, it wouldn't end well. Instead of fueling the fight his ego was putting up, he created mental space between himself and the train of thoughts and emotions coming from it. Using the mindfulness practice of being an observer of his own thoughts, he was able to step back and effectively disengage from the emotions. This allowed him to see the situation with more clarity. He was also able to take responsibility for what had happened and begin more quickly working toward a solution.

In Roy's situation, his ego could have made a bad situation worse. It could have made it personal, driven by fear rather than focused on solutions. His protective ego could have directed the blame elsewhere. Mindfulness training combined with an understanding of ego helped Roy make the best of a bad situation.

Ego not only makes us vulnerable to behaving badly in the face of setbacks and criticism, it prevents us from learning from our mistakes. Our ego has a strong orientation to protect us from harm. But in doing so, it creates a defensive wall around us that makes it difficult to appreciate the rich lessons we glean from failure. It can also make it easy for others to take advantage of us.

Ego Makes You Susceptible to Manipulation

Some years ago, we worked closely with the private finance division of a global bank to instill more mindfulness in their leadership team. One of the senior leaders had a very large ego. When he walked into a room, you could feel the size of it. He had a long list of accomplishments and good reason to be proud. But it was clear to us, and to everyone else, that he took credit for every success and valued himself above the team. It was also clear that when there were problems, he looked for someone to blame. Making himself look good was his primary focus, and he didn't seem to care who he stepped on along the way.

It was obvious to us that others in the organization were aware of his inflated ego. We could see how easily they were able to manipulate him in certain situations. If they wanted a project to go in a certain direction, they would explain to him how it would make him look good—and he would do it. If they wanted to avoid something, they would tell him it would make him look bad—and he would avoid it. They were able to get him to make decisions and take on tasks influenced by their praise or caution.

Because our ego craves positive attention, it can make us susceptible to manipulation. And the bigger our ego is, the bigger the risk of being manipulated will be. An inflated ego makes us predictable, because it drives our behavior in obvious ways. And when people know it, they can play to it and become puppeteers of our actions. When we're a victim of our own need to be seen as great, we end up being led into making decisions that may or may not be good for ourselves, let alone our people and our organization.

Ego Narrows Your Field of Vision

Anish Melwani, CEO of LVMH Moët Hennessy Louis Vuitton Inc., North America, shared how ego can narrow our field of vision because of confirmation bias. He contends that if we bring a big ego to work, it makes us search for, interpret, favor, and recall information in a way that confirms our preexisting beliefs or hypotheses, while giving disproportionately less consideration to alternative possibilities. "Confirmation bias is often about ego," he said. "We all hate to be wrong and we generally want other people to validate our ideas and positions." As Anish described it, we end up seeing things the way we want to see them, and this confirms our belief in what we want to see. It can become a loop that's difficult to disengage from.

Ego narrows our vision and makes it hard for us to see and accept new opportunities. Because of this narrowing vision, we fall victim to the limitations of our own success.

Marshall Goldsmith, coach and author of the best-selling *What Got You Here, Won't Get You There* calls this the "success delusion."[9] Many leaders we've worked with suffer from it. Psychologist B.F. Skinner, the first social scientist to identify radical behaviorism, famously found that dogs, pigeons, and all other animals, including humans, tend to repeat behavior that's rewarded.[10] When rewarded for something once, we unconsciously persist in the behavior that led to the reward, regardless of whether the behavior is functional or dysfunctional. This may sound mundane and simplistic, but it's the basis of the success delusion.

As we rise up the organizational ladder, our success can lure us into thinking that we're great. We tend to believe that we're the sole architects of our success. We subconsciously conclude that our past actions and behaviors led to our success, so those actions and behaviors must be the ingredients of success. As a result, we repeat these ingredients, believing they will bring more success. But there is no causal logic behind this thinking. Instead, it's just our ego confirming biases through rewards and creating the delusion that we know the one way—the right way—to succeed.

The moment we give in to the ego's success delusion, we narrow our vision and limit our potential. The moment we believe that past successful behavior will lead to present and future success, we've stagnated. We become blinded by our own success and fail to question ourselves and our behavior. We fail to see that the world is changing, people are changing, the organization is changing, and the demands on us as leaders are changing, and past action does not always lead to future success.

The success delusion is a crossroads that many leaders face around the age of forty. In our conversations with leaders, this is the age when some start to feel that they are stagnating. They realize that the strategies that got them to where they are will not take them to where they need to go. They must let go of past behaviors and reinvent their way of leading. But this is easier said than done. Keeping our ego in check is not easy.

Ego Corrupts Your Behavior and Causes You to Act against Your Values

Your ego is constantly looking for ways to improve your status and power in conscious and unconscious ways. And although the ego's desire to protect us and ensure our survival isn't inherently bad, if left unchecked, the ego can cause us to act against our better judgment. It can twist our values. It can warp our better natures. And unfortunately, becoming a leader is not always a good thing for our kinder, considerate selves.

Studies have found that power tends to corrupt our behavior. While people usually gain power through traits and actions that advance the interests of others—such as empathy, collaboration, openness, fairness, and sharing—when they start to feel powerful or enjoy a position of privilege, those qualities begin to fade. The more powerful they are, the more likely they are to engage in rude, selfish, and unethical behavior.[11] Studies show that people in positions of power are three times as likely as those at the lower rungs of the ladder to interrupt coworkers, multitask during meetings, raise their voices, and say insulting things at the office. And people who've just moved into senior roles are particularly vulnerable to losing their values compass.[12]

Think of the management teams at Wells Fargo, Uber, or Volkswagen, all of whom have come under scrutiny for unethical behavior. It's easy to look at them and believe they were inherently bad people driven by greed and willing to cause harm to others. But that conclusion is overly simplistic. Remember that human beings are inherently kind. We have positive intentions for one another. But sometimes our intentions are derailed by ego, driving us to take harmful actions. We believe that the members of these management teams did not wake up every morning asking themselves how they could inflict harm on others. More likely, they were in the grip of their ego's desire for more status and power, and they lost touch with their better selves.

When we're caught in the grip of the ego's craving for more power, we lose control. We become slaves of our own ego. And almost unwittingly, we end up doing things that are not aligned with our values. And because we are not always in touch with our true selves and thus our values, it becomes easier to make poor or egoistical choices. This does not excuse bad behavior. Acting in ways that are completely self-serving and causing harm to others is not okay. But with our ego-driven focus of getting more wealth, status, and power, at least we can understand where it comes from. Which, in turn, can help us in reflecting on these examples and, potentially, making better choices.

We're all influenced and easily caught up in our ego's desires. It's just a matter of degree. In the words of Jennifer Woo, CEO and chair of

The Lane Crawford Joyce Group, Asia's largest luxury retailer, "Managing our ego's craving for fortune, fame, and influence is the prime responsibility of any leader." Not only does managing the ego make us better and more effective leaders, it also makes us better human beings.

Having a big ego is a significant problem in leadership. It makes you vulnerable to criticism, susceptible to manipulation, limits your vision, and corrupts your behavior. Unfortunately, getting to the top can often make the situation worse because of a phenomenon known as the "CEO bubble."

The CEO Bubble

A newly appointed CEO we interviewed shared an interesting observation. He noticed that since his promotion, people had started laughing a little harder at his jokes. He also noticed that people seemed to generally agree more often with his comments in meetings and the once-candid conversations he used to have with his pre-promotion peers were now not so candid. When offering thoughts and suggestions, his reports now seemed to hold back. But of course, rising to the top doesn't actually make us funnier or smarter.

Instead, as we rise in ranks, we acquire more power. And with increased power comes increased insulation. We end up in a bubble, where we're praised and supported more often than before. Hal Gregersen, executive director of the MIT Leadership Center at Sloan School of Management, says too many CEOs and executives are in a bubble, one that shields them from the reality of what's happening in the world and in their businesses.[13] The result is that you can get caught up in a space that's not very healthy for you or for your organization.

When we're in the CEO bubble, we don't get the tough feedback we need to improve our thinking and behavior. Also, we don't reap the benefits of the 360-degree perspectives that a quality team can provide. Consequently, we lose wisdom and perspective. We become more narrow-minded. And we're left with a version of reality that's of our own making. As a result, we may slowly stagnate in our beliefs and strategies. If we don't consider the perspective of others, we're left to unconscious biases, our own inflated sense of self, and fixed beliefs. To be most effective, we must break free from the bubble.

But breaking free from an inflated ego can be hard. It requires selflessness and courage. The first step toward breaking free is to continually question yourself. Question your behavior, your beliefs, and your strategies. Look at yourself in the mirror every day with an open mind. Never assume that you have found the eternal answer to being a leader, because you haven't. Leadership is about people, and people change every day. If you assume you have found the universal key to leading people, you've just lost it.

The next step is to support, develop, and work with people who won't put you in a self-inflated, egocentric bubble. Hire people who are smarter than you are and who have the confidence to speak up when you may be wrong. This, of course, requires that you have the self-confidence needed to respond without ego and fear, a trait we'll touch on later in the chapter. Less self-confident leaders tend to hire people less smart than themselves; people they can influence and manipulate. Anish Melwani shared with us how he hires people based on their courage to speak their opinions. People who have the courage to disagree with the boss help develop a culture of positive dissent and productive openness. This can lead to greater collaboration, improved results, and increased opportunities for self-growth. A significant step in creating this sort of openness—and applying selfless self-leadership—is grounded on fostering a true sense of humility.

Humility

Great leaders are generally not the types of people who publicly pat themselves on the back and trumpet their accomplishments. On the contrary, we've found that great leaders exude a strong sense of humility. Humility and selflessness are closely linked. You cannot be selfless without humility, and humility without selflessness is false humility.

Humility is not just a noble attitude; it's a realistic perspective on individual worth. Because of the delusion of success, we as leaders can create unrealistic perspectives on how much we really matter in the bigger picture. In the scheme of things, even the best CEO is only one out of thousands of individuals contributing to a company's success. Furthermore, the company's success is heavily determined by market trends and large-scale global forces. Any company is merely the result of an interconnected string of events, actions, and intentions.

If you think your company is successful mainly due to your own efforts, ask yourself a few questions: Who trained and mentored you? Who schedules your meetings and manages your calendar? Who built and who maintains the car that takes you to work? How many people in your organization are doing a great job every day? We're so interconnected with others, it's impossible to know who caused or created what. Understanding this reality awakens a healthy sense of humility. And with this humility, a sense of gratitude to those who contribute to our success comes naturally. In this way, humility helps us better recognize and acknowledge others' contributions. It makes us more appreciative and attentive to others, which increases interconnectedness and engagement.

Serhat Unsal, CEO of the global company Dawn Foods, has noticed how humility becomes increasingly important the higher you rise in position or rank. "As a leader," Serhat explained, "your end goal is to succeed as a team. This means you need to give other smart, ambitious people the space to contribute." The more senior you are, the more senior your reports are. And the more senior your reports, the more they expect respect and inclusion. In this case, your role is to be more of a listener and less of a manager. Your role requires being open to various viewpoints and includes a willingness to act as a catalyst for others' success. To do so, you must be able to put your ego aside and embody a genuine sense of humility.

Edouard-Malo Henry, group head of compliance of global bank Société Générale, shared with us how humility is a quality that must be developed by regularly bringing it to mind. Before he enters a meeting, he has created a habit of mentally recognizing the efforts and skills of everybody in the room. "When considering how many hours of work, good intentions and experience my colleagues bring to the table at any meeting, I am humbled and grateful. This short recognition enables me to show up more humble and appreciative and better at listening rather than providing answers."

As Edouard-Malo explains, humility is an inner process. And when exercised, it shapes how you show up. Humility is a direct way of keeping your ego in check and developing a healthy sense of selflessness. It does not mean completely dissolving the self, because every leader needs to have a healthy sense of self and a healthy self-confidence.

Self-Confident Selflessness

A general concern many leaders have about the concept of selflessness is that it will make them pushovers. That's not necessarily the case. To be successful, leadership selflessness has to be combined with strong self-confidence. We call this combination self-confident selflessness. Self-confident selflessness makes you stand up and follow through with your ideas, while not being hampered by ego-attachment and pride.

Self-confident selflessness is illustrated in figure 4-1. We covered the details of each quadrant in chapter 1, but a brief review may be helpful.

In this matrix, you have selflessness versus selfishness on one axis. On the other axis, you have self-confidence versus diffidence. In the lower left quadrant, you lack self-esteem, yet you're overly concerned with your own interests—it's all about you. In the lower right quadrant, you have a strong sense of self-confidence but you're driven by selfish goals and desires. In this quadrant, leaders can achieve great results, but at a steep cost to team satisfaction and loyalty. In the upper left quadrant, you're a

FIGURE 4-1

The selflessness matrix

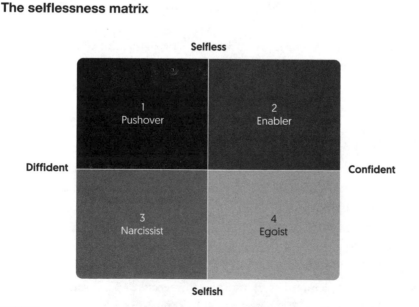

pushover, with a strong possibility of burning out or being taken advantage of by others.

The upper right quadrant represents the sweet spot—a powerful combination of selflessness and self-confidence. You're not worried about being taken advantage of, because you have the confidence to speak up for yourself if needed. At the same time, you have a strong focus on the well-being of your people and organization. You lead for the long run. You don't worry about receiving praise. It's not about you—your ego doesn't crave recognition. Therefore, you give credit for achievements to others. This allows you to bring inspiration and inclusion. As an enabling leader, your mission is to contribute to the greater good.

Research by Jeremy Frimer and Larry Walker from the University of British Columbia found that the most successful leaders were the ones who had a healthy balance between selflessness and confident care for themselves.[14] Calling selflessly self-confident leaders "moral exemplars" and "ethical giants," Frimer and Walker examined the motivations and "personal strivings" of award-winning leaders. Through extensive assessment and analysis, they found that the most successful exemplars lead through what they termed "enlightened self-interest." That is, they lead with both strong personal ambition *and* strong moral conviction—two seemingly contradictory motivations. Previous studies had seen "the self's basic interests being fundamentally at odds with the person's moral compassions," but Frimer and Walker found that the two worked together to create "brilliance with wisdom" and "power with conscience"—the ultimate combination for exceptional leadership.

Leadership is a journey, and we all change as we go through it. If we don't change, we don't progress. The same is true when it comes to selflessness. Our interviews indicate that many senior leaders have a strong combination of selfless self-confidence, but that they have not always been that way. Selfless self-confidence is a balance that most of the leaders we interviewed found that they needed to develop over the years. Many of them indicated that the self-confidence had always been there, but balancing it with selflessness had been an ongoing journey. The starting point is valuing selflessness not just as something good to do for others but as something inherently good for you as a leader—something that you can do to be healthier, happier, and more of the leader you want to be.

Training Selflessness

Selflessness can be realized and cultivated with training. It's a realization and attitude that we can enhance due to neuroplasticity—our ability to shape our neural makeup. As a result, the more we experience life from a selfless perspective, the more selfless our mind becomes. The goal is to train our mind so that selflessness becomes our default mode. Here's a short practice to get you started (see "Training for Selflessness"). It begins with the basic mindfulness practice you did in the previous chapter and builds from there.

Training for Selflessness

1. Set a timer for five minutes.

2. Sit on a chair, comfortably, with a straight back and relaxed neck, shoulders, and arms. Close your eyes and breathe through your nose.

3. For a minute, direct your full attention toward your breathing. Simply observe your breath neutrally. Don't try to control it. Allow your mind to stabilize and settle.

4. Now, let go of the focus on the breath and instead focus on identifying the observer.

5. Who is observing the breath? Where is this sense of "I"? Can you find it? Is it solid? Is it changing? Is it static and in the same place all the time?

6. Continue to search for the observer until the timer goes off.

7. When the timer sounds, let go of the training.

8. Take a moment to reflect on your experience.

Quick Tips and Reflections

✓ Commit to practicing selfless training on a regular basis as recommended in the app (see the appendix for information).

✓ Every time you use, or are about to use, a self-referential term, pause and consider whether using a more inclusive term would be beneficial.

✓ Consider ways in which your ego gets in the way of your leadership, and think of one concrete step to overcome its limitations.

✓ Consider what "humility" means for you; if it is a value, consider one thing you will do to cultivate greater humility in your leadership.

✓ Consider where you are in the selfless leadership matrix and where you would like to be; commit to one action that will help you move in that direction.

5

Lead Yourself with Compassion

The airline industry has got it right: when there are pressure issues in the cabin, they instruct us to put on our own oxygen mask first—to help ourselves—before helping others. This wisdom is equally important in leadership. In shouldering the responsibility of leadership, we take on a great deal of pressure. Self-compassion helps us lead ourselves in a way that mitigates this pressure and increases our leadership performance.

However, in our research and interviews, we have found that many leaders are rather tough on themselves. Their minds can go into a mode of negative self-talk and self-judgment. Noelene Mason, principal of Malibu School, a large special education school in Australia, shared with us how the first years she was in leadership roles were hard. "In my early years, I felt as though the only feedback I received was about my deficits, where I needed to improve, and what I was doing wrong. My perception of myself was that I was good but never good enough. I always felt I had to put on a mask, a coat of armor, because I had to appear strong and in control all of the time."

Noelene's problem wasn't that she was an incompetent leader. In fact, she kept progressing in her career and being offered more senior positions. Her challenge was her own internal voice, telling her that she wasn't fully competent. But as we discussed in previous chapters, the voice in our head is just a voice, and if we decide to ignore it, it loses its power over us. And this is what Noelene came to realize. Through a mindfulness training program, she learned to stop listening to the negative self-talk, to have stronger self-acceptance: "Today, I am allowing myself to be who I am, and I find I am enjoying being with other people. And people seem to enjoy more being with me. Letting go of my inner voice, has made me a much better leader."

Our research has shown that on average, higher-ranking leaders have greater levels of compassion for themselves than midlevel managers. From our interviews and discussions, it appears that they've had the discipline of caring for themselves and sustaining high performance throughout their career progressions. Our conclusion: leading yourself with compassion is a vital enabler for successful leadership.

Many people dismiss self-compassion, because they think it conflicts with their ambition or hard-driving attitude, which are qualities that they believe have made them successful. But being self-compassionate doesn't imply that you shouldn't be ambitious or push yourself to succeed. Self-compassion is about how you care for yourself to better succeed.

Self-compassion involves taking care of your body and your mind. This chapter includes strategies to help you sleep better, digitally disconnect, and take mental breaks. We then look at how to maintain more balance in your mind, increase kindness, and leverage the power of purpose.

Care for Your Body and Mind

Taking care of your mind and body includes the basics of finding time to exercise and making a commitment to a healthy diet. Being physically active and eating properly are foundations for high performance and improved well-being—a fact well understood by most leaders. Through our own research, we've found three additional factors critical to a healthy mind that are less appreciated by busy leaders: the need for quality sleep;

the need to disengage from compulsive technologies; and the need to make time for mental breaks.

Get Enough Quality Sleep

Although all aspects of good health are important, our research shows that sleep is often one of the first "luxuries" compromised by leaders. When there are not enough hours in the day, they steal some from the night. Many leaders stay up late to catch up on email or finish other tasks. According to our research, this tendency is widespread, regardless of gender and level of leadership. We found that 68 percent of leaders get between five to seven hours of sleep per night, with only 28 percent getting seven or more hours of sleep on a typical night.

This is a problem. Sleep is not a luxury.

According to the American National Sleep Foundation, adults between the ages of sixteen and sixty-four should be getting between seven to nine hours of sleep per night.[1] If they don't, they pay a steep price. Scientific studies have conclusively shown that sleep deprivation is a key issue underlying a long list of mental and physical disorders.[2] Even light sleep deprivation has been proven to negatively impact logical reasoning, executive function, attention, and mood.[3] Worse, severe sleep deprivation can lead to depression, anxiety, and symptoms of paranoia.[4] In the long run, sleep deprivation is a main contributor to the risk of dementia and Alzheimer's disease.[5] Now the most surprising fact: while humans can survive multiple weeks without food and up to a week without water, they can only go a few days without sleep.[6]

Our research found that leaders with a disciplined approach to self-compassion sleep more. In fact, the majority of C-suite executives we spoke with get seven to eight hours of sleep per night. Despite intense travel and demanding schedules, they are all disciplined about not compromising on sleep. Some block their calendars from a certain time in the evening. Others have asked for support from their spouses, executive assistants, and colleagues to keep a healthy sleep regimen.

It used to be a badge of honor to brag about how few hours you sleep, but many of the leaders we interviewed share openly with their colleagues that they get sufficient sleep. Take a moment to reflect on your own sleep habits. Do you get seven or more hours per night? If not, consider testing how getting more sleep could enhance your performance and well-being. For the next two weeks, make a commitment to yourself to get at least seven hours of sleep every night. After two weeks, see if you notice any difference in your well-being and focus.

Of course, it's one thing to make a commitment to go to bed early and another to actually get seven or more hours of quality sleep. For many leaders, going to bed is only part of the problem. The other part is getting high-quality, restorative sleep. Fortunately, a good night's sleep is not a random event; it's a trainable skill. The following are some guidelines for improving the quality of your sleep:

- **Catch the melatonin wave.** Go to bed when you're just starting to feel drowsy (usually between 10 p.m. and 11 p.m.). Melatonin, a natural hormone released from the pineal gland deep inside your brain, makes you relaxed, drowsy, and ultimately fall asleep.[7] If you learn to notice it and go with its flow, you'll enjoy falling asleep and have better-quality sleep during the night.[8]

- **Avoid screens.** Turn off TVs, smartphones, and laptops at least sixty minutes before bed. Why? Each of those screens emits high levels of blue light rays.[9] That blue light suppresses your pineal gland, and, in turn, the production of melatonin.[10] It's almost like your brain reads the blue light as if the sun is still up, when in reality the sun has probably been down for hours and you should be sleeping.

- **Enjoy only perceptual activities sixty minutes before bed.** Too much thinking is another enemy of late-evening drowsiness. Conceptual activities like intense conversations, replying to emails, working, or reading can arouse your attention and suppress your natural sleepiness. In contrast, perceptual activities like doing the dishes, going for a walk, or listening to music can help you better catch the wave of melatonin as it rises.[11]

- **Avoid eating two hours before bed.** Most people know to avoid caffeine in the hours before going to bed, but in fact, eating anything can negatively impact your ability to get good sleep.[12] Eating activates the flow of blood and sugar in the body, keeping your body and mind alert and awake. Not the ideal state for a good night's rest.

- **Practice two minutes of mindfulness when you go to bed.** Practice focus training while sitting on your bed, followed by two minutes of relaxed breathing while lying on your back, then turn on your side and let go of your thoughts and concerns.

As you begin to enjoy the benefits of more and better sleep, consider ways you can wean yourself from the compulsive interruptions created by today's most popular technologies.

Practice Disciplined Disconnectedness

The rise of technology in our lives puts us at serious risk of shattering our ability to be present with other people and diminishing our well-being. The dopamine rush released when checking texts, emails, or social media on our phone, tablet, or computer drives us to compulsively check these devices. Without thought or plan, we click through messages, update our status, or read the latest irrelevant factoid. To better understand the scope of the problem, consider the following statistics from Deloitte's annual "Global Mobile Consumer Survey":[13]

- The time it takes for us to first pick up our phones in the morning continues to shrink—more than 40 percent of respondents check their phones within five minutes of waking up.

- During the day, we look at our phones forty-seven times on average.

- Once the day is over, more than 30 percent of professionals check their devices five minutes before going to sleep—and about 50 percent of professionals check their phones in the middle of the night.

- During leisure time, 89 percent of respondents check their phones, 93 percent while watching TV and 87 percent while talking to family and friends.

Keep in mind what we noted in chapter 3: your prefrontal cortex actually shrinks the more often you let yourself be interrupted by disruptive technologies like instant messaging, email, and social media. The fact that we actively choose to check our phone while talking to family and friends indicates that it has indeed become compulsive behavior. If you're wondering whether this applies to you, try this quick test. Turn off your phone and leave it off for the next two hours. While it's off, notice how often you feel the desire to check it. How does it feel to be disconnected? Are you feeling a little anxious? If not, you're a rarity in today's hyper-connected world. If so, you're like most leaders—too strongly tethered to today's most distracting, addictive tools.

Our compulsive phone habits impact our social relations both at work and at home. Sherry Turkle, professor of the Social Studies of Science and Technology at MIT and author of the bestselling *Alone Together*, has found that the mere presence of a phone during a conversation creates a "distance" between the people attending a meeting or taking part in a social activity.[14] Even if the phone is not used—and even if it's lying face down—it impacts the quality of social interaction. This raises a number of important questions for you as a leader. How often do you have your phone on the table in front of you when you have a one-on-one conversation? How often is it visible during meetings? How often do you hold or use your phone when you're with family and friends? If you're like many people, the answer to all these questions is "too often."

We stand to gain by assessing and redefining how we let technology influence our work and life—especially in terms of when we're connected and when we're not. Harvard Business School professor Leslie Perlow, author of *Sleeping with Your Smartphone*, conducted an in-depth study of the effects of digital disconnection at Boston Consulting Group, a global management consulting group. Even in such a fast-paced and high-pressure environment, the study showed that the consultants who disconnected from their mobile devices for a few hours every week experienced better internal communication, increased learning, and improved delivery to their clients.[15]

In today's business environment, disconnecting requires discipline and the application of a few basic principles. The following are a few tips for disconnecting from compulsive technologies and more compassionately leading yourself:

- Define phone-free zones at home and at work.

- At work, keep your phone out of sight when you're engaging with others.

- When you're sitting at your computer, keep the phone out of sight so it doesn't trigger compulsive checking. Or simply turn it off for periods of time.

- At home, find a hidden location for your phone; a place you can keep it without it attracting your attention.

- Treat your bedroom like an airline flight cabin. On a flight, your phone must be in "airplane mode" or turned off. The same should go for your bedroom.

As leaders, much of our success at work—and in life—depends on how well we're able to engage with people, including our colleagues, employees, customers, and suppliers. We need to both hear them and influence them; understand them and guide them. By shutting off compulsive devices that steal our attention, we not only free ourselves from the control of technology, we strengthen our personal and professional interactions in a way that improves relationships and accelerates success.

Take Time for Mental Breaks

Much like a good night's sleep, taking regular breaks is seen by many leaders as a "luxury." But in reality, taking breaks is an impactful, simple, and pleasant way of increasing your focus and lengthening your attention span. Air-traffic controllers, more than most professionals, understand the importance of focus and attention. Sitting in their control towers, literally watching over thousands of lives, there is no room for distractions. To maintain this superhuman level of attention, air-traffic controllers are legally required to take fifteen-minute breaks every hour.

In a 2013 *Harvard Business Review* article, "To Strengthen Your Attention Span, Stop Overtaxing It," best-selling author Daniel Goleman describes the importance of breaks to maintain mental performance throughout long working days. "Top performance requires full focus," he wrote, "and sustaining focused attention consumes energy—more technically, your brain exhausts its fuel, glucose. Without rest, our brains grow more depleted. The signs of a brain running on empty include, for instance, distractedness, irritability, fatigue, and finding yourself checking Facebook when you should be doing your work."[16]

Chris Schmidt, CEO of Moss Adams, a US-based accounting firm, takes short mental breaks between every meeting or big task. During these breaks, he gazes on the Seattle-area mountains through his office windows for a minute or two, thinking of nothing. This helps him continually refresh his attention during long, stressful workdays.

Many of us are so busy that we forget to take a break. Often, the only break we do take is for lunch. And even that "break" is often only the minutes it takes to grab food and bring it back to our desk. Take a moment to consider two quick questions: How often do you take breaks during a work day? What keeps you from taking more breaks? Interestingly enough, the main barrier between ourselves and taking breaks is not our organizations. In fact, most organizations recognize the value of breaks—many even encourage them.

It turns out that the greatest enemy of breaks is most often ourselves. Here are a few steps for making the most of what little time you have for taking mental performance breaks throughout your workday:

1. Let go of your work activities. Close your eyes or keep them open, whichever you prefer.

2. Direct your full attention to your breath.

3. For three breath cycles: Breathe in while noticing your breath; breathe out while relaxing your shoulders, neck, and arms. Breathe in while focusing fully on your inhale; breathe out while focusing on the exhale. Breathe in while enhancing the clarity of your attention; breathe out while maintaining clarity.

4. Let go of the exercise. Return to your work with renewed relaxation, focus, and clarity.

The benefits of allowing your brain short regular breaks from the stress and rigors of work are numerous. Your brain is re-energized, your mind is more focused and clear, your body is more relaxed, and you break the spell of constant distractions. If you do have to skip breaks, it's not the end of the world. Just remember, the more you take them, the more rested and effective your mind will be. Think of it this way: a day without breaks is for the mind what running a marathon without water is for the body—unnecessarily exhausting.

Taking care of the basic needs of body and mind should be a priority for every leader. Unfortunately, too many of us compromise our health to meet the demands of our jobs. Although we may be able to sustain an unrelenting pace in the short term, eventually not taking care of ourselves will catch up with us. To avoid this fate, be kind to yourself and make self-care a priority. From this foundation, the next step is to cultivate more balance in your mind.

Equanimity—a Mind in Balance

We are all bipolar to some degree. We move up and down a scale between euphoric, elated states and depressed, despondent states, depending on the latest results or news. But it's dangerous to get too high or too low based on daily events. This is especially true if we begin to get attached to the states of euphoria or excitement that success can bring. Attachment of any kind has its downside, but a strong attachment to an elated state often means that feelings like sadness, frustration, and disappointment will come more easily. It's like a pendulum—the farther you swing in one direction, the farther you'll swing back in the other direction. Equanimity is a form of accepting the good just as you accept the bad and vice versa: they're both transitory states that will pass.

Does this mean you need to become someone who doesn't enjoy the ups and downs of life? Quite the opposite. It means you can relish the things you truly enjoy without developing an all-encompassing desire or addiction to those things. It also means you can respond more skillfully to things you don't like without becoming angry or aggressive. Remember, you are only letting go of your *attachment* to pleasant experiences, not the experiences themselves.

This sort of mental balance creates an overall state of contentment and happiness that averages out to be much more positive than having peaks and valleys that are euphorically high or painfully low. It also supports strong self-leadership and people leadership skills.

Equanimity is a mental calmness, composure, and evenness of temper. It is a mind in balance, despite both positive and negative events. In this way, equanimity is the middle ground between attachment and aversion to the events, interactions, and feelings we experience in life. It's the art of viewing life's successes and tragedies as ebbs and flows without getting pulled up or down. Equanimity is an important component of self-compassion and in leading ourselves, because it teaches us to be in balance with things as they are, to be clear minded and accepting of life's vagaries.

To better understand how a balanced mind can inform leadership, we talked with Manish Chopra, a senior partner at McKinsey & Company who has trained extensively on maintaining mental balance. We asked him how equanimity has impacted the way he leads.

"As a leader," he said, "you get your fair share of difficult situations on a daily basis, primarily because other people's difficult situations are brought to you for resolution." This is a reality that all leaders can understand. Everyone's problems become your problems. Manish continued, "Equanimity has helped me find ways to manage difficult situations differently than I did before. So whether it's the loss of a client, a delay in career progression, or a difficult personal situation with a direct report who needs a more empathetic ear—these are all instances that I dealt with differently in the past by being overly reactive. Now, I'm more balanced in each situation and able to provide more thoughtful, effective responses."

We then asked Manish if by becoming more equanimous, leaders lose their taste for business success. In other words, does a balanced mind temper the drive for achievement? "If anything, the opposite has happened," Manish countered. "My aspirations have gone up, not down. I feel more available to myself for trying things that I otherwise wouldn't have attempted before. Building equanimity frees up mind space for other productive pursuits. And with continued practice, effort and output actually go up."

The ability to better manage difficult situations—along with an increased degree of ambition—is a benefit to leaders at all levels. But having a balanced mind is not something you can just believe in. It's not possible to say, "Well, I choose not to be attached to that feeling of being overly elated or excited." You can't talk yourself out of feeling euphoric. If you're feeling elated, that's what you're feeling. Instead, your ability to maintain balance is determined by how you train your mind to respond to different situations in life.

A challenge for all of us as leaders comes when we succeed, for instance, in selling a big order or closing a major deal. We naturally get excited. Unfortunately, after we have been elated for a short time, our mind has a tendency to swing in the opposite direction as the enjoyment wears off. Furthermore, after we have tasted that experience, we crave to feel it again. This is due to the release of dopamine in our brain. It's like trying to drink saltwater to quench our thirst: we just end up getting thirstier.

Another neurotransmitter, serotonin, has a wide-ranging impact on the mind and body, primarily serving to inhibit impulsive behavior and increase relaxation and clarity.[17] Serotonin and dopamine are closely connected. When they're in balance, we can enjoy good food, or a glass of wine, or a big win at work, without becoming addicted. Serotonin offsets the negative effect of dopamine, enabling us to be more resilient in the face of adversity. The more you train yourself to resist automatic impulses, the more balanced your dopamine and serotonin levels become.

This is important, because we as human beings naturally desire things. A study by Wilhelm Hofmann, a professor at the Booth School of Business at the University of Chicago, found that the average adult spends eight hours a day desiring things they don't have in the moment.[18] Our main desire is food. This is followed by sleep, then media use, then sex, social contact, and leisure. We are, indeed, desiring beings. And when we desire, we're by definition out of mental balance, because we're craving something that we do not have. The following are a few tips for working toward increasing balance in your mind:

- When you feel an impulse toward elation or euphoria, pause for a moment to let your mind find balance and grounding.

- Consciously identify the events at work that bring you instant gratification. Now identify the events that bring discomfort. Be aware of your reactions to these tasks, and temper those reactions by purposefully limiting or delaying the gratification of the experiences you like, while more actively confronting the experiences you dislike.

- Train balance by being aware of your reactions to everything you experience: good, bad, and neutral. Notice the experiences you like and those you do not like; situations in which you experience attraction and situations in which you experience aversion.

- Just being aware of these reactions will lead to change. When you become aware of a desire, the desire will lessen as it's replaced by awareness of the desire. When you become aware of resistance, the resistance will lessen as it's replaced by awareness of it. If something is pleasant and nice, you observe it neutrally without giving it more value or holding onto it. If something is unpleasant, you observe it neutrally without wanting it to disappear.

Maintaining a balanced mind—and, by extension, leading yourself with compassion—requires discipline. Discipline is about having the strength to do what is good for you in the long term. Discipline is about avoiding impulsive behavior that generates short-term gratification but in the long run is not healthy or helpful. In this sense, true happiness is not to be in an elevated state of euphoria, but rather to be in balanced state that allows you to accept the ups and downs of life. Being balanced eases self-doubt. It boosts resilience. And it increases kindness for yourself and for others. Having a balanced mind means that you are happy with what you have without clinging to it; that you value success without grasping for it. And that is truly one of the most compassionate gifts any leader can give her- or himself.

Practice Kindness

Sue Gilchrist, regional managing partner for Asia and Australia, of the global law firm Herbert Smith Freehills, has been a senior leader in the legal industry for two decades. In this highly competitive environment, people are trained to be critical, and there's a lot of pressure to be "right . . . always." This feeds into a culture where people work very hard for long hours and strive for perfection. People also tend to ruminate on challenges and assume their decisions or actions will be held up to be judged and criticized. This is a common trait in the legal business, as well as in many other industries.

But, of course, we're all human—and humans make mistakes, plus there may well be more than one "correct" approach to a challenge. When we perceive that we have made a mistake, we often hold on to that mistake, obsessing over it and harshly judging ourselves. We let the inner critic free. This can inhibit thinking and in particular, creative thinking.

The important thing to keep in mind is that this inner critic is self-created; it's a construct of our mind. With a well-trained, compassionate mind, however, we can learn to dismantle this critic and reframe perceived mistakes. Understanding this, Sue supported the implementation of a mindfulness program at Herbert Smith Freehills to help her lawyers enhance performance, lessen self-judgment, and create more self-compassion. Observing her own team, she noticed that the training gave them the insight and tools needed to help overcome their inner critic and reframe perceived mistakes or imperfections in a more productive way. What would normally be a self-critical voice saying, "How could I miss that particular detail?" can be reframed as, "It was important to focus on the substantive arguments at this early stage. We'll get to finessing all of the details next." The benefit of a team working on this together is that the compassion quotient within the team increases along with everyone's feeling of psychological safety.

Reflect for a moment on how you treat yourself when you make a big mistake or experience a setback. If you're like most successful leaders, you're probably pretty tough on yourself. And yet, if you dive into self-criticism, hide in embarrassment, or ruminate for a long time on your perceived shortcomings, it isn't helpful. When things go wrong—and especially when we fail in front of others—we can become our own worst enemy. But with self-compassion, there are other alternatives.

Being kind to yourself is the ability to acknowledge that *you are good enough*. Yes, you are a human being with flaws and imperfection, but you're doing your best. When you make mistakes, it's important to stop and learn from them. But once you've learned the appropriate lessons and done what you can do to fix any negative consequences, it's time to move on. It's time to let go.

Researchers from the University of Arizona conducted a study to find the impact of self-compassion on people who have been through a crisis.[19] "Higher levels of self-compassion," they wrote, "were associated with less emotional intrusion into daily life." In essence, people who are high in self-compassion tend to experience distressing events without becoming overwhelmed or stuck. They view themselves and their actions empathetically, which allows them to see both the highs and the lows of life as part of the human experience. More resilient, they're better able to take responsibility for events and more easily bounce back from a setback.

Self-acceptance, especially of mistakes, is the cornerstone of self-compassion. Take a moment to reflect on how often your inner critic shows up, creating self-doubt and lowering your sense of self-worth. Are there certain situations in which that judging voice is more likely to arise?

Now make a conscious choice to pause the next time your inner critic pops up and try the following steps:

1. Acknowledge that your inner critic has made an appearance.

2. Pause and breathe.

3. Remind yourself that you're doing your best.

4. Pause and breathe.

5. When you're ready, let go of your inner critic and move on.

We all make mistakes. None of us are perfect. But what separates average leaders from exceptional leaders is the ability to quickly move on from life's inevitable missteps.

But the benefits of kindness don't end with defeating your inner critic. Once you commit to caring about yourself, you gain greater capacity to care for the people you lead. And according to research, being kind to others is one of the most effective ways to become happier yourself.

Numerous studies indicate that being kind to others positively impacts our happiness and well-being.[20] This was in direct contrast to popularly held beliefs—which are often amplified by our consumerist culture— that when it comes to happiness, we should focus on ourselves. In an extensive longitudinal experiment, researchers found that doing acts of kindness for others consistently makes people happier than focusing on themselves.[21] The results of this study contribute to a growing research base that supports the benefits of what's termed "prosocial behavior." In striving for happiness, you may be tempted to treat yourself, but treating your colleagues yields even better results.

But let's face it. Being explicitly kind to others is not the norm in many organizations. It goes against the grain of conventional wisdom, which suggests that if we want to feel better, we need to treat ourselves to a nice dinner, a massage, or some new gadget. But these types of self-indulgences provide only short-term relief. This is because, as explained in chapter 2, true happiness always comes from within—from what we *give* to the world. In contrast, fleeting pleasure comes from outside—from what we *get* from the world. When we as leaders treat both ourselves and other people with more kindness, we feel better about ourselves, improve outcomes, and create a more humane culture.

The Power of Purpose

An important aspect of self-compassion is purpose. Developing a sense of purpose in what we do makes us get up in the morning filled with energy, passion, and meaning. A sense of purpose provides the drive we need to carry the responsibility of leadership.

But purpose isn't a given. It's something we must create by finding meaning in what we do day-to-day, month-to-month, and through the years. A great example of that is the story of Nand Chaudhary, CEO of Jaipur Rugs.

Founded in 1978, Jaipur Rugs is a social enterprise that connects rural artisans in India with global markets, empowering impoverished communities and preserving traditional craftsmanship. We asked Nand what he saw as the ultimate role of a leader. He answered instantly: "The main role of a leader is to be connected with oneself and to have a sense of purpose. And from that, to bring people within the organization along on that purpose."

He then offered a personal story. When he was in college, he had a very strict business professor. One day, the professor burst into the classroom, called out Nand by name, and told him to stand. Alarmed, his mind raced, trying to pinpoint exactly what he had done wrong. The professor took out a term paper and told the whole class, "See this boy? He's given the best answer in his paper." The question: What is the purpose of business? Nand's answer: "Business is the creator and preserver of civilization."

Nand has carried this strong sense of purpose from college through decades of business practice. About Jaipur Rugs, he likes to say, "We don't sell carpets; we sell a family's blessing." Today, his organization provides a sustainable livelihood to more than forty thousand artisans across six hundred villages in five states in India. While enormously successful, Jaipur Rugs is an inspiring case study in how a purpose-driven leader can catalyze social innovation, foster a disruptive business model, and support marginalized communities.

Many business experts make the case that purpose is a key to exceptional performance, while psychologists describe it as the pathway to greater well-being. Doctors have even found that people with purpose in their lives are less prone to disease.[22] Purpose is increasingly being touted as the key to navigating the complex, volatile world we face today, where strategy is ever changing and few decisions are obviously "right" or "wrong."

Finding your purpose as a leader is not always easy. Many industries do not have the same inherent "feel-good" purpose like Jaipur Rugs. But purpose should not only be looked for in what the company does. It should also be looked for in what you do. Your way of leading your people has a massive impact on their lives, and with that, the lives of their families. As a leader and as a colleague, you have an opportunity for having big and positive impact on others. And in that, you can look for purpose.

What do you want to bring to the people you lead—and to their families? How can you influence them to be truly happier and more connected to others? How can you help them find purpose in their work and life?

Nand's company Jaipur Rugs does not just sell carpets; it is in the business of creating societal change. You are not necessarily in the finance or consulting or pharma industry: you are in the people-impact industry. You have the power to influence for good.

Ask yourself frequently: What do you want to bring to your people and to your organization? How can you bring more benefit? And as described in the previous section, by treating your people to something positive, you stand to gain happiness for yourself too. It's a win-win.

Training Self-Compassion

Self-compassion is something you can practice and enhance. Do it at the end of any mindfulness practice session you do. It only takes an additional minute. Follow the steps in "Training for Self-Compassion."

Training for Self-Compassion

At the end of a mindfulness practice session, for the last minute do the following:

1. Recall an experience you have had, where you felt deeply cared for and loved.

2. Hold this experience in your mind, without analyzing or thinking about it. Simply sit with the experience that you are cared for.

3. If useful, visualize that you are filled with the love and warmth from anyone that cares for you.

4. To end the practice, repeat these words for yourself: May I be happy, may I be healthy, may I bring happiness to the ones I meet today.

Quick Tips and Reflections

✓ Commit to practicing self-compassion training on a regular basis as recommended in the app—see appendix A for information.

✓ Commit to one thing you will do to take better care of your body and mind (e.g., get better sleep, set up phone-free zones, take mental breaks).

✓ The next time you experience something really good or something really bad, use it as an opportunity to cultivate balance in your mind, as neither type of experience will last.

✓ Make a commitment to be kind to yourself and your "inner critic"; consider ways that you can befriend it or reframe it so it doesn't rule your mind.

✓ Reflect on what purpose means for you and how developing a greater and broader sense of it could be beneficial.

PART TWO

Understand and Lead Your People

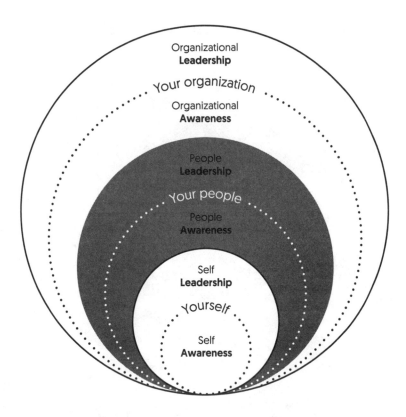

Organizational **Leadership**

Your organization

Organizational **Awareness**

People **Leadership**

Your people

People **Awareness**

Self **Leadership**

Yourself

Self **Awareness**

Catering to the intrinsic motivation of your people is what unleashes the greatest performance. If you help them be happier at work, they will have more energy. If you help them find meaning, they will have more drive. If you help them feel connected, they will have more commitment. And if you allow them to contribute in meaningful ways, they will feel appreciated. When you manage to lead for these foundational human drivers, your people will be more fulfilled, collaborative, and productive.

If you don't lead for peoples' intrinsic motivation, they will at best lack engagement and fulfillment. At worst, they will be unhappy and actively resist. Without a clear understanding of what motivates people, even technically gifted and well-intentioned leaders can unknowingly create an indifferent—or even hostile—work environment.

MSC leadership enables intrinsic motivation. Mindfulness, selflessness, and compassion are universal languages that are understood by everyone. They are innate human qualities in which status and authority do not get in the way of true human connectedness. Mindfulness makes your people feel seen and heard. Selflessness gives your people space to develop and do what they do best. Compassion helps your people feel safe and connected. MSC leadership is the easiest and most effective way to bring out the best in your people.

But just knowing and understanding MSC leadership won't get you far. You must live it, breathe it, and embody it. It must be more than just words or intentions. It must be translated into daily actions and behavior.

The next chapters and their practices will provide you with a clear road-map for leading your people with MSC leadership.

Good leadership starts by really understanding your people. You must understand what they think, what they feel, and what matters most to them. Only then can you enable their engagement, commitment, and performance. But this can be a challenge. To help facilitate your under-standing of others, part 2 opens with a chapter that will deepen your knowledge of human behavior and motivation. Chapter 6 answers the following questions: How can you better understand your people? How can you manage your mind in a way that creates less unconscious bias and helps you see the potential of your people?

The next three chapters in part 2 explore how to apply MSC leadership to the way you lead your people. Chapter 7 looks at how mindfulness helps to create better presence and trust. Chapter 8 explores how selfless-ness helps to get yourself out of the way and give space to your people. And chapter 9 examines how compassion—not to be confused with em-pathy—can create more kind, caring work environments.

6

Understand Your People

To lead your people, first you must understand them. You must understand what matters to them, what they think, and what they feel. Only then can you lead them for more meaning, happiness, and connectedness.

But there are challenges. First, we don't see other people as they are, but as distorted through our own perceptions and unconscious biases. And second, they're not what they say and think, but rather what they experience and feel. Take a moment to test your own unconscious biases. Imagine you receive a message that your company has just hired a new chief technology officer.

- According to your first instinct, is it a man or a woman?

- How old is the new CTO?

- What race is the new CTO?

- How tall is the new CTO?

- What car is the new CTO driving?

Did you imagine that the new CTO was a short Brazilian woman in her sixties, driving a big Ford pickup truck? Or did you imagine a tall Caucasian man in his early forties, driving a Tesla?

We all have unconscious biases. Our minds are constantly creating our perception of reality. And as leaders, that is a problem, because we don't see our people as they are but as we are. To lead others effectively, we must learn to open our mind and avoid mental rigidness and judgment.

To meet the second challenge, we must understand emotions and how to skillfully manage them. Effective leadership is not about addressing reports and team members through their rationality, but instead through their emotions. It's only once we learn to connect with emotions—starting with our own—that we have the potential to become truly inspiring and engaging leaders.

This chapter starts with understanding our biases and how we can overcome them by cultivating a beginner's mind. We will then explore our emotional nature and the dark side of responding with empathy. Finally, we will look at how to manage emotions from an MSC leadership mind. But to start, we look at one of the biggest barriers to understanding others: our unconscious biases.

Unconscious Bias

We all have preconceived ideas, judgments, and biases that affect how we see others. Unconscious bias is a challenge for leaders because it makes us reflexively pigeonhole our people and prevents us from seeing their potential and what really motivates them.

See if you can relate to an experience of a senior director whom we worked with at a global financial services company. She was frustrated with a member of her team who often complained about other departments, the weather, missing information, and so forth. As a result, she had formed a perception of him as a chronic complainer—as a glass-is-half-empty pessimist who liked to focus solely on the negative.

One day, during a team meeting, the individual opened a discussion on how information was shared within the team. Before he could finish his sentence, the senior director shook her head, thinking, "Here we go again." She cut him off and asked to move to the next item on the agenda.

Bewildered, the rest of the team stared at her.

The individual had presented a constructive strategy to overcome a significant issue they were all experiencing. But the senior director dismissed it out of hand. Certain of her preconceived bias, she'd stopped listening as soon as she heard the slightest hint of a complaint. It was only after everyone at the meeting objected that she realized the downside of her own fixed mindset. She'd almost lost a time- and money-saving solution—one that would benefit the entire team—because she couldn't see beyond her initial judgment of this one employee.

Unconscious biases prevent us from seeing what's right in front of us. For example, studies have demonstrated how unconscious biases impact hiring decisions. In one such study, researchers created fictitious resumes to respond to help-wanted ads and randomly assigned either African American– or white-sounding names. Those with white-sounding names received 50 percent more callbacks for interviews and callbacks were more responsive to resume quality for white names than for African American ones.[1]

Unconscious bias prevents us from seeing people as they are and from hearing what people are truly saying. They make us see the world as we are, not as it is. This is an important point. In truth, we don't see others and our world as it is. Our minds create our reality. From a neurological perspective, when we see something for the first time, we create a mental image of it. The next time we see the same thing, or something similar, within split seconds the mind brings up the mental image—and that is what we see.[2] This is called *habitual perception*.

Our mind loves to put people, objects, and ideas into boxes—neat and orderly containers we can understand in an instant. On one hand, this can be very useful. It makes us effective in navigating a complex reality. Life would be overwhelming if we didn't organize and label things. Think about it this way: you wouldn't get much done if every time you saw someone you had to think about who they were and how to relate to them.

On the other hand, this tendency also has a downside. The way you see your people is much less determined by who they are and much more by your history. In other words, your mind—like the senior director's—has programmed you to interpret reality in a certain way. This includes the people who populate your reality. Clearly, such an approach is not beneficial to your ability to truly understand your people. If you see your people in only one way, your expectations of them will be limited.

Consider what unconscious biases you might have about your team members or other colleagues. What fixed ideas are playing in your mind when you meet with them? Do you tend to listen more attentively to men or to women? Do you listen more attentively to younger or older individuals? Take a moment to think of five of the most important people you interact with, and ask yourself what unconscious biases you have of them. Once you acknowledge and understand these biases, you can begin to see individuals and problems from a clearer perspective—from what we call the "beginner's mind." And this allows you to overcome those biases and more effectively engage your people.

The Beginner's Mind

A beginner's mind is the ability to avoid the trap of unconscious bias and habitual perception. A beginner's mind is the ability to see every person and situation—and ourselves—with fresh eyes. To see what is really there instead of what we expect to see.

With mindfulness, we train our mind to see with fresh eyes, moment by moment. We're literally training ourselves to be fully awake and alert to everything we perceive and not to give in to our unconscious biases.

Having a beginner's mind is not easy for anyone, but it can be especially difficult for leaders. Victor Ottati, a psychology professor at Loyola University Chicago, has found that people who perceive themselves as experts in a certain field have an enhanced level of close-mindedness.[3] Social norms allow experts to adopt a relatively rigid, dogmatic orientation. As leaders, we're generally perceived as experts, at least in managing our organizations. This makes us more close-minded—which our people readily accept because of hierarchy. It's a non-virtuous circle.

John Hansen, senior vice president at the LEGO Group, shared with us how, in the early years of his leadership, he was on a learning curve for avoiding unconscious bias. He applied a beginner's mind to his people, especially in situations where friction seemed to arise between him and them: "I found that the friction was most often due to misunderstandings, rather than actual opposing points of views." Out of this insight, he developed a habit to cultivate a beginner's mind to better see things from the other person's point of view: "I found that the most effective way of getting on the same page was to ask questions. Now, it is a habit for me; whenever there is tension or misunderstandings, I try to keep asking questions, rather than giving answers, until there is a shared understanding."

Mindfulness makes us more open-minded.[4] Mindfulness training helps us develop the ability to view other people with fresh eyes. When we train our minds in mindfulness, we open our minds to seeing and experiencing more of what is going on both internally and externally, which helps us recognize when we're putting someone in a box. It also raises our awareness of the stories we create in our mind about other people. Of course, it is essential that we make use of and learn from experience, but we need to balance this experience with an open mind. Facts may have changed, circumstances might be new, and people might surprise us.

To better understand our people, curiosity is an essential and powerful tool. When a team member comes into your office and shares a challenge, force yourself to pause and invite curiosity. Ask more questions; provide fewer answers. And when you ask questions, listen closely to the answers, and then ask more questions.

You can also influence how your people behave through the way you treat them. When we relate to others while expecting them to be a certain way, our expectations can shape their behavior and performance.[5] In other words, if you choose to see your people as high performers, it has the potential to lead to better performance.

Don't be misled by how obvious or simple this idea sounds. One of the most difficult things for us to do as human beings—especially as smart, successful leaders—is to alter our views about people and situations we have experienced before. Especially in stressful situations, we all know how hard it can be to take the time to ask questions rather than shoot out answers, because the mind is wired to identify and process information based on pattern recognition.[6] It takes effort for us to challenge ourselves not to assume that we know what someone is about to say or that we have seen that problem before and the answer is the same. But if we don't, we can miss information and fail to engage our people.

Arne Sorenson, CEO of Marriott, knows that if he is not present and curious about the people he is with, he learns nothing. In addition, it would fail to convey his genuine interest in them. When Arne tours Marriott hotels around the world, presence and curiosity are what help him to truly understand and connect with people in the organization, the overarching business, and its challenges. Being mindfully curious helps him overcome the CEO bubble described in chapter 4.

Make it a habit to ask at least one meaningful question of anyone you're with. Not only will you know that person better, she or he will also know you care. But being curious and overcoming unconscious biases is only part of the journey toward better understanding others. The next step is understanding emotions.

Understanding Emotions

Emotions drive behavior in the office, often much more than we're aware of. To be more effective leaders, we need to become more attuned to our own emotions as well to those of the people around us. This may come as a surprise, but as leaders we're not as rational as we think, and we're not leading rational beings so much as leading their emotions.

We all want to believe that we're rational beings, but we're not. We think we react rationally, but we don't. And this means we expect our people to behave rationally, but they don't. They can't. That's not how we're wired; that's not how they're wired. Understanding this enables better leadership.

Emotions steer much of our behavior and daily decision making, often in unconscious ways.[7] For example, across twenty-six countries, the amount of sunshine recorded on a given day and the stock market performance on that day are positively correlated.[8] If we were truly rational beings, sunshine would not impact how financial markets operate. But it does, and so do many other factors, some that we are aware of but many that we are not.

It's like an iceberg; the majority of the mass is hidden under the surface. And it's this unseen mass that determines what direction the iceberg floats. Similarly, in situations of stress and pressure, people typically act less rationally, because they're driven by emotions such as fear or anxiety.

Paul Zollinger-Read, chief medical officer at the UK-based global healthcare organization Bupa was a medical doctor before joining Bupa. His experience of working with patients, who are stressed and anxious because of their illnesses, has proven very valuable for him in supporting his employees when they are under pressure. "I have learned that when conflicts or collaboration issues arise in professional teams, it is often really not about the subject matter, but rather the emotional state of the people in the team. When we feel under pressure, we act with less mental clarity, and problems arise." Because the problem is not the subject matter, but the emotional state of people, Paul focuses on that rather than on the perceived problem. "Giving people's emotions space, attention, and care, can solve a lot," he shared with us.

To be clear, emotions are neither good nor bad. Emotions have a purpose and are essential for normal human functioning and socializing. And as leaders, it's imperative that we understand the role of emotions, so we can connect with our people, not just on strategy and tasks but also on a fundamental human level. It's only when we create emotional resonance between ourselves and our people that we enable true connectedness. Whether we're aware of it—and whether we want to accept it or not—true engagement happens when people feel connected on an emotional level. Why? Because emotions are both universal and contagious.

Emotions Are Universal

Paul Ekman, professor emeritus at the University of California, San Francisco, and author of the best-selling book *Emotions Revealed*, is arguably the world's leading expert on emotions. For years, he traveled the world while researching human emotions across cultures. He concluded that everyone has five universal emotions—enjoyment, fear, disgust, sadness, and anger—regardless of genes, upbringing, or culture.

In other words, when it comes to emotions, we are all alike.

Ekman spent years developing an "atlas" of emotions to support others in being able to understand and navigate them better.[9] According to this atlas, the five universal emotions can be experienced to different degrees. For instance, anger can move from annoyance to frustration, exasperation, argumentativeness, bitterness, vengefulness, and end in fury. Additionally, our emotions serve an evolutionary purpose. Sadness is a cry for help. Fear makes us flee, freeze, or fight to avoid danger. And anger provides us with the drive to deal with difficult situations.

Ekman also found that our emotions present themselves in our facial expressions through incredibly rapid facial movements. These facial expressions, called *micro expressions*, last somewhere between one-fifteenth and one-twentieth of a second and are exceedingly difficult to consciously control. But although these expressions may only last an instant, other people pick up on them and are influenced by them consciously or unconsciously. Thus we carry our emotions on our face, no matter how much we may try to conceal them.[10] These emotions are expressed through the forty-three muscles in our face. Enjoyment requires the fewest muscles and anger the most.

Emotions Are Contagious

In the office, our mood impacts the moods of those around us, whether we're aware of it or not. Research has found that people in the same meeting end up sharing moods within two hours, regardless of whether that mood is good or bad.[11] It happens because of a group of neurons in our frontal lobe called *mirror neurons*. Mirror neurons are activated when we see others taking action or experiencing a feeling. These actions or feelings are then reflected inside our own brain.[12] When we see someone smile, we're compelled to smile. When a baby laughs, we laugh. In the workplace, mirror neurons connect us through our shared neurological experiences. When one person in the office is criticized unjustly, everyone feels it. When one person receives deserved praise, we all experience it. We're deeply connected in this way, much more than many of us truly appreciate.

As a leader, your emotions have a bigger impact on others than do the emotions of the people you lead. Daniel Goleman, science journalist and author wrote: "The continual interplay of mirror neurons among members of a group creates a kind of emotional soup, with everyone adding his or her flavor. But it's the leader who adds the strongest seasoning. Why? Everyone watches the boss."[13] It's no wonder that a moody leader creates stressful and fearful environments, while a happy leader makes the team see everything in a more positive light. An upbeat leader has the most positive impact on productivity.[14] That's something to smile about.

Leading by recognizing, and acknowledging people's emotions allows for true connectedness and following. The question is, how do we do it? In many leadership training books and programs, the answer is empathy. But empathy can be detrimental in leadership.

The Dangers of Empathy

To enhance engagement, many leaders are told they need to be more empathetic. Empathy is the skill of understanding and recognizing others' feelings and perspectives. As a leader, that skill is obviously important. You cannot effectively lead someone you don't understand. You can only motivate and influence a person when you know how he or she feels. There are good reasons that experts like Daniel Goleman have hailed empathy as a core competency of good leadership. Empathy increases life satisfaction, emotional intelligence, and self-esteem.[15] People with high empathy have larger and more fulfilling social networks, are more social themselves, volunteer more readily, donate more to charity, and are more likely to help others in need.[16]

Empathy is an enduring individual characteristic that's relatively stable over time and across a life span.[17] It can be increased through mindfulness training.[18] Not surprisingly, Amazon's search engine returns more than fifteen hundred books with the word *empathy* in the title, with many of them also including the words *leadership* and *management*. Research into the neurology of empathy, however, provides a more nuanced picture—at least from a leadership perspective. Empathy has some pitfalls that every leader should understand.

Empathy Can Lead to Poor Decisions

Empathy can be a poor moral guide. Yes, you read that correctly. Empathy often helps us do what's right, but it also sometimes motivates us to do what's wrong. Research by Paul Bloom, professor of cognitive science and psychology at Yale University and author of *Against Empathy*, discovered that empathy can distort our judgment.[19] In his study, two groups of people listened to the recording of a terminally ill boy describing his pain. One group was asked to identify with and feel for the boy. The other group was instructed to listen objectively and not engage emotionally. After listening to the recording, each person was asked whether they would move the boy up a prioritized treatment list constructed and managed by medical doctors. In the emotional group, three-quarters of participants decided to move him up the list against the opinion of medical professionals, potentially putting sicker individuals at risk. In the objective group, only one-third of the participants made the same recommendation.

This study demonstrates how empathy triggers our altruistic impulses, resulting in poor judgment that could harm many people for the benefit of one person. As leaders, empathy may cloud our moral judgment. It encourages bias and makes us less effective at making wise decisions.

Empathy Can Hamper Diversity

Studies find that humans empathize more easily with people similar to themselves.[20] Even animals that resemble us receive more of our empathy. Just think of a baby seal with it big round eyes, as opposed to a chicken. Which would you more readily kill and eat? They are both living beings with the instincts to avoid danger and death. Yet we discriminate. We're more likely to kill and eat the chicken with its small, cold eyes and feathers. Similarly, we easily empathize with our neighbor whose car is stolen and less easily with the homeless person on the street.

Much in the same way, we unconsciously empathize with colleagues who are similar to us. We tend to offer them better assignments and better positions, all unknowingly. Empathy can also mislead us to hire and promote those like ourselves. It can create an organization that suffers from lack of diverse perspectives limiting problem solving and creativity.

Empathy Can Be Too Narrow

It's hard to truly empathize with more than one or two people at the same time. Try it. Take a moment to have true empathy with two people close to you. Right now. Feel their challenges. Feel what they feel.

Difficult? Maybe impossible.

The mind—or heart—simply can't hold such different emotions at the same time. Empathy for one can be difficult; for two, even more so. As a leader, we often need to consider the different perspectives and concerns of multiple people at the same time. Empathy is simply too constricting to help us effectively navigate multiple perspectives and concerns.

Empathy Can Lead to Distress

Taking on the suffering and troubles of others is tough. For a moment, imagine being an emergency room doctor, treating victims of traffic accidents, violence, and other horrific injuries. You see people hurt, some even dying. You see the pain of relatives losing loved ones. Hour after hour, day after day.

A well-known reaction to this type of situation is empathetic numbness, simply shutting down our emotional reaction to others. As a result of seeing all this carnage, doctors shut down their emotional life. Too much empathy in some situations can lead to distress. A US study found that 60 percent of medical professionals suffer from or have suffered from burnout. A third of them have been affected to the point of having to take a sabbatical from their jobs.[21]

As leaders, there are many times when members of our team will face tough situations. They may lose a big client. They may not get the promotion they wanted. They may get into a conflict with another member of the team. If we take on the disappointment, anger, frustration, or impatience of the people who report to us, we will become exhausted. Empathy in leadership can drain us.

Empathy Is Fleeting

Empathy can make us passionate and fierce—for a moment. Studies have found that this energy often dissipates before we can take any meaningful action.[22] Feelings are fickle. Social media offers a great example of this phenomenon. A photo of a young refugee child washed up on a European shore inspires millions of Facebook users to donate millions of dollars on the day the photo appears. But in the days that follow, something else has captured our attention, and the refugee crisis is all but forgotten. Few took long-term action.

Empathy is good, but it must be combined with constructive action to have real impact. Empathy without the skill and discipline to stand back, judge objectively, and act accordingly is worth little. Supporting an employee who has had a death in his family is important, but it's the discipline to check in, repeatedly over time, that makes the real difference.

So if empathy is not the answer to skillfully lead emotional beings, what is? The answer is MSC leadership.

Managing Emotions with MSC Leadership

Emotions are just energy in motion, in our body and our mind. There is nothing inherently good or bad, positive or negative about emotions. When we're mindful, we're aware of these emotions—this energy—as it plays out during the day. Being aware of these emotions is the first step to managing them.

A natural human reaction to emotions is to either suppress them or act them out. Suppressing our emotions is like trying to hold down the lid on a boiling pot of water. At some point, it will boil over. And in the process, it drains our energy and narrows our perspective. Acting out our emotions, whether aggressively or passive-aggressively, might feel good in the moment, but in the long run, it usually leads to disappointment, regret, or shame. Think of emotional suppression and acting out as being on opposite sides of a seesaw. Putting your weight on either end throws everything off balance.

Because emotions are fueled by our reactions to them, the greater our reaction, the more energy our emotions build. The mindful approach to emotions is to cut short the reactions of suppression or acting out by developing the ability to embrace emotions as they arise. This means looking our emotions in the eye and not reacting to them. Facing our emotions requires courage and mental strength, the courage to endure the discomfort of raw emotion and the strength to stay with this discomfort as long as it lasts.

This in turn requires a healthy level of selflessness and nonattachment to our emotions. If we can distance ourselves from our emotions, we can observe them more objectively. With training, observing our emotions can be like watching a movie: you're not the movie, and the movie is not you. In the same way, your emotion is not you, and you're not the emotion. You may *have* anger, but you *are not* anger. The anger is just a part of your current experience.

Another core reason selflessness can help us better manage our emotions is because we can avoid taking things personally. When something upsetting happens to us, our ego has a natural orientation to look for someone to blame. But although bad things can happen to us, we are the only one who can control our reactions. You cannot make me angry. You can do something that I react to with anger, but ultimately, how I react is not in your control. I alone can choose how to respond.

If we face emotions neutrally and without ego, they lose their grip. It may take seconds or minutes, but it passes. Managing our emotions like this, over time, dismantles their power.

Mark Twain once said, "I have lived through some terrible things in my life, some of which actually happened." Emotions seem so real, so concrete. In truth, they're like bubbles waiting to be popped. And when we learn to pop them—to manage our own emotions—we're better able to connect with others rather than merely react to their emotions. And instead of having just empathy, we wisely use it to respond with compassion.

Empathy is the tendency to feel others' emotions and take them on as if you were feeling them as well. Compassion is the ability to understand others' perspectives and use that as a catalyst for supportive action.[23] LinkedIn CEO Jeff Weiner describes the difference as follows: "To show empathy is to see someone suffering under the weight of a great burden and respond by putting the same burden on yourself. Compassion is the act of alleviating the person from the burden." The two have very different outcomes.

Helena Gottschling, chief human resources officer of the Royal Bank of Canada, shared with us how she uses emotional resonance and compassion to support her people. In the recent past, a leader came to her, upset about a decision that had negatively impacted him. He felt that he'd been treated unfairly—and he was very vocal about his concerns.

Helena could have responded by justifying the decision, offering a detailed, rational argument for the change. But as she explained to us, "In that moment, I knew he wouldn't have reacted well to an explanation. He was caught in the grip of his emotions."

So instead, she listened intently to him. She wanted to understand his perspective and give him the space to feel heard. She was careful not to offer any indication that she agreed with his arguments, while still demonstrating a genuine concern for his feelings. After giving him time and space to express his frustration, she invited him to take some time to look at the situation from another point of view. "I asked him to consider other people's perspective, to think about the team expectations. Then I assured him we'd follow up after he had some time to reflect." By resonating with the leader's emotions, Helena was able to diffuse a passionate, overly charged situation. Then, by applying compassion, she was able to provide him with a concrete next step toward trying to actively address the situation.

Emotional resonance and compassion are invaluable for leadership and relating to others, particularly in challenging work situations. Rather than taking on others' emotions and problems, with compassion you can help them diffuse the issues and move on.

When we manage our own emotions and manage to resonate with those we lead, we enhance connections and engagement. In subsequent chapters, we will look in greater detail at how to lead others with mindfulness, selflessness, and compassion.

Quick Tips and Reflections

✓ Consider what biases—conscious or unconscious—you may have about people you work with; pick one that you are going to make a conscious effort to overcome.

✓ Challenge yourself to be more curious, ask more questions, and consider other possibilities and perspectives; experiment with having more of a beginner's mind in your daily work.

✓ Consider what emotions you regularly bring to the work environment; reflect on how these emotions influence your colleagues.

✓ The next time you experience a difficult emotion, pause and face it; find the courage to be uncomfortable with the discomfort until you are ready to consider an appropriate response.

✓ Consider the downsides of empathy and how you can be more aware of avoiding the traps you might be susceptible to.

7

Mindful Leadership

We're social beings. We all want to be connected—not just digitally but in fundamentally human ways. Because of this desire, leadership cannot be a transactional activity. It's about creating human connections to strengthen engagement and increase productivity. As leaders, we have a choice. We can utilize the built-in structures of command and control and engrained power dynamics to enhance productivity. Or we can facilitate true connectedness, meaningful work experiences, and human flourishing to enhance engagement, happiness, and, in turn, productivity. The latter is an enormous opportunity we cannot take lightly.

Consider the experience of Narendra Mulani, chief analytics officer, Accenture Analytics. Narendra joined the firm in 1997 with significant experience relative to many of his colleagues, who had been hired directly out of college. At that time, he noted the strong sense of unity and cohesion in the culture. It was as if everyone knew how to operate in the Accenture mindset to the point that people seemed to know what others were thinking.

But now in Accenture—as with most other large organizations—the days of near mind-melding cultural cohesion are long gone. Organizations today are increasingly digital, global, virtual, and in a state of constant change. As a result, human connection and cohesiveness is deteriorating.

Yet, as Narendra told us, "You need something that gives you a common language and allows you to collaborate, trust, and work together, because we all come with such different experiences. It's made me aware that everyone wants to connect. Even in this digital world, personal connections are everything."

We all have an innate urge to feel connected and part of a whole. For leaders, this human need to feel connected is critical to better understanding and managing people. In global teams—despite distance, digitalization, and disruption—mindfulness can become the glue that creates true human connections.

Nathan Boaz and Rahul Varma, global leads of Accenture's leadership development and talent organizations, are implementing global initiatives to help leaders care for their people like family, with a deeper sense of belonging and connectedness. In our conversations with them, they shared their philosophy and strategy. "We are working to develop a truly human experience within the company, where everyone brings their whole self to work. One of the foundations for this is that our leaders show up fully present, attentive and focused, when they engage with their people and teams."

In this chapter, we'll share how you can lead your people with mindfulness to build more effective teams and realize increased levels of engagement, trust, and performance.

The Power of Presence

Some years ago, we worked with a country director of a multinational pharmaceutical company. This director was receiving negative 360 reviews on engagement and leadership effectiveness, putting him under pressure from the company's board. Although he tried to change, nothing seemed to work. His frustration grew, and so he started tracking the time he spent with each of his direct reports. Every time he received feedback that indicated he wasn't an engaging leader, he would pull out his data and state: "But look how much time I spend with everyone!" He didn't know what to do.

As a last resort, he got in touch with us.

We started him with ten minutes of daily mindfulness practice and showed him how to apply it to his everyday leadership activities. After a couple of months, people began commenting on a big change in their experience of working with him. They found him more engaging, nicer to work with, and more inspiring. He was surprised and elated by the results. The real surprise? When he pulled out his spreadsheet that tracked time with direct reports, he saw that he was spending on average 21 percent *less* time with his people.

The difference? He was actually *there.*

He came to understand that being in a room with someone is not the same as being present with someone. He recognized that previously when someone came into his office, he would often be occupied with other activities or thinking about other things. Most of the time, when he thought he was listening to others, he was in fact mostly listening to his own inner voice. This reality was obvious to the people he was with and left them feeling unheard and frustrated.

If you're not familiar with your inner voice, it's the one that often provides a running commentary of what you're experiencing. It often says things like, "I wish he would stop talking." Or, "I know what she's going to say next." Or, "I've heard this all before." Or, "I wonder if Joe has responded to my text?"

To truly engage other human beings and create meaningful connections, we need to silence our inner voice and be fully present.

According to a Chinese proverb, presence is the greatest gift you can give another. It is the intensity of attention you pay to other people. And it greatly determines the outcome of an interaction. Mindfulness stands in stark contrast to being scattered and distracted. A lack of mindfulness comes across as impulsiveness and lack of focus. It doesn't leave a positive impression.

Presence is a universal language with a two-way benefit. According to research from Harvard University, you are happier when you are present, and the ones you are with experience a greater sense of well-being.[1] In leadership, being mindfully present is foundational for connectedness, engagement, and performance.

Bain & Company conducted a large research project to pinpoint key traits of effective leadership.[2] A survey of thousands of employees revealed thirty-three important characteristics, such as creating compelling objectives, expressing ideas clearly, and being receptive to input. But the one trait that stood out as the most essential was *centeredness*—the ability to be mindfully present in a situation so that you can bring your best traits to bear, moment to moment.

In this light, it is not surprising that a study by Professor Jochen Reb of Singapore Management University found a direct correlation between leaders' mindfulness and the well-being and performance of their people.[3] In other words, the more a leader is present with his or her people, the better they will perform.

In our survey, more than a thousand leaders indicated that more presence would be an optimal strategy to overcome such challenges as stress, complexity, information overload, and conflicts. We all know it, but we forget it in the busyness of work.

Like most senior executives, Dominic Barton of McKinsey & Company has a daily schedule of back-to-back meetings. All of these meetings are important, all include complex information, and most require far-reaching decisions. Under these conditions, being present moment to moment, meeting after meeting, is a challenge. But in Dominic's experience, presence is not a choice. It's a necessity. "When I'm with people during the day, I'm doing my best to be focused, I'm present with them," he told us. "Part of this is because I get energy from being with people. But the other part is because if you're not focused, if you're not present, it's discouraging to the other people. They lose motivation. If you're not present, I think you may as well not have the meeting. It can sometimes be difficult to do, but it's always important."

The person currently in front of you does not know what you were dealing with a moment ago, and there's no reason he or she should. It's your responsibility to show up and be fully present to effectively utilize the limited time you have with each person you are with.

Dominic believes being mindfully present requires discipline and skill. It takes discipline to stay on task—not letting yourself be affected by nagging challenges or distracted by mental chatter. And it requires skill to have the mental ability to stay laser focused and present. When he's present throughout his day, he finds it deeply gratifying. Being present becomes the cornerstone to getting the most out of every moment with each person.

Lead with Mindful Presence

Through our many years of working with leaders around the world, we've discovered a number of strategies that answer the question "how to" with respect to leading with mindful presence. The foundation for developing leadership presence is to practice mindfulness, as described in chapters 2 and 3. Mindfulness practice is the mental gym that trains your neural networks for presence.

Just setting an intention to be more present with your people is not enough. Although you may have great intentions, if you have not developed the mental fitness to let go of distractions and overcome the mind's natural tendency to wander, you will have only limited success. After you have cultivated a greater ability to "be here now," here are two ways you can apply mindfulness toward enhancing leadership effectiveness: creating personal "touchpoints" and doing less by being more.

Creating Personal Touchpoints

When Douglas Conant was appointed CEO of Campbell Soup Company in 2001, he identified presence as his guiding leadership principle. After his ten-year turnaround of the company, it received some of the highest employee engagement levels in the *Fortune* 500. In his decade as CEO, Doug developed rituals for physically and psychologically connecting with people at all levels in the company. He did this by explicitly being present. He coined the term *touchpoints* and later wrote a book of the same name. *Touchpoint* is his word for the short moments of presence you can create with each individual you meet at work.

Every morning, Doug allocated a good chunk of his time to walking around the plant, greeting people, and getting to know them. He would memorize their names and the names of their family members. He would take a genuine interest in their lives. He also wrote handwritten letters of gratitude to recognize extraordinary efforts. And when people in the company were having tough times, he wrote them personal messages of encouragement. During his tenure, he sent more than thirty thousand such letters.

To Doug, these behaviors were not just strategies to enhance productivity, they were heartfelt efforts to support his people. He was being truly present, mindfully present. These efforts can't be faked. Faking presence—and concern for others—is worse than not being present at all. People will know. In fact, if presence is inauthentic, it will negatively impact connectedness, engagement, and performance. Therefore, cultivating the right intentions is important.

Before taking action, reflect for a moment on why being present is important to you. How do you think it would benefit you as a person and as a leader? Be clear about your intentions, and then consider what steps for being mindfully present with your people you can bring into your daily ritual. It doesn't need to be a big initiative. Start simple. Begin with yourself, your behaviors, and those with whom you directly engage. You may even be surprised at the extent of benefits that arise simply from being more fully present.

Do Less—Be More

Individuals rise up through the ranks of organizations often because they are good at solving problems. Although this ability is very useful, always coming up with solutions can get in the way of connecting with, engaging, and empowering others. Gabrielle Thompson, senior vice president at Cisco, has found that when an employee comes to her with a challenge, sometimes it needs a simple solution. But often, the problem just needs to be heard: "Many situations simply need an ear, not action. Oftentimes problems don't need solutions, they need presence and time." As leaders, having the ability to be fully present and listen with an open mind is often the most powerful way to solve issues.

As noted in chapter 6, in many instances, mindfulness can help us create the emotional resonance needed for a person to feel heard, understood, and valued. As a leader, our role can simply be to create the safe space for people to air their frustrations and process their problems. Through mindful presence, you become the container in which they have space to process the issue, without you stepping in to solve, fix, manipulate, or control the situation. Presence in itself can help resolve issues. This kind of presence not only has the potential to solve problems but can also create greater connection and engagement.

A simple but effective mindful leadership mantra: Do less—Be more.

The above strategies are specifically derived from a mind perspective, but leadership presence is further cultivated and enhanced when it is embodied.

Lead with Physical Presence

Exceptional leaders influence the environment around them without saying a word. What are you communicating nonverbally with your posture, body language, and gestures? What effect are these physical actions having on your colleagues, your team, or others around you? Think about the way you feel when you're in the presence of colleagues or other leaders who inspire you. How did they carry themselves? What gestures did they use?

Mindful leadership can be solely about being mentally present, but it can also have a physical component. The people we are with know when we're mad, sad, glad, or anxious without us saying a word. This is because emotions, sensations, and reactions manifest themselves physically—whether we like it or not. Our bodies communicate far more to our employees, colleagues, and clients than we might think.

Embodied leadership presence is a sense of being fully present in your body. It comes out of strong mindfulness, combining focus on what you do with awareness of yourself and your physicality. Embodied presence is tangible. When you have it, others feel it. It creates leadership from the inside out. And not through intellectual understanding or by presenting a theoretical model, but by connecting to one's own body.

We've all experienced leaders with embodied presence. It feels like charisma. But really it's a presence based on centeredness. Centeredness increases our physical presence, it opens our perspective to interconnectedness, and it helps us see the big picture. When we're present and centered, we open ourselves to challenges. We can acknowledge and face difficult situations without the noise and frustration created by fear, bias, or judgment. We have heightened awareness, greater perception, and greater confidence.

Loren Shuster, chief people officer at the LEGO Group, explained that when he has very important meetings or presentations, he takes five minutes to ground himself in his body. He visualizes coming fully alive in each cell of his body. As he explained to us, "When you're not grounded, when you're not connected to your body and surrounding environment, you don't have a strong sense of direction or purpose. You're just floating. The smallest thing can distract you. This grounding technique helps me clear my mind, recharge my energy, strengthen my instincts, and calm my emotions." After this five-minute practice, he walks differently, he talks differently. With more gravitas. With more weight. With more vigor. And as a result, he's able to be more fully present mentally *and* physically with those around him. It grounds him in the room like a rock. Gaining this type of physical embodiment—this type of centeredness involves three basic factors: posture, space, and engagement.

When we have embodied presence, our posture shifts. Rather than slouching, crossing our arms, and literally closing in on ourselves, we assume a more balanced, uplifted, open, and inclusive posture. This includes sitting up straight, with our arms open. As shown in many studies, this shift in posture can influence how we think, behave, and communicate.[4] In the same way that we can catalyze qualities like confidence through assuming a bold posture, we can induce qualities like awareness, focus, inclusion, and compassion through an uplifted, dignified posture. The act of sitting up and opening up has a positive effect on the chemistry of our brains. It cultivates our capacity for higher functioning thought processes. It gives us access to wisdom that comes from heightened awareness, compassion that comes from increased openness, and confidence that comes from the strength of vertical alignment.[5]

To achieve this type of posture and its benefits, stand straight, shoulders pulled back and squared, with your arms at your sides. Think of your body as being on an axis, with everything centered and vertically aligned but not rigid. When sitting, assume a similar posture: back straight, shoulders back, with your torso aligned. Position your feet squarely in front of you, evenly spaced, and flat. Place your arms on armrests or extended in front of you, squared with your body but distinctly open. Adjust as appropriate to achieve an overall feeling of alignment, openness, and expansiveness. Ideally, you want to feel a sense of readiness and vigor but still be comfortable.

If you begin to slip into a closed or sagging posture, ask yourself: What shape is my body taking? Where is my attention focused? Am I being inviting and engaging for the people I am with? The answers to these questions will help you regain your physical presence and strengthen your embodied leadership.

During particularly difficult conversations, you may find yourself crossing your arms or legs, slumping forward, and physically closing in on yourself. But when the body contracts, so does the mind. As the mind contracts, the prefrontal cortex—the home of executive functioning skills—begins to shut down, with the more primitive parts of the brain taking over. This limits your capability for high-level, logical thinking and puts you into a reactive mode that limits your potential responses. If you realize that you're physically shutting down, you should revert to a more centered, welcoming posture—vertically aligned, shoulders squared, arms open. This will help you regain the clarity, focus, and thoughtfulness needed to resolve difficult problems.

We're all more likely to follow and be engaged with someone who is present with us, physically and mentally. And one of the big reasons is that presence is the foundation for creating trusting relationships.

Presence and Trust

Who would you trust most, someone who looks you straight in the eyes and is fully present with you or someone whose attention is scattered? The answer is obvious. Fundamentally, we are more likely to trust people who are present with us.

Presence is a foundation for trust. And trust binds individuals together—it binds employees and leaders together. Trust provides us with a sense of safety and a sense of meaning, and it significantly contributes to our overall sense of happiness. Trust is a significant contributor to an employee's sense of purpose, engagement, and performance. Paul J. Zak, professor of economics, psychology, and management at Claremont Graduate University and founding director of the Center for Neuroeconomic Studies, has spent ten years studying the role of trust in organizational performance. He's found that, compared with people at low-trust companies, people employed at high-trust companies report 74 percent less stress, 106 percent more energy at work, 50 percent higher productivity, 76 percent more engagement, 60 percent more job satisfaction, 70 percent more alignment with their company's purpose, 29 percent more satisfaction with their lives, 40 percent less burnout, and 13 percent fewer sick days.[6] The importance of trust in today's workplace should not be underestimated.

The organization Great Place to Work and *Fortune* magazine produce a yearly list of the "100 Best Companies to Work For," in which trust comprises two-thirds of the criteria. Their survey shows that trust between managers and employees is the primary characteristic of a "best workplace." And this sense of trust shows in each company's bottom line. These companies beat the average annualized returns of the S&P 500 by a factor of three. Similarly, the advocacy group Trust Across America tracks the performance of America's most trustworthy public companies, finding that the most trustworthy companies also outperformed the S&P 500.[7]

And CEOs recognize that trust is an issue foremost in the minds of their employees. The 2016 PwC global CEO survey reported that 55 percent of CEOs think that a lack of trust is a threat to their organizational growth. In 2014, just two years earlier, this number was 37 percent.[8] Hold this number against the results of the Edelman Trust Barometer global annual survey of 2017, which found that 63 percent of employees said that CEOs are "not at all, or somewhat credible."[9] Similarly, Ernst & Young's *Trust in the Workplace* found that only 46 percent of employees place trust in their employer.[10]

Trust matters. In business and in leadership.

When we have a trusting relationship with colleagues, we don't need to convince others of our intentions. And in a trusting organizational culture, much of the bureaucracy and politics can be avoided. In fact, studies show that trust affects economic and social development by enabling better functioning of organizations.[11] Trust bypasses many unconscious and cultural processes and allows us to get things done faster. To paraphrase Anish Melwani, CEO of LVMH Moët Hennessy Louis Vuitton Inc., North America, trust is the currency of influence. If we want to influence a colleague or team to do something, their trust in you is what makes it happen.

And of course, the converse is true. When there's a low level of trust, the opposite happens. We build control mechanisms and increase bureaucracy on individual levels, organizational levels, and throughout society. All of these mechanisms slow interactions and reduce productivity. On an interpersonal level, the impact of low trust is subtler, but even more detrimental to the speed of getting things done. An extensive study at Google confirmed this fact. For three years, Google studied 180 of its internal teams to find the secret ingredient of high-performing teams. As a company that focuses on hiring the smartest of the smart, the people at Google were confident that the common ingredient of the successful teams would be sheer cognitive horsepower. In other words, they believed the teams with the smartest people on them would also be the highest performing.

But they were wrong.

The researchers found that *who* was on the team mattered less than *how* the team members interacted.[12] Presence, trust, and a sense of psychological safety turned out to be the key determinants of team performance. The research found that teams with high levels of trust generated more revenue for the company, were rated as effective twice as often by their leaders, and had a much better retention rate.

As the leader, you have a great impact on the level of trust in your teams. If you have integrity and people know what you stand for, trust increases collectively. You must be authentic. But equally important, trust starts with how you show trust in others. John Hansen, a senior vice president at the LEGO Group, has a guiding principle for developing trust with his people: "Whenever I interact with my colleagues, I always trust they have the best intentions. I choose not to even consider that the opposite could be the case." John adopted this approach from a leader he once worked for who was always fully trusting of John. "It was truly liberating and motivating. I felt he had my back and that I had the freedom to solve problems and also to fail, without being judged. His approach gave me the space to learn and become what I am today." Trust starts with your trust in your people. And your ability to be fully present when showing that trust in them.

Quick Tips and Reflections

✓ Reflect on your experience with your "inner voice"; consider how often it distracts you from being more fully present with others.

✓ Consider what leading with mindful presence means for you; commit to one thing you are going to try in order to bring more presence into your leadership.

✓ Make a commitment to find ways to better connect with members of your team and people in your organization; when you have these moments, make them matter.

✓ Consider what embodied presence means for you and how enhancing your physical presence—posture, space, positions—could be beneficial for your leadership.

✓ Reflect on the level of trust in your work environment and specifically, people's trust in you; commit to one thing to enhance trust and create more psychological safety.

8

Selfless Leadership

The ancient Chinese philosopher Lao Tzu wrote, "A leader is best when people barely know he exists, when his work is done, his aim fulfilled, they will say: We did it ourselves."[1] Selfless leadership is about being invisible. It's about recognizing that leadership is not about you. Selfless leadership is about fundamentally understanding that your success is based on your ability to skillfully develop the potential of your people.

Selfless leadership requires restraint. It requires holding back from micromanaging people and processes. Non-action can be the most powerful action for a selfless leader. This is not to say that selfless leaders sit back and do nothing. Of course, a leader's role is to provide vision, strategy, direction, and guidance. But for selfless leaders, it's done in a much different way than traditional top-down, power-based management.

Selfless leadership starts with the ability to be fully present with your people and cultivate an environment of trust. In other words, it starts with the solid foundation of the M in MSC. With a platform of mindfulness, a selfless leader can coach and influence people by leveraging experience and knowledge. Selfless leadership is about having the wisdom to develop and grow your people so they can shine and thrive with your support. It's about becoming a truly enabling leader who helps her or his people perform in ways that could not be achieved through direction and management.

As leaders, we must rise above the constant flow of activity and keep our larger goals in sight. We must move from our natural tendency to be effective managers toward becoming inspiring, engaging leaders. If we try to be involved in every detail, we become a bottleneck. Instead, we need to be a catalyst for energy flow. We do this by allowing others to do their jobs and enabling them to have a sense of meaning and purpose.

In this chapter, we'll explain what we mean by selfless leadership and explore some of the benefits it offers. We'll then examine some of the barriers to selfless leadership. Finally, we'll look at the most important qualities you can develop to more selflessly—and effectively—lead your people.

Being of Service

Shimon Peres, former president of Israel, said at his Nobel Peace Prize award ceremony: "Leaders have lost their way, leadership is about being a servant, not a ruler." As we explored in chapter 4, the power that comes with leadership can be fuel for our ego. If mismanaged, ego takes over, and our leadership becomes about ourselves rather than about the people and the organization that we've been selected to serve. As leaders, being of service is our true power. And servant leadership is a natural application of selfless leadership. It comes out of the insight that leadership is not about us but about serving the people and organizations we lead.

Robert Greenleaf, former AT&T executive and author of *Servant Leadership*, makes a distinction between legitimate power and hierarchical power. Legitimate power is the power others offer you, which is based on what you offer them. Legitimate power is earned, not given. And it's often placed in other people in an organization besides the formal leaders. Legitimate power is different than hierarchical and authoritarian power that has been assigned by a rank or a title. And in Greenleaf's view, this legitimate power comes from acting as a servant to others.[2] The notion of "servant" leadership can be slightly misleading, because it suggests that your role is to serve your people. Alternatively, selfless leadership is about being of service as opposed to just being a servant. This includes being of service to yourself, so that you can set effective boundaries. If leaders are focused solely on serving everyone else, they won't be able to take care of themselves. And this means they're unable to serve anyone well. In the same way, if a leader puts individual needs above the needs of the company, everyone will suffer, because the company's performance will decline. In this way, selfless leadership requires more than being a servant to your people. It requires the balance and perspective to understand how to be of the best service to your people in a larger context.

Being of service means showing up moment to moment with an intention to support your people and your organization in the best way possible. Ted Kezios, global head of benefits for Cisco, meets with each of his team members every week and asks, "How can I help you do your job?" For Ted, being of service can include coaching people on how to address a challenging issue or helping them remove barriers. But being of service can also include providing tough feedback to support their development.

ARaymond, a French traditional industrial production company, is not necessarily the kind of business one would expect to adopt a selfless leadership orientation. In 2008, when the financial crisis hit, CEO Antoine Raymond realized that the loyalty and engagement of his people was the most important asset for the company's survival. "An enterprise is made of people," he told us. "And the success of the enterprise depends on the engagement of people. Each and every role is important. Everybody counts. Everybody deserves respect. So we invest in training our people in servant leadership, nonviolent communication, and mindfulness. This helps us create a collaborative network and an enterprise based on meaning. These intentions are shared by 100 percent of the people in the enterprise."

Antoine realized that true connectedness, meaning, engagement, and loyalty is not nurtured through top-down leadership but by putting people first. As a result, in the years since 2008, ARaymond has invested in training the entire leadership team to apply more selfless leadership and to be of service to its employees, changing the culture and truly engaging its global workforce.

Similarly, John Cheh, CEO of 57,000-employee Esquel Group, based in China and one of the world's leading producers of cotton shirts, views selflessness as a key to creating harmony. Organizational harmony is a mantra for him, both in the company and in the communities that the organization serves. For John, harmony should be a core objective for any company: "I see an emergent economic model that rejects the assumption that capitalism and selfless service are mutually exclusive. The reality is, many of the world's great organizations have discovered that the more we put aside our selfish motivations, the greater the harmony within our organizations. And the greater the harmony, the more successful we become. This makes it clear, at least to me, that service and selflessness will lead to businesses that are more profitable and productive."

Having a sense of harmony ensures that people in the organization are happy and that they find their work meaningful. With this sense of meaningfulness, people become more productive. In a sense, selfless leadership becomes a virtuous circle, offering benefits for leaders, employees, and the larger organization.

One clear manifestation of John's drive to create harmony in Esquel Group is to link employees' income with rising productivity. "We invest in technologies that raise employees' productivity and their income. Not only does this create stronger social cohesion and engagement, it contributes to the society at large by increasing communal wealth."

Research shows that financial inequality can stunt economic growth, decrease loyalty, and stifle trust.[3] Reducing the income gap engenders mutual respect between leadership and employees. If leaders are not earning respect—and the legitimate power that comes with it—then the employees will not be engaged and productive. In this light, John sees selfless leadership as more than a moral responsibility—it's a business imperative.

In our research, selflessness was rated as one of the most important qualities in leadership. When it's not all about the individual leader, people have more trust, feel more connected, and are more engaged. Surveying fifteen hundred workers in Australia, China, Germany, India, Mexico, and the United States, the research group Catalyst found that selfless leadership strongly enhances people's engagement. More specifically, the research showed that people's sense of "belonging" was increased by more than 25 percent; their sense of recognition of their unique contribution was increased by more than 30 percent; and their citizenship behaviors increased by 27 percent.[4]

These numbers prove an important point: selflessness isn't just a nice philosophy—it drives business results.

But, as you'll soon realize, developing a selfless leadership approach isn't easy.

Barriers to Selfless Leadership

Very few leaders would come right out and say, "Leadership is all about me." Yet when it comes down to it, many leaders act in selfish and self-serving ways. In chapter 4, we explained that this is not because leaders are bad people. In fact, the vast majority of leaders are good people doing their best to help their organizations succeed. Instead, the tendency to act in selfish ways is rooted in two fundamental challenges of the mind: the first is our fear-driven ego, and the second is our limited ability to understand how interconnected we truly are.

Ego and Fear

Selflessness in leadership makes sense in theory, but it can be difficult. When we let go of a strong sense of self—when we give our people more latitude, when we offer praise to others, when we take the blame ourselves—our ego suffers. The ego feeds on recognition, praise, influence, and fame. When it doesn't get those inputs, it shrinks. But it doesn't do so without resistance. That resistance often manifests itself as fear.

Fear is a big barrier to bringing selflessness into leadership. The fear of not being recognized. The fear of not being acknowledged. The fear of not being successful. On the surface, these fears may appear as a subtle physical or mental tension. But when analyzed, they can often be traced to a deep existential fear catalyzed by the following question: "What if I'm not successful?" This question can consciously or unconsciously drive the mind toward bigger issues: "If I'm not successful, my boss may be unhappy with me, my company may fire me, my family will abandon me, and I'll end up in the gutter—alone, poor, and unhappy."

The point is that fear can cause our mind to magnify small anxieties and turn them into deep existential fears.

To overcome this tendency, Michael Rennie, global leader of Organisation Practice for McKinsey & Company, has a ritual before every high-stakes event. He sits for a moment, allowing the fear to appear. He observes it with acceptance, letting it simply be. As he lets his fear be, without reacting to it or suppressing it, the fear gradually loosens its grip on his mind. In this way, neutral awareness of the fear neutralizes the fear. Over time, repeating this exercise will dismantle even the deepest existential fear.

Interconnectedness

One of the most powerful illusions we all have is that we're independent beings capable of creating our own reality, making our own decisions, and determining our own fate. The truth is, this is a complete fabrication. None of us could survive on our own. Take a moment to consider a single piece of fruit that you may have enjoyed in the last day or two. Think about how that piece of fruit came into your hand. Consider the farmer who planted and watered the seeds. The person who picked it when it was ripe. The inspector who ensured it was safe to eat. The truck driver who delivered it to the store. The grocer who placed it in an aisle. And even the cashier who accepted your payment for it. And this is just a piece of fruit. The same chain of events—and interconnectedness—is true for everything around us.

This raises an important truth. Regardless of how independent we think we are, we survive thanks to many visible and invisible people.

And that's just in relation to our physical survival.

Now consider your work, your career, your success. Sure, you may recognize the mentor who provided you with guidance. And hopefully, you recognize the people on your team and other colleagues who you rely on to do your job. But our interdependence goes well beyond the individual contributions we can see. Just as in the case of the piece of fruit, everything we do relies on others. But if we haven't worked on dissolving our ego, we might still be caught up in the illusion that we are the sole architect of our own success. Nothing could be further from the truth. We have not survived, will not survive, and will not be successful without all the visible and invisible beings who support us in the millions of ways that our minds rarely appreciate.

Consider for a moment all of the things you have that you need to survive and be successful. We survive, and thrive, through our ability to work together, to collaborate and cooperate to support one another.

Although you may think you rationally understand this concept, more than likely you still have a good-sized ego that wants to cry out, "But look at everything I've accomplished!" Fair enough. You wouldn't be a leader if you didn't have many achievements. But to think that you accomplished these feats on your own limits your leadership potential by keeping you from cultivating the best in others. And, yes—others may not notice how much you did, or do, for them, and they may not give you credit. But this is a core tenet of selflessness: to not crave recognition and credit. In this way, selfless leadership goes against the traditional top-down leadership approach and provides greater opportunities for your people to learn, develop, and improve.

Grow Your People

Selflessness in leadership includes a strong commitment to helping your people grow. And not just by allocating funds for training, but by having a personal commitment to pass on your best insights and intentions. This is true even if it means helping them become smarter and more capable than you.

Morgan Tan, Hong Kong president of global cosmetic firm Shiseido, realized that her twenty-five years in business had given her a unique position to pass on experience to her people. She has made employee development her prime purpose as a leader. Morgan recognizes that she achieves exponential impact by passing on her experience rather than trying to do everything herself. "In my experience, really effective leadership is having the capacity to switch between being a mentor and coach," she told us. "This gives less experienced employees valuable feedback, insight, and support, while passing down wisdom and institutional knowledge." In this way, Morgan sees herself as less of a leader and more of a person shaping and expanding others. The mentor approach to leadership has transformed her into more of a catalyst and less of a manager. This leadership style makes organizational success about the other people working with her, and not about herself.

Morgan constantly looks for opportunities to put her people on stage instead of herself. She looks for recognition and credit that can be passed on, instead of receiving it herself. This approach offers two clear benefits. First, less attention on herself helps keep perspective of what is important. Second, and more important, is the huge satisfaction she feels in seeing her people grow, excel, and shine. In the long run, this leadership style prepares Morgan's managers to be great leaders in the future, both within the company and in broader society. In this way, it serves a much bigger purpose than just focusing on the company's performance and bottom line.

Selfless leadership is about acting as a teacher, a mentor, and a guide. It's about giving your people room to flourish and shine. Think about it this way: If you fill the room, they can't take the space. And when you leave, you'll leave behind a big empty space. It's wiser to empty that space up front and let your people take it for you. One way to do this is through the application of skillful action—and in many instances, skillful non-action.

Skillful (Non)Action

In Chinese, the word for leadership includes two characters. The first can be translated as "lead, command, or direct," and the second can be translated as "guide or shepherd." Take a moment to reflect on your own leadership style. How much time do you spend commanding versus guiding? What's the right balance?

Serhat Unsal, CEO of Dawn Foods, has a clear answer to this question: "In good times, we must be humble and spend most of our time mentoring and listening. That way we develop trust, increase engagement, and build skills. But when times get tough, we must be more directional. At this point, we need the trust, engagement, and skills that were encouraged during the good times." With a selfless leadership style, as described by Serhat, the key is to be mostly in the guiding and mentoring mode and as little as possible in the authoritarian mode. Finding the right balance between the two states is often more about the actions we don't take than the actions we do take.

As leaders, we're compelled to solve all the problems we come across. This is, after all, how we advanced to become leaders. But when we reach a certain level, non-action becomes an important action. Roy Harvey, general manager at EA Sports, finds that some problems are best solved by not solving them. As he explained, "With some problems, the best thing to do is nothing." According to Roy, sometimes wisdom emerges in the form of not taking immediate action. "The easiest thing to do when you become aware of a problem is to push for an immediate fix. But often, when we're looking for a solution, we're actually looking in the same direction the problem came from. Instead, we have to look in a different direction. We have to look to others. We have to look inside ourselves. Or we just have to let things be. Non-action can give us the space to do that." Over the years, Roy has been amazed to discover how many problems solve themselves or become obsolete if we leave them alone for a while.

There's always an endless list of problems to solve and actions to take. There's always more to do than we can do. But often, it can be more productive to refrain from action and instead do nothing. When we get caught up in reacting to every problem, we risk becoming a victim of action addiction. We get addicted to being busy, to checking off boxes, to clearing to-do lists. Doing so provides us with a sense of being useful and productive. But somewhat perversely, the more we look and feel productive as we race through the day—jumping from task to task, reading emails, messaging in a flurry of activity—the less productive we really are. It's an illusion that negatively impacts us as leaders, as well as the people we lead.

Selfless leadership is the wisdom of refraining from action and to instead pause, clear the mind, and to take only the most important actions. It's more effective to move one big rock every day than a thousand pieces of gravel. If you get buried in activity, if you become a victim of action addiction, your attention is scattered, and your work becomes unfocused. Nothing good comes from this, except maybe a huge pile of gravel. But, as Roy observed, many problems will solve themselves or go away, or may be better addressed by others on your team. With the right engagement and direction, ten of your people can achieve much more than you can alone. It's simple math. In leadership, you must have the courage to endure the discomfort of unsolved problems. You must have the patience and resilience to avoid knee-jerk reactions.

Striving to be selfless, to enable your people to take the lead with guidance rather than direction, can create challenges. Jennifer Woo, CEO and chair of The Lane Crawford Joyce Group, a multibillion-dollar luxury goods company in Asia, shared how a senior leader in the organization found it frustrating that she did not seem to provide strong directives. He was used to having an authoritarian, top-down boss who told him what to do. Jennifer continually encouraged him to be more self-directed and independent, with her guidance as needed. He didn't like this. He mistook selflessness for weakness and lack of direction.

In this way, selflessness and ideas like non-action seem to work against traditional leadership beliefs. But as Jennifer has found, today's constant disruption requires a more holistic, less linear approach to leadership. In a disruptive world, leaders must break free of their own ego bubble and create a work environment that is relevant to their people. However, if leaders are action-addicted micromanagers, everyone suffers. And while Jennifer has experienced challenges in helping some people understand the benefits of a selfless leadership style, she has seen that it is worth it in the long run. "At first, some people are confused when I refrain from taking directive action. But quickly they realize it leaves a space for them to step in and create their own approach and direction. Initially it is uncomfortable for both myself and others, but when we get into the habit, it is liberating for both parties."

Let Go of Status

PepsiCo president and chairman Indra Nooyi had a great leadership lesson on the day she got the news of her appointment in 2001. Understandably, she was pretty excited to go home and share her big news with her mother. But things didn't go exactly as she hoped:

> "I've got great news for you," I shouted. She replied, "It can wait. We need you to go out and get some milk." So I go out and get milk. And when I come back, I'm hopping mad. I say, "I had great news for you. I've just been named president of PepsiCo. And all you want me to do is go out and get milk." Then she says, "Let me explain something to you. You may be president of PepsiCo.

But when you step into this house, you're a wife and mother first. Nobody can take that place. So leave that crown in the garage."[5]

Her mother's lesson was that you may have a very important role, lots of responsibilities, a big paycheck, a fancy house, and expensive cars, but if you start to think you are something really special, you'll become your own worst enemy.

In most corporate cultures, we create identities based on our status. When we enter a meeting room, we're conscious of our role and our place in the hierarchy. We then choose our seat based on those factors. The most senior leader often sits at the head of the table, with assistants sitting on the side. This positioning often happens unconsciously and represents the ego's way of reconfirming its sense of status and identity.

When we create these identities, however, we're also creating a separation between ourselves and the people we work with. If I see myself as of higher status than the person I'm talking with, there's separation. The same is true, of course, if I see myself as of lower status. And separation is never conducive to establishing a true connection with others and helping people find meaning and purpose. If we as leaders identify with our superiority, we can't truly connect with the people we lead. Similarly, if we identify too ardently with our own organization while working with clients or collaborative partners, we create another barrier.

For many of the leaders we interviewed, the connections between people matter far more in business than anything else. Through decades of experience, they've found that their ability to truly connect with people is the key ingredient for ongoing, long-term business relationships. In their experience, selflessness is the key to creating this type of relationship. Many of them described how they engage with their people as "a person to a person"—as two equal human beings interacting on an equal level—rather than as a leader to a subordinate.

To prepare each day, to help shed status and ego, leaders can follow a morning ritual. Before entering your office or a client's office, sit in your car for a few minutes and reflect on your identity. Like peeling an onion, pull away the layers of self-created identity. Let go of your leadership status. Let go of your identity as a businessperson, lawyer, or consultant. Let go of your belief systems, of your constructs like gender or age. At the end, you'll be left with a sense of agile and focused presence. This practice helps remove separation and enhance unity. It helps you rid yourself of the barriers ego normally erects between yourself and others.

This doesn't mean there's no place in leadership for status and hierarchy. Our leadership status is an important lever in those few cases in which we need to make a tough choice, a critical decision, or a clear call. In these types of cases, our status, our power, is critical to making people accept our choices and follow our decisions. But this power must be used sparingly, combined with selflessness and an open interest in listening to diverging perspectives.

Give Credit, Take Blame

Wenli Wang, partner in charge for the San Francisco office of Moss Adams, a US accounting firm, is passionate about supporting the growth and development of her people and believes that sometimes people need to be put in uncomfortable situations to grow. She looks for chances to create development opportunities for members of her team and has a clear message for them: "If you succeed, you will get all the credit. If you fail, I will take all the blame."

She shared a story with us about a team member who had made a mistake. And it was a big one. Mistakes in any profession are not good, but for an accounting firm, mistakes can have long-term negative implications. Wenli sat down with the team member and talked through what had happened and what could be learned from it. There was no blame assigned, only a true intention to understand and see what could be done. Then she sat down with the team member and called the client. Wenli let the client know that she had made a mistake and apologized for the error. She shared how she was able to find a solution and fix the issue to "make the client whole." That's selfless leadership in action.

To be truly selfless leaders, we shouldn't look for credit for every success. On the flipside, as selfless leaders, we shouldn't fear taking the blame for failures. Following this advice sounds simple, but it's not. It's difficult.

If we avoid praise, our ego fails to gain the recognition it craves. And when the blame hits, it's painful. The fact is, selflessness isn't easy. But it's the job of leaders to keep their egos in check. That's the only way their people can grow, thrive, and do great work.

When we create a safe space for failing—one in which we shoulder the blame—our people can take bigger risks and be more creative. They'll feel a greater sense of trust and autonomy that leads to increased commitment. And only when they feel comfortable experimenting—and failing—can they learn how to be more successful. IDEO, the world-renowned design firm, coined the slogan "Fail often in order to succeed sooner." With a similar objective, accounting software company Intuit gives out special awards for the best failures of the year. Cofounder Scott Cook explained that it teaches people to take risks in order to generate the next great idea. Creating this type of safe space begins with developing a sense of radical acceptance.

Radical Acceptance

A senior consultant on Michael Rennie's team at McKinsey & Company, shared a story. He was asked to organize a meeting between Michael Rennie and the CEO of one of McKinsey's largest clients. He contacted the CEO. He booked the meeting room. He notified other McKinsey team members. He aligned everyone's calendar, ordered the refreshments, and finalized all the specifics. But he overlooked one detail—he forgot to invite Michael himself.

At the meeting, the CEO waited impatiently, but Michael never showed up.

After what felt like an eternity, the CEO got up and shouted, "Screw all of you. If you're not going to show up to meet with me, I'm not waiting around to meet with you." He then stormed out of the room.

When the consultant realized the magnitude of his mistake, he didn't know how to tell Michael. This was a big client. This was a big mistake. And it could signify the end of the account, the relationship, and then maybe his career.

When he told Michael, it didn't go quite as expected. To his surprise, Michael laughed. It wasn't that Michael didn't take the situation seriously—he did. But it had happened. And it couldn't be reversed. It was what it was. Getting upset about it wouldn't help anyone or anything.

Radical acceptance is the wisdom of not making a bad situation worse. And selflessness helps us have radical acceptance, even in situations that are truly bad. With selflessness, our ego is curbed, leaving few buttons that can be pressed. We keep the ego in check, so it doesn't get the best of us. In the scenario above, selflessness allowed Michael to keep his head clear and focused, to see the humor in the situation, and to thoughtfully approach the mistake. With this clear, thoughtful approach, Michael and the senior consultant were able to sincerely apologize to the client and make up for the mistake—which was nothing more than an innocent slip-up. Without selflessness, Michael's ego would have instigated anger and likely led to a panicked overreaction.

Acceptance is easy to talk about. It makes sense in theory. But when you're in the middle of a crisis, when your key performance indicators are plummeting, when there's pressure from all sides, when you're not getting enough sleep, that's when your capacity for acceptance will be tested. It sounds hard . . . and it is. But there is good news. All the qualities needed for selfless leadership—humility, calmness, and acceptance—can be cultivated through training.

Training Selfless Leadership

Selflessness is a basic quality. It's not spiritual. It's not weird. It's not even emotional. It's merely a realistic assessment of yourself and your role in the world, and it can be trained.

Like any training of the mind, selflessness can be developed due to neuroplasticity, our ability to develop and strengthen new neural pathways. To strengthen these selfless neural pathways, all you need to do is experience a state of selflessness and abide in that state for a short period of time on a regular basis. As you practice in this way, your brain subtly takes on the quality of selflessness and rewires itself accordingly. The following is a short practice for developing selflessness (see "Training for Selfless Leadership"). It takes five minutes and is best done at the end of the day when you have a quiet moment.

Training for Selfless Leadership

1. Set a timer for five minutes and find and comfortable posture, ideally in a seated position.

2. For a few moments, pay attention to your breath while relaxing your body and mind.

3. Now, consider the people who made today possible for you:
   - Those who attended the meetings you attended
   - Those who helped organize your time
   - Those who contributed to the projects you are involved in
   - Those who made it possible for you to have something to eat
   - Those who expressed appreciation for you
   - Anyone else who made today possible for you

4. Consider how deeply interconnected you are with others. Only through others are you able to be you and achieve what you achieve.

5. Allow a realistic sense of humility to arise. You're only a little piece in a larger interconnected play of events. The world will keep spinning even if you're not around. Life will go on. Sit with this humility for a moment.

6. Take a moment to be grateful to all of those who contribute to your ability to live your life the way that you do. For a minute or two, simply sit with a sense of gratitude.

A strong sense of selflessness is a powerful tool when we lead others. Properly understood, selfless leadership can increase engagement, loyalty, creativity, and happiness. Harnessing this power requires being of service to our people and our organizations. Selflessness is more than just a word or an intention, though. It must be reflected in tangible actions that improve how people are treated and valued within an organization. And this can only happen when we as leaders learn to manage our egos, nurture safe spaces, and foster radical acceptance.

Quick Tips and Reflections

✓ Commit to practicing selfless training on a regular basis as recommended in the app—see appendix A for information.

✓ Reflect on what "being of service" means to you; consider one tangible way you could be of more service to your people.

✓ The next time conflict arises, take a moment to pause and ask yourself: How might my ego be getting in the way? Consider other ways of seeing or experiencing the situation.

✓ At the end of each day, take a moment to reflect on one contribution someone made to support your success, and send them a note of gratitude.

✓ Commit to one thing you are going to do to support the development and growth of your people through intentionally applying more selflessness in your leadership.

9

Compassionate
Leadership

In 2016, John Stumpf, now the former CEO of Wells Fargo, was called before Congress to explain a massive scandal. For more than four hours, Stumpf fielded a range of question about why the $1.8 trillion bank he led had set up 2 million false accounts, and, after it was discovered, fired fifty-three hundred employees as a way of redirecting the blame. The recordings of the hearing are a shocking, but illustrative case study of how leaders are at a risk of being corrupted by power.

We've already mentioned how power statistically makes leaders less considerate and more rude and unethical. The studies done in this field by researchers like University of California, Berkeley, professor Dacher Keltner are conclusive.[1] But even more worrisome is that neuroscience seems to find that power, if not managed well, structurally changes the brain, leaving leaders with a deficit of empathy and an inability to put themselves in others' shoes.

Stumpf's appearance before Congress shows a man who had made it to the top of the world's most valuable bank—and who has been left with an utter lack of ability to have compassion for other people. Even though his actions caused fifty-three hundred people to lose their jobs, he seemed incapable of acknowledging their pain. Yes, he apologized. But he didn't seem remorseful. Rather, he seemed a little taken aback by the whole thing, as if he really didn't understand what all the fuss was about.

The behavior of John Stumpf can be explained through the research of neuroscientist Sukhvinder Obhi, from McMaster University in Canada. In his study, Obhi put people with various levels of power under a transcranial-magnetic-stimulation machine to measure their mirror-neurological activity—the neurological function that indicates the ability to understand and associate with others.[2] Interestingly, he found that power impairs our mirror-neurological activity. In other words, power dismantles our ability to see and understand others' emotions and perspectives. Obhi concluded, "Anecdotes abound about the worker on the shop floor whose boss seems oblivious to his existence, or the junior sales associate whose regional manager never remembers her name and seems to look straight through her in meetings. Perhaps the pattern of activity within the motor resonance system that we observed in the present study can begin to explain how these occurrences take place and, more generally, can shed light on the tendency for the powerful to neglect the powerless."[3] Power, even on a neurological level, disconnects us from the world and leaves us in our own bubble.

In 2009, the British neurologist and parliamentarian David Owen published an article in *Brain* titled "Hubris Syndrome: An Acquired Personality Disorder?" that described the same issue. Owen defined the hubris syndrome as a "disorder of the possession of power, particularly power which has been associated with overwhelming success, held for a period of years."[4]

One CEO we interviewed was very open about this problem. For more than a decade, he had been the CEO of a large global consumer goods brand. During that time, he found that his job had impaired his empathy. The constant pressure, the heady activity of dictating a strategy, and the need to make tough decisions with tough implications for others had made him unconsciously pull back from emotional involvement. He noticed it in relation to his colleagues, friends, and even his children. Empathy used to be a dominant trait of his personality. He would instinctually know how others felt and naturally demonstrate concern for their feelings. But in recent years, he had noticed how empathy was simply not part of his thinking or behavior. He was matter-of-fact about it but also remorseful.

Through our interviews, we heard variations of this time and again. It's not that power makes anybody want to have less empathy. It simply results from the mental mechanics of taking on great responsibility and pressure, which can rewire our brain to disconnect from caring about other human beings. But it does not have to be this way. It shouldn't be this way. Such rewiring can be avoided—and it can also be reversed. Compassion is the way.

By developing and training our compassion, we can counter the empathetic loss that results from holding power. But equally important, compassion is the key that enables truly human connections with our people. This leads to opportunities for people to experience a deeper sense of meaning, contributing to their happiness.

Of the over one thousand leaders we surveyed, 91 percent said that compassion is very important for leadership, and 80 percent would like to enhance their compassion but do not know how. Compassion is clearly a hugely overlooked skill in leadership training.

This chapter explores the qualities of compassion, how compassion and wisdom go hand-in-hand, how you can become a more compassionate leader, and how to train your mind to increase compassion. Let's start by diving in to a greater understanding of compassion.

Compassion in Leadership

Compassion is the ability to put oneself in others' shoes and in doing so better understand their challenges and how best to help them. Compassion is the intent to contribute to the happiness and well-being of others. With the numerous challenges faced by today's workforce, compassion has become increasingly important and recognized as a foundational aspect of leadership.

Historically, compassion was not promoted as a cornerstone leadership quality. Many viewed it as being a soft skill not well suited for leaders. Compassion, it was thought, made you appear weak and overly emotional.

Before jumping in to the more practical aspects of compassion, let's first clarify a few misconceptions about the term. Compassion is hard, not soft and fuzzy. In tough business environments, compassion requires strength and courage. Compassion is an intention that does not necessarily change your actions; instead, it changes the way you conduct your actions. Just think of the difference between firing someone with compassion rather than out of frustration. One is constructive, the other may be experienced as cruel. And make no mistake, firing someone can be compassionate if it's done with the intent to help the other person learn and flourish in their next job.

Research by Professor Shimul Melwani, from the University of North Carolina's Kenan-Fliegler Business School, found that compassionate leaders are perceived as stronger and better leaders.[5] In other words, if you dare to be compassionate, you'll appear stronger, have increased levels of engagement, and have more people willing to follow you.

When we as leaders value the happiness of our people, they feel appreciated. They feel respected. And this makes them feel truly connected and engaged. It's no accident that organizations with more compassionate leaders have stronger connections between people, better collaboration, more trust, stronger commitment to the organization, and lower turnover.[6]

Simply put, compassion is core to effective leadership.

Qualities of Compassion

Compassion is a single word for the intention to benefit others. But in that intention lie four distinct qualities. Together, these four qualities make up the meaning behind the word *compassion*. The first quality is the wish for others to be happy. The second is the wish to alleviate the suffering of others. The third is the joy of seeing others succeed. And the fourth is the ability to see all others as of equal worth.

These four qualities are closely connected; they mutually enhance and support one another. The following sections explain the four qualities and show how they can be used in leading people and organizational strategy.

Wishing Others Happiness

Years ago, Narendra Mulani of Accenture discovered the unspoken truth relevant to any leader: All people are alike in that they want to be happy and avoid problems. Narendra realized that if he could help his people be happy, he would not only do the right thing but also help them meet their most basic desire. Narendra started viewing his global teams as an extended family. He made it his leadership responsibility to actively support them in finding more happiness. Through this approach, Narendra cultivated stronger loyalty, increased job retention, and improved performance.

Narendra initially struggled with the apparent mismatch between compassion and tough, but necessary, actions. But with time, he came to realize that tough feedback, as harsh as it seems, can be given with a clear motivation of being of benefit to the receiver. "To people, this is their life," he explained to us. "You have to make the right decisions for the business, but you have to make sure that people understand the reasons. I'm not going to mince words. They need to hear it from me; they need to understand it and absorb it. I have to tell them the reasons why. But I also need to tell them what they need to work on, how they can improve, or point them in a better direction." In this way, compassion is about the motivation behind the action. Difficult feedback can be intended to be helpful and constructive to a person, when offered with compassion, or it can be intended to belittle or devalue a person, when offered in anger or spite.

When we develop a healthy, positive motivation for what we do, it changes our actions and behaviors. Narendra learned that motivation can play a significant role even when tackling a situation as difficult as letting people go. With compassion as his motivation, the dynamic of the conversation changed, both for himself and the person he was letting go. And most often, despite the difficulty of the conversation, compassion helped him attain better results. Narendra found this realization also applied to his clients: recognizing his clients' desire to be successful and happy motivated him to be present with compassion. As a result, he became better at listening and understanding their needs, which helped him create better solutions. He now makes a habit of pausing before a meeting and asking himself what would make the individual client happy and truly benefit his or her organization. Instead of checking incoming texts or emails, he takes a moment to ask himself the following question: How can I be of benefit to make this person and organization successful and happy?

When did you last ask yourself how you could bring happiness to the people you lead or the clients you serve? How do you think it would change your interactions with them?

Wishing to Alleviate Suffering

The second characteristic of compassion is the wish to alleviate the suffering of others. Balancing the care of the individual with the care of the organization is a difficult part of leadership: the two goals don't always go hand in hand. And without care, they may remain diametrically opposed. As part of the job, you have to tell people when they aren't doing a good job. You have to let go of people to serve the larger objectives. Sometimes people are sacrificed to further the advancement of the organization.

In tough times, like large-scale layoffs, leaders risk growing numb to the individual's suffering. When the 2008 financial crisis hit US accounting firm Moss Adams, then COO Chris Schmidt (now CEO) faced a challenge. Either the firm would make significant cuts, or the firm would risk financial failure. The decision was clear, though difficult to make. As Chris explained to us, the question he and his partners had to ask themselves was: "How can we do this in a way that inflicts as little pain as possible on the people who'll leave, as well as the people who'll stay?" As a firm, they offered generous severance packages and job replacement support. This compassionate approach allowed Chris to stay more humane, in touch with himself, and more present and authentic with his people.

When you make decisions that adversely impact others, how do you feel about it? The next time it happens, try to develop a compassionate attitude and intention toward the people involved. Then notice how it changes the dynamics of the experience.

Enjoying Others' Success

The joy of celebrating the success of others is an invaluable leadership quality. Yet despite our best intentions, our ego often gets in the way of celebrating the achievements of others. But leaders can't survive on their own—they can't count on having the best ideas or strategies all on their own. They need collaboration. They need teamwork. To get the best out of others, leaders must develop a genuine motivation to support and celebrate the success of their people.

Marriott has embedded this motivation and practice into every element of their culture. At Marriott, there are no employees, only associates—over 400,000 of them. Career progression is a strong focus at Marriott.

Many top executives and property managers started as waiters or front desk trainees. There is an elaborate system for mentoring, supporting, and training people for promotions. Marriott truly wants to see their people succeed in work and in life. Because of this support, Marriott has made *Fortune*'s list of the "Best Companies to Work For" every year since the list was created.

Marriott CEO Arne Sorenson spends about two hundred days a year on the road, visiting associates at hotels. He doesn't just appear at a brief town hall meeting, but walks around and meets associates at the front desk, in the kitchen, or on the guest room floors. His objective is to listen to their thoughts; to understand their work, hear their concerns, and laud their successes. Marriott has a simple business philosophy: *If we care for our associates, they will care for our guests, and the business will take care of itself.*

When it comes to compassion, Arne doesn't just talk the talk; he follows through with action. After 9/11, when the global travel industry plummeted and Marriott went from a 75 percent to a 5 percent occupancy rate, he waived the thirty-hours-per-week requirement for benefits and health coverage. This lessened the worries of Marriott associates and allowed them to focus on their jobs rather than fearing for the future. Arne sees this culture as critical to the company's overall strategy. The culture he and his leadership team have created drives loyalty, which drives retention, which drives better service, which drives customer experience, which drives revenue. Marriott's internal data shows that properties that score higher in associate engagement have better financial results.

As in Marriott's case, the wish to see others be successful is a strong and sound strategy. How do you think such a strategy would help you and your business if you took more joy in others' success?

Seeing Others Equally

Mark Tercek, former managing director at Goldman Sachs and current CEO of The Nature Conservancy, sent shockwaves through the environmental world when he announced a partnership with Dow Chemical Company. Mark believes that when we're passionate about ideas but faced with opposing forces, we often turn to aggression and rejection. "It's really easy to vilify people or groups you see as being on the opposite side of an issue. It's easy to see them as evil or morally compromised." But this approach leads to polarization, a situation in which collaboration and communication are abandoned.

A core element of compassion includes the ability to see others as truly equal. It's the realization that we are all alike in our desire to be happy and not suffer. With this understanding comes a lack of preference for one person to be happier than another. When you see everyone as equal, the ones who cause you problems are valued the same as the ones you love. This may seem like a big ask, but as a leader, it's a fundamental quality to embrace. It means supporting diversity and inclusion and putting the organization's needs before one's own personal preferences.

Seeing others equally allows us to be open. It allows us to find common ground instead of fixating on opposing opinions. Mark found that seeing others equally enabled him to dismantle his own automatic rejection of organizations and people who seemed at odds with his beliefs or goals. It allowed him to seek common ground and be open for constructive collaboration. By embracing a partnership with one of the world's largest chemical corporations, The Nature Conservancy has been able to impact that organization's environmental agenda in profound ways.

Mark was accused of indifference and a lack of values. But seeing others equally is far from being indifferent. It comes from a clear mind and a clear comprehension of reality as it is. Fighting against the things we don't like in life will only marginalize us.

By default, the human mind categorizes experiences into three buckets: things we like, things we dislike, and things we are neutral about. Out of liking comes craving and desire. Out of neutrality comes indifference. Out of disliking comes aversion and rejection. Seeing others equally dismantles this entire categorization scheme and allows us to make more objective and reasoned choices.

All four qualities of compassion are powerful and have clear applications to leadership. To better develop each quality, we've included training practices for each in appendix B. But before going further, here's an important question to consider. Is compassion ever misplaced in leadership? We asked this question as we interviewed hundreds of executives, and the answer was clear. Compassion is always important. But with one caveat—it must be paired with wisdom and sound judgment.

Wise Compassion

Compassion doesn't mean you're always trying to please people and give them what they want. As mentioned in chapter 1, to ensure we make sound decisions that benefit the bigger picture, compassion must be complemented by wisdom. Compassion and wisdom together can provide a clear leadership framework, as illustrated in the compassion matrix we introduced in chapter 1 (figure 9-1).

The top left quadrant in the matrix represents a state in which we have compassion but can't discern the impacts of our actions. As a result, we risk doing disservice to the cause we intended to support. People and organizations solely focused on compassion risk acting out of naïveté and making well-intentioned mistakes.

The top right quadrant depicts the successful combination of compassion and wisdom. It is constructive compassion. We act to be of benefit to others, while closely discerning the impact of our actions. Leaders like the ones mentioned earlier in this chapter operate in this quadrant, balancing compassion with a skillful focus on organizational success.

FIGURE 9-1

The compassion matrix

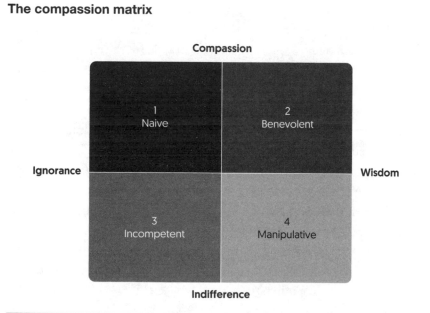

A lack of compassion and wisdom falls in the bottom left quadrant. Without compassion, we're indifferent. And without wisdom, we are unlikely to be able to get much done. Very few leaders and organizations are in this space, simply because success is close to impossible.

Similarly, the bottom right quadrant is also a dangerous place. The necessary skills and expertise for success are in place, but leaders in this quadrant lack wholesome intentions. Leaders operating in this space can be manipulative. They may be effective in delivering short-term results. In the long term, however, people will not follow their lead.

Take a moment to consider where in the matrix you would place yourself. Where would you place the leaders in your organization who are closest to you?

We've examined the qualities needed to be a compassionate leader and how to balance compassion with wisdom. Now let's take a closer look at how to actually become a compassionate leader.

Become a Compassionate Leader

When we're mindful, we remember to lead with compassion. When we have selflessness, we're thinking less about ourselves and more about others. With mindfulness and selflessness as foundations, we can train to increase our level of spontaneous compassion. The more time we spend training our mind in compassion with the practice at the end of this chapter and those in appendix B, the more our brains will rewire for spontaneous compassion.

But even though compassion benefits us as leaders, benefits our people, and benefits our organizations, it's not always easy to maintain. In the leadership survey we conducted for this book, we asked leaders what got in the way of being compassionate. The biggest culprits were workload, demands from others, and competing priorities. Stated another way, busyness makes it hard to have space for compassion in daily work. Other research corroborates our findings. A study from Brain Mind Institute, School of Life Sciences, École Polytechnique Fédérale de Lausanne, showed that the more pressure we feel, the less we pay attention to the needs and emotions of others.[7]

In other words, when we get too busy, our attention goes to our head, rather than to our heart. The Chinese word for busyness illustrates this; it consists of two characters, one meaning "killing" and the other, "heart." When we get too busy, we lose our heart. And in the lives of most leaders, this is a real challenge. But it's one that can be overcome.

The Compassion Compass

A Chinese proverb says, "There is no way to compassion, compassion is the way." Bringing compassion into any interaction you have and asking how you can be of benefit to others is the way to compassion. It is neuroplasticity in action.

Compassion is something we create by applying it to every interaction we have. In this way, it can become the compass that directs your intentions, attention, and actions. Whenever you engage with someone, ask yourself: "How can I be of benefit to this person?" Ask this of yourself every time you meet clients, stakeholders, colleagues, family, or friends. Let it be like a mantra that drives your intentions, moment by moment, in meeting after meeting.

John Chambers, former CEO of Cisco, knew that compassion was more than the right thing to do—it also had positive impact on his organization. He set up a system to ensure he was informed within forty-eight hours of any employee, anywhere in the world, who experienced a severe loss or illness. Once notified, he would personally write a letter and extend his support to that person. In this way, he instilled a top-down appreciation of the value of human care and compassion throughout the company. This type of compassion can be considered *wise egoism*.

Wise Egoism

Compassion is wise egoism because when we are kind to others, we are happier.[8] Compassion is one of the most important contributors to our own well-being. It's a true win-win no matter how you look at it. If you want *others* to be happy, show compassion. If *you* want to be happy, again, show compassion.

Compassion is also the antidote to negative mind states and in particular the emotion most destructive to our well-being and health—anger. Anger leads to an increased risk of cardiac events, an increased risk of serious illnesses, and, statistically, an increased death rate.[9] Anger can be likened to holding a piece of burning coal in your hand. It hurts you, not the one you feel anger toward.

But dealing with anger can be tricky. We interviewed a senior director of a global professional services firm who shared a story of how anger trapped him while he was with an important client. The client, a head of state of a large country, started their first meeting by unconditionally criticizing the senior director's firm. Instead of staying calm and constructive, he fell into the trap of righteous indignation—something he regrets to this day. The senior director ended up scolding the head of state and, as a result, lost the contract.

Though anger can feel good in the moment, it's a trap. It narrows our perspective of reality and makes us focus single-mindedly on the cause of our anger. When this happens, we lose sight of the big picture. Our minds are literally distorted.[10] Needless to say, this is not a good place from which to make important decisions.

Compassion is the direct antidote to anger and righteous indignation. The more you train to increase your compassion, the less space there will be for anger. Why? You can't have both in mind at the same time.

Training Compassion

Compassion can be trained through a number of time-tested practices. Research has found that just a few minutes of practice a day will help your brain rewire for increased compassion and that with regular training, you can experience increased positive emotions, increased mindfulness, a stronger sense of purpose, and increased happiness.[11] Compassion training has been shown to significantly alter the neural networks of our brain in such a way that we react to the suffering of others with spontaneous compassion, instead of distress and despair.[12]

Each of the four qualities of compassion can be trained individually. You will find the instructions in appendix B. But they can also be trained all at once with a single practice called giving and taking—*Tonglen* in Tibetan. The practice is simple, yet powerful, and has been practiced for thousands of years, passed from generation to generation, in China, India, Japan, and Tibet.

In short, the practice is about recalling a person you care for who is having a tough time and visualizing that you give compassion and take away their problems. You can do this exercise in a minute, or take as long as you like. Here is a short *Tonglen* practice for you to try. You can also use the app; see appendix A for more information.

Tonglen Practice

---

1. Set a timer for four minutes.

2. Sit comfortably and relaxed, and focus your attention on your breath for a moment to let your mind settle.

3. When you have centered yourself, recall a person dear to you, someone who is experiencing challenges at the moment.

4. Be clearly aware of the challenges and how it must feel for the person experiencing them.

5. With each exhale, imagine you breathe out everything this person needs: warmth, strength, and compassion. Breathe out everything that is positive and imagine it enters the other person.

6. While you continue breathing compassion on each exhale, with each inbreath, imagine that you remove all suffering, pain, regret, and hurt from the person—but without you taking it on. Imagine that you're simply removing her or his pain.

7. When you're ready, let go of the person and return your attention to your breath.

8. When you're ready, let go of the practice.

You can do this practice as a sitting practice, taking a few minutes, or you can do it as a micro practice anywhere you are, in the office, at home, or on the road. When you enter a meeting or pass someone in the office, notice the expression on her or his face. Our faces carry any pain, hurt, and regret we might be experiencing. Look for it. And when you see it, breathe compassion into them in one outbreath and imagine that you remove their pain with your inbreath. Try it a few times, and see how this changes your state of mind and actions.

We all want to be happy. We all want to do good unto others. Every time you do this exercise, even if it's just for a few seconds, you connect with your deepest and best human characteristics. You truly connect with yourself and with others.

Quick Tips and Reflections

✓ Commit to practice compassion training as presented above or recommended in the Mind of the Leader app—see the appendix for information.

✓ Make compassion the compass of your intentions for anyone you engage with; for any interaction, ask yourself how you can be of benefit to the person or people you are with.

✓ Commit to one practical application of compassion in your leadership to increase genuine happiness, reduce unnecessary suffering, celebrate others' success, or see others equally.

✓ Consider where you are in the compassion matrix and where you would like to be; commit to one thing you can do to move in that direction.

✓ Reflect on what wise egoism means for you and in what situations you would want to have this as your guidepost.

PART THREE

Understand and Lead Your Organization

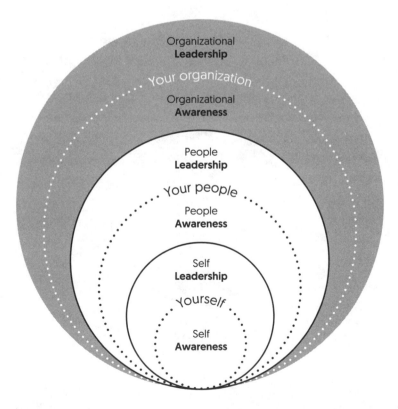

T he mind creates our behavior. Our behavior shapes the people we lead. And the people we lead create the cultures of our organization and thereby determine its performance.

Finding purpose or happiness or engagement can be difficult when working in an organization that views employees as mere tools for profit. Organizations instead need to become people-centered. This requires creating an organizational culture that caters to intrinsic human drivers, like connectedness, meaning, and happiness. Caring for people as a core business strategy is an effective way of enhancing collective performance.

Most organizations talk about the importance of people, but few create cultures in which people are truly seen as the core of the company. Mindfulness, selflessness, and compassion are powerful building blocks for creating that kind of culture. With MSC leadership in place, people will be at the center of your organization, and their basic human needs to be connected, have meaning, be valued, and be happy will be met—all to the benefit of your organization and the wider community.

A cultural transformation toward a more people-centered organization has to start with leadership teams embodying the change. It's about action, not words. This transformation includes modeling desired behaviors as well as revisiting and revising work practices, policies, and procedures in line with new ways of working.

In part 3, we'll explore how mindful, selfless, and compassionate leadership behaviors are critical to creating and sustaining a truly people-centered organization. Like the previous parts, this part starts with a chapter on understanding your organization. Showing the impact that organizational culture has on organizational results, this chapter considers what we as leaders can do to develop cultures that enable engagement, enhance meaning, and increase connectedness and happiness. Chapter 11 follows with a look at how to create a more mindful culture and enhance organizational focus. Chapter 12 then examines how to instill a culture of selflessness and reduce unhelpful divisions and hierarchies. Finally, chapter 13 explores how to embed compassion in your culture, making people feel cared for, respected, and valued as part of the organizational tribe.

10

Understand Your Organization

Peter Drucker famously claimed, "Culture eats strategy for breakfast." And it's true. Cultures shape organizations in a way similar to how thoughts shape our behaviors. Cultures aren't visible, but they're powerful. If we as leaders want to guide our organizations toward greater success, we need to understand culture and how to influence it.

Culture, as elusive as it may seem, is stronger than the bricks of any company's headquarters. Culture is created, maintained, and expressed by the many minds making up any organization. You can tear down an office and build a new one in a month. But you can't change a culture that quickly. You can design an office to be just the way you like it, but you can't design a culture to be exactly the way you want it. You can own a building, but you can't own a culture. And if you move your organization into new offices, the environment will be new, but the culture may remain the same. Consider research that finds that 90 percent of all desired organizational change initiatives fail because organizational culture is not sufficiently taken into account.[1]

A culture is created by the people inhabiting it. It's layered in the minds of those people. It's layered as emotions, values, and principles. As discussed in chapter 2, most of the time these emotions, values, and principles exist below our level of awareness. We can't see them. And most of the time, we have no idea that we're being influenced by them. Consequently, we all shape a culture we're part of, but often with values and behaviors we're not aware of.

At the same time, we're shaped by the cultures we inhabit. We are far more influenced by those around us than we might think. Researchers have found that the culture we're part of shapes our brain structures and functions.[2] Living in a Western culture, like that of Europe, the United States, or Australia, makes our brains more individualistic and causes us to see business interactions as more separated or compartmentalized. In contrast, living in an Asian culture shapes our brains to be more collectivistic and causes us to process information in a more inclusive manner.[3] This strong reciprocal relationship—the individual as both the shaper of culture and shaped by culture—happens because we're social beings - constantly driven to pick up on social cues and orient our behavior accordingly.

As leaders, the responsibility for shaping organizational culture rests on our shoulders, because people's brains are wired to see and respect hierarchies.[4] Human brains are oriented toward understanding where we fit in social structures and looking to those who appear to be dominant or in charge for guidance on how we should behave. As noted by author Daniel Goleman, although everyone has the ability to influence a culture, "it is the actions and behaviors of the leader that matter most because everyone watches the boss."[5]

In fact, being a leader is a much greater responsibility than most of us realize. Through our behavior, we have a powerful impact on one of the most prevalent cultures in many people's lives. Since most us spend far more time working than on most other elements of life—and because we're social beings heavily influenced by those around us—what happens at work influences nearly every aspect of our life.

The simple fact is, culture matters. Because of this truth, we as leaders have a responsibility to shape culture in ways that are beneficial for the organization and the people in it. This chapter shows how culture rules organizations and how we as leaders can influence it. It will also show why putting people at the center of your strategy and creating a truly human culture is important for organizational performance.

Influencing Organizational Culture

Edgar Schein, professor at the Sloan School of Management at MIT, is highly regarded for his research on organizational culture and leadership. Schein has identified three levels of organization culture: visible artifacts; espoused values and beliefs; and invisible, unconscious values and beliefs. Schein contends that leaders are the primary source of organizational culture because of their ability to influence the invisible, unconscious values and beliefs that are the ones most difficult to detect, define, or manage. Because of this, he believes leaders' primary responsibility should be to understand how cultures are created and influence it in ways that will be beneficial for the organization.[6]

For most leaders, this process begins with establishing a set of core values. Typically, these values represent the highest ideals of how leaders would like to influence individuals' behaviors and functions at work. It's necessary for people to know what a company values so they can determine whether their own values are aligned with the company. It's also important for leaders to be able to articulate which behaviors are in line with desired values and which ones aren't, so they can help shape individual behaviors to align with the collective whole.

It would be wonderful if influencing culture was as easy as creating a set of aspirational values and then letting the culture take shape on its own. If that were the case, most organizations would be great places to work, with high levels of engagement and trust. Publicly stated corporate values are universally positive and are all very similar. According to a study by James Archer, the twenty most common corporate values are: integrity, respect, innovation, teamwork, excellence, customer focus, trust, diversity, accountability, openness, quality, honesty, passion, safety, community, service, collaboration, responsibility, people, and commitment.[7] If all organizations lived by these twenty values—well, we wouldn't have issues with unhappy employees and plummeting engagement scores. Influencing organizational culture goes deeper than articulating a set of values and posting them on the wall.

Far too often, leaders fail to connect espoused values to workplace realities. The most common reason for this disconnect is that most leaders are not aware of the realities of daily life. Instead, most leaders operate on habitual autopilot, seeing what they want to see and hoping that simple words will fix complex problems. This disconnect also occurs because the stated values are inconsistent with other important business objectives. Consider the case of Wells Fargo that proclaims that it values "ethics" and doing "what's right for customers." Yet in 2016, more than five thousand employees were fired when it was discovered that, due to heavy pressure from supervisors to meet quotas, they created more than 2 million fake accounts collecting at least $2.6 million in fees from unwitting customers. Or consider Volkswagen's proclaimed value of being "responsible for people, the economy, society, and the environment." Yet in September 2015, the US Environmental Protection Agency announced that Volkswagen had intentionally programmed its clean diesel engines to activate certain emission controls only during laboratory emissions testing, thereby defrauding both regulators and consumers.

In both these cases, we can safely assume that individuals were knowingly operating against espoused values. But in many other cases, people operate with the best of intentions, and yet the organization's values still conflict with employee actions. Take the case of United Airlines, which aspires to be the "Friendly Skies." In early 2017, millions of people watched an online video of a security guard dragging a sixty-nine-year-old bruised and bloodied passenger off a plane due to established procedures for overbooked flights. In retrospect, it's easy to see how that policy could lead to unintended outcomes; but clearly in creating the policy, leaders didn't consider the potential negative consequences.

Although it may be easy to believe Wells Fargo, Volkswagen, and United Airlines are extreme cases, they're not. Value statements are often turned into attractive posters and put on websites, but they're not always apparent in daily operations, in how people are rewarded, how policies and procedures are established, or how decisions are made.

Although establishing a culture that aligns with core values and creates a stronger sense of engagement and purpose is a challenge, it's not as complex as it may seem.

Just put your people first.

The People-Centered Culture

As we've explored throughout this book, human beings are neurologically driven to want to feel connected and valued. Since we spend so much time at work, many of us look to fulfill these basic needs by searching for purpose and connection at work. These needs are on one side of the engagement equation. On the other side, most organizations talk about how much they value their people. In theory, there shouldn't be any problems with engagement: people want to feel valued, and organizations say they value people.

Although many factors contribute to dismal levels of employee engagement, one of the biggest drivers is rooted in what companies actually value. In the past quarter century, it hasn't been employees. Or even customers. It's been shareholders.

The year 1976 was a turning point for publicly traded companies. The shift was ignited by the article "Theory of the Firm" in the *Journal of Financial Economics*.[8] Arguing that companies were owned by—and responsible to—their shareholders before anyone or anything else, the article started a steady movement that changed the general perception of corporations' roles and responsibilities in society. Shareholder wealth became more important than employee health. This change has had a significant impact on both societies and companies. There are two primary problems with this "shareholders first" thinking. The first is a widespread focus on short-term results at the cost of long-term benefits. The second is a lack of incentive for corporate social responsibility.[9] Both problems tend to come at a cost for the general employee and do not foster people-centered cultures.

A senior leader of a national retail chain in Australia, shared with us her experience of a "shareholders first" orientation. When business was going well, it was great to be a leader in the organization. But when times were tough, shareholders still expected short-term returns. To maintain these returns, the company made sacrifices. Employees were laid off or put under unrealistic pressures. When shareholders' wealth is the main objective of companies, the tendency is for management to lead for short-term gains. And short-term gains often come at a cost for the people in the company.

In *Capitalism at Risk: Rethinking the Role of Business*, Harvard Business School professors Joseph Bower, Herman Leonard, Lynn Paine argue that boards must focus on company health before shareholders' wealth.[10] Only by doing so can companies regain trust from employees, and, in turn, attain long-term sustainable performance. In our fieldwork and research, we see this trend gaining traction. There's a slow but growing movement among executives toward focusing on the long-term health of organizations and creating people-centered cultures.

People-centered organizations value "people first," because it's people who make the company successful. Marriott is a great example of this approach. When you stay at Marriott hotels, the overall experience is that the people in the company enjoy their jobs. Companies like Marriott realize that when people feel valued and cared for, they do their work with stronger intrinsic motivation, meaning, and engagement. They go that extra mile simply because they *want* to contribute to something that's meaningful to them.

As we've examined in several chapters, genuine happiness comes from a sense of purpose, from true connections with others, and from an ability to contribute. Too many organizations try to address the challenges of employee disengagement and dissatisfaction by focusing on external gratification with incentives like bonuses, raises, funkier office environments, and free food. Although these benefits are nice, they represent short-term injections of pleasure, not lasting happiness. Consider the research discussed in chapter 2, which showed that people with higher salaries are not happier than people with lower salaries. If we were driven only by financial rewards, we should be happier the more money we make. But we're not. Instead, if we as leaders want to uncover ways of solving today's challenges with engagement, we must look deeper—we must look at what drives us, our people, and all the employees throughout our organization.

Base the Culture on Foundational Human Drivers

To increase engagement and productivity, we as leaders need to focus on our people's foundational motivations. To create lasting engagement, we must look at the internal drivers of our behaviors, not just external factors like money and perks. If we lead with the goal of helping people create an intrinsic sense of happiness—of meaning, connection, and contribution—in their work, they'll leave the office every day with a sense of fulfillment. And if we as leaders create an environment where employees feel a true sense of concern for their well-being—where we are truly present—they'll become more willing, more enthusiastic, and more collaborative team members. These characteristics are in stark contrast to the all-to-common organizational cultures of busyness, rushed interactions, and competitive pressures.

This is why creating people-centered cultures is the most logical response to today's organizational crisis of soaring employee disengagement and widespread job dissatisfaction. A people-centered organization solves these issues by putting people first. It reverses the power dynamic. And it puts the responsibility for engagement and meaning on the company rather than on the employee.

The key idea here is rather than thinking of people as being assets of the company, it is the recognition that people *are the company*.

This may not seem like such a radical idea, but it is a big departure from traditional management thinking that treats people more like parts in a machine. When work requirements were relatively simple, leaders could count employees the way they counted tools. If they had five hammers and five people to use them, they could calculate the number of widgets they could produce per day. Although this may have been successful in the past, in today's much more complex and competitive environment, it's no longer sufficient. Simple, repetitive jobs are done by machines. And treating knowledge workers like tools will not inspire them to create, innovate, and collaborate. New ideas can't be pulled or purchased from employees—they must be offered willingly. An intrinsic sense of happiness, of meaning and connection, promotes a willingness to innovate.

Just to be clear, this people-centered approach involves much more than just saying, "Our people are our most important asset." Many leaders already say this. But actually putting people first and creating a culture where human beings are truly valued is, sadly, a radical shift in how most organizations operate. But it's a shift that needs to happen if organizations want sustainable performance. And one that we believe is enabled by creating a mindful, selfless, and compassionate culture.

Create an MSC Culture

Real change starts with leadership. If you as a leader don't walk the talk, no one else will. This is particularly true for a people-centered organization—and certainly for developing an MSC culture. Creating an MSC culture requires you as a leader to visibly demonstrate the behaviors described in this book. Saying you *want to be* mindful, selfless, and compassionate isn't enough: You must *be* mindful, selfless, and compassionate.

Chris Schmidt, CEO of US accounting firm Moss Adams, is passionate about the benefits of mindfulness for himself as a leader and for his organization. When he introduced mindfulness into the organization, he started with the executive committee and the firm's managing partners. It was obvious to him that it was critical to start with leaders before engaging the rest of the organization. This would allow mindfulness to cascade down from the leadership through the various inter-organizational divisions and teams. "Any significant organizational initiative requires leadership support," he told us. "If leaders aren't onboard, the organization is unlikely to become more mindful. Also, mindfulness triggers a lot of discussions about the organization's working culture. How do we manage interruptions? How do we minimize distractions in meetings? If leaders aren't actively involved, it limits the positive change that can come from these discussions."

But Chris discovered something even more impactful in helping create a more mindful culture. He realized he needed to be more explicit with people about how he was using mindfulness, moment to moment, to help his performance and effectiveness. For example, when a group came to him with a difficult issue to solve, he told them he would first take a mindful pause. "I wanted to ensure that my mind was calm and clear before responding to their request," he explained. "That way, as I told the team, my response would be thoughtful rather than reactive." By modeling mindfulness in action, he was better able to demonstrate its benefits.

Culture change and values must be modeled, not just posted on the wall.

A Truly People-Centered Organization

A great example of an organization that matches aspirations with actions to put people first is Barry-Wehmiller. With more than eleven thousand employees and revenue of $2.4 billion in 2015, it is a highly successful global supplier of manufacturing technology and services. Although most organizations measure success based on revenue, Barry-Wehmiller's leaders measure success based on "the way we touch the lives of people." Its mission statement reads: "We are in business so that all of our team members can have meaningful and fulfilling lives."

And this isn't just an empty slogan.

In the book *Everybody Matters*, chairman and CEO Chapman shares stories of how executives at Barry-Wehmiller guide policies and decisions based on putting people first.[11] For example, during the 2008 financial crisis, Barry-Wehmiller's revenue declined. While many other organizations laid off employees to save costs, Barry-Wehmiller chose a different approach. Chapman asked, "What would a caring family do in tough times?" The answer: everyone in the organization made a sacrifice so that no one would experience undue suffering. To help spread the pain, Chapman and his team initiated cost-saving strategies, including asking everyone to take one month of unpaid leave. These measures ensured that no one had to lose his or her job. In 2010, Barry-Wehmiller emerged from the recession with record revenues—and levels of commitment and loyalty unparalleled in its industry.

The example of Barry-Wehmiller shows what a truly people-centered approach to business looks like. When the overriding business goals include ideals like trust and compassion, the outcome is financial success. Chapman believes it's a leader's responsibility to "create an environment where people can discover their gifts, develop their gifts, share their gifts, and be recognized and appreciated for doing so—which creates an opportunity for them to have a more meaningful life, a life of purpose in which they feel valued and get a chance to be what they were brought onto this earth to be."

An overarching belief in caring for every human being in your organization is a powerful shift in values with a direct, positive impact on the organization's culture. Be careful, though, not to confuse this people-centered approach with being soft. Recognizing that people must be at the center of corporate strategy is not just about being kind and good—it enables true engagement and thereby high performance. To do otherwise is a recipe for disengagement, dissatisfaction, and, ultimately, suboptimal performance. Think about it. Do you really want your customers served by people who don't feel valued? Do you want your equipment and tools handled by people who don't believe you care about them?

Although you may not choose to go as far as Barry-Wehmiller, caring for people is the starting point for addressing organizational disengagement and dissatisfaction. It's the first step toward creating happier, healthier, and more productive work environments. A truly people-centered business strategy requires a hard look at traditional approaches to leading organizations. It requires a rethinking of organizational values, operations, policies, and, of course, leadership models. But when good intentions are put into action, the increase in engagement, commitment, and innovation will benefit your organization—and the bottom line.

In the following chapters, we will explore how to cultivate a more people-centered organization through bringing more mindfulness, selflessness and compassion into the culture.

Quick Tips and Reflections

- ✓ Reflect on the culture of your organization; can you identify three aspects that create barriers to people being able to perform at their best?

- ✓ Reflect on the core values of your organization and consider whether they need to be reinforced or revised to better guide desired behaviors and outcomes.

- ✓ Consider how central people are to your strategy and what putting people more at the center of your strategy would look like.

- ✓ Commit to one thing you will do to influence positive change in your organizational culture for it to become more people centered.

- ✓ Consider ways you can create a more "human" work environment, where people can realize more of their potential.

11

Lead for a Mindful Organization

Nathan Boaz, senior managing director of leadership development and talent strategy at Accenture, and his team have a vision of eliminating what is known as "attention deficit trait" in the firm. They want to create a focused culture. He says, "We know that the single biggest impact on our people's well-being and performance is how their direct manager is operating. And if I see my supervisor take a break and go practice mindfulness for ten minutes, and I see her putting her phone down and giving me her full attention and deeply listening and really engaged with me, that's so powerful. And that's going to leave an impression on me that says, 'Wow! That's what is expected here!'"

The starting point for creating a people-centered organization is presence. When we are fully present with other human beings, we have the greatest potential to work more effectively together, to respectfully challenge one another, to learn from one another, and to leverage greater collective potential. Presence is the foundation of a mindful organization. When people are collectively calm, focused, and clear minded, then the organization is more effective, connected, and higher performing.

For Nate, this logic is compelling: "Every time I look at what's blocking people from doing what they love to do, focusing on the most important things in their lives—spending more time with their family, loved ones, friends, or doing energizing work—it's usually something in the mind. It's counterintuitive, but when we get people to calm down, slow down, and declutter, they become more innovative, productive, and fulfilled. And it all starts with being focused—individually and collectively."

Leading for a mindful organization can be challenging. We have worked with many leaders who have found such benefit for themselves in practicing mindfulness that they would like to introduce it into their organization. But just introducing a mindfulness program does not create a mindful organization. Creating a truly mindful organization requires not only rewiring individual minds but also reprograming how people collectively think, work, and behave. This takes time and conscious effort.

A mindful organization is one where mindfulness is embedded in the culture, where it becomes part of the DNA. In a mindful culture, work is organized in a way that is conducive to being present with one another, being focused on the task at hand, and having awareness of self and others. Presence, focus, and awareness are generally seen as skills for individuals, but they are just as relevant for a culture. And developing a culture with these qualities embedded in it enhances connectedness, commitment, and performance. The mindfulness matrix introduced in chapter 1 can be used to describe the mindfulness level of an organizational culture. Reflecting back on the matrix, where would you say your organization is in terms of collective focus and awareness?

This chapter specifically looks at mindfulness in an organizational context and how organizational mindfulness can be enabled. But first let's explore some examples of organizations that have integrated mindfulness into their culture to achieve strategic objectives.

Performance, Creativity, Change

We would love to be able to point at one specific organization and say that it's a truly mindful organization. But that would be wishful thinking. In our work with hundreds of organizations, many have been mindful in some ways, but in other ways, not so much. Just as mindfulness is a practice for individuals, so too is it for organizations. It's an ongoing practice that takes training, time, and a level of commitment. In addition, mindfulness does not make all problems and challenges go away; instead it changes how we approach those problems and challenges. Some organizations do stand out by having developed mindfulness in distinct aspects of their culture. Three good examples are Accenture's mindful performance culture, Ogilvy's mindful creativity culture, and Citrix's mindful change culture.

Accenture is a hyperkinetic, hypercompetitive organization of more than 425,000 people serving clients 24/7. It's an always-on, high-pressure, high-impact consultancy environment where attention is constantly under siege. Attention to detail, attention to the client, and attention on the task determines the success of consultants and staff. But with people's overall attention skills decreasing, leaders at Accenture realized that their performance culture was under threat. As a result, they started offering mindfulness training programs to teams and individuals to create a more mindful performance culture. How well did these programs work? Accenture evaluated results from their offices across twenty countries in Europe and the Americas and found a 30 percent increase in focus, a 25 percent increase in prioritization skills, a 34 percent increase in mental clarity, and a 23 percent decrease in multitasking behaviors. All in all, these results indicate a significant increase in the mindful qualities and mental effectiveness necessary to deal with distractions and serve clients with increased focus.

Ogilvy, the global advertising agency, faces the eternal catch-22 of creative industries: needing to be creative on demand. To succeed, people must learn to be creative not just when inspiration strikes but on a regimented schedule marked by deadlines. They're also required to be creative in the midst of a constant stream of distractions and competing priorities. One national Ogilvy CEO wondered how his division could maintain its edge, bolster its creative culture, and continue to offer out-of-the-box solutions to clients. He had already implemented all the technological tools that he could find to reduce distractions and enhance creativity. To find a more impactful, long-term solution, the CEO and his leadership team decided they needed to look inward instead of outward. The entire division took part in a four-month mindfulness training program to revamp their working habits, create new collaboration guidelines, and establish daily group practices of mindfulness. With mindfulness, they were able to reduce mental clutter and distractions. The training also helped them achieve collective alignment on how to support everyone's creative processes. This meant respecting others' need for solitude, understanding how to give feedback, and knowing when it's appropriate to interrupt someone. This helped them significantly enhance creativity throughout their day.

To enhance its service offerings to customers, Citrix, a multinational software company, acquired a very successful startup with a culture of entrepreneurship and risk taking. As soon as the deal was done and the honeymoon period was over, the usual problems with acquisitions kicked in. The formerly autonomous startup suddenly belonged to a large multinational business with its own policies and distinct culture. It was a culture clash. Many people resisted, revolted, and, in some cases, secretly worked against the interests of Citrix. Chris Prince, the head of learning and development for Citrix, understood the underlying problem: it stemmed less from resistance to Citrix than from basic human resistance to change. He understood that it was natural for people to resist being forced to do things in new ways. As a solution, Chris introduced mindfulness training across the entire organization, which helped people acknowledge and face their resistance. They were then able to deal with it where it resided: in their minds. As a result, a strong culture of mindful change was developed throughout the organization. This enabled Citrix to successfully manage through the acquisition with greater efficiency, less angst, and less resistance.

As these three examples demonstrate, mindfulness is not just a quality in itself. It can be a strategic vehicle to enable a targeted creation of desired cultural attributes. Whether the goal is to improve performance, increase creativity, enable change, or any other organization-wide enhancement, mindfulness offers a foundation for change and a conduit for sustainable improvement. At its root, an organizational culture is made up of the minds that create it, embrace it, and implement it. Mindfulness is a type of training that allows us to reshape and rewire our minds. When we collectively rewire our minds to change how we work, we transform our culture. It's that simple.

In our experience, in addition to offering mindfulness training programs, three keys to creating a more mindful culture are enabling greater organizational focus, managing organizational distractions, and embedding mindfulness in daily work activities.

Enable Organizational Focus

Through working with organizations in various industries all over the world, we've found four consistent challenges to maintaining focus for both leaders and employees. Leaders and employees are under pressure, always on, information overloaded, and working in distracted environments. We call it the "PAID" reality. The problem with the PAID reality is that it's a multipronged attack on our attention. It makes us multitask and turns us into action addicts. Multitasking and action addiction, as explained in chapter 3, destroy our focus and ruin our prioritization skills. Instead of focusing on the big issues, the high-value actions that drive performance, we keep ourselves occupied and become overwhelmed with busywork—small, easily accomplished tasks.

When this is a widespread characteristic of an organization, the organization as a whole lacks focus. Many distracted minds equals a distracted culture. Having a clearly defined mission statement or an explicit strategy is not enough to counter this problem. It can only be accomplished by training and rewiring the brains of individuals in the organization in a way that increases attention and reduces the appeal of distractions.

Some years ago, the Carlsberg Group undertook a series of significant reorganizations and layoffs. Leaders and employees alike were left with new responsibilities, ongoing changes, and a strong feeling of uncertainty. Understandably, this generated significant levels of distraction within the organization. Then CIO Kenneth Egelund Schmidt observed how individuals, teams, and the organization failed to focus on the long-term plan. "Groups of people were working in different directions and reacting to every bit of news that came their way," he lamented. "Entire teams would get caught up in low-priority projects for days before realizing that they were on the wrong path." As a result of this turmoil, people at Carlsberg became severely stressed, which only made them more reactive. Collaboration faltered. Distraction became more widespread. Performance suffered—all part of a downward cultural spiral.

Kenneth decided it was time to act. He believed that he needed to reinstate a collective focus and enhance well-being. For a year we worked with him and his teams to first develop their individual skills in mindfulness and then to create more focused and mindful collective work habits. Assisting Carlsberg for a year helped us gain greater insight into the anatomy of organizational focus and prioritization. Individual focus and prioritization is about doing the right things rather than trying to do everything. Similarly, organizational focus is a collective focus on doing the right things rather than doing lots of things. In this sense, it's a high degree of shared focus and awareness toward realizing well-defined goals and objectives. In a mindful organization, leaders and employees have greater clarity on collective priorities and, therefore, greater organizational focus.

Organizational focus allows individuals and teams to make better decisions about what to do—and often more important, what not to do. It facilitates constructive conversations among colleagues when priorities conflict, providing clarity and reaching consensus based on the overarching goals and objectives of the organization.

As a leader, your role in securing organizational focus is to continually help your people have clarity. What are the right tasks to do at the right time? Do these tasks serve the larger objectives of the organization? Depending on employees' level in the organization, their function, and job requirements, this clarification may need to happen once a month, once a week, or even daily. It must be done not only at the individual level but also for all teams across all functions.

Based on our years of experience helping organizations develop stronger organizational focus, here are a few practical tips that you as a leader can implement in your organization.

Cultivate Mindful Meetings

Meetings are low-hanging fruit in a journey toward creating a more mindful culture. According to a survey reported in *Industry Week*, two thousand managers claimed that at least 30 percent of their time spent in meetings was wasted. And similarly, according to a 3M Meeting Network survey of executives, 25 to an alarming 50 percent of meeting time was viewed as wasteful.[1]

Meetings in most organizations tend to be unfocused for a number of reasons. First, with back-to-back meeting schedules, the beginning minutes are generally wasted, because people are late or mentally lingering on the meeting they just left. Second, many meetings lack collective focus because it is culturally accepted to bring and use phones and laptops in meetings, creating distractions. Third, if people have too much going on and are over-whelmed by busyness, they will have a difficult time being fully present, especially if the meeting objectives and agenda are not crystal clear.

After we worked with Carlsberg's people to bring more organizational focus to their culture, they were able to decrease their average meeting time by 30 percent. What was most interesting about this result is that reducing meeting time was not a core objective of the initiative. The reduction in meeting time happened naturally as people became more focused and less distracted. They were simply able to get more done in a shorter amount of time. Here are some simple guidelines for creating more mindful meetings.

At the beginning of each meeting, invite everyone to join in one minute of silence before getting started. Although for some people a moment of silence can seem strange, in our experience, it can become quickly adopted as people appreciate the benefits of having a moment to settle in. This simple one minute can be key to helping everyone mentally arrive—versus just being there physically—in the meeting with a little more focus and presence.

During the meeting, have a collective agreement that phones and laptops are off or put away unless specifically required. If even one person is busy writing emails, texting, or reading the news during a meeting, it has a negative impact on the collective focus. It is also important that meeting objectives are clear and that someone is leading the meeting and ensuring everyone sticks to the agenda. This helps everyone stay more on task and engaged.

Toward the end of the meeting, establish a collective discipline of ending five minutes before the scheduled end time—often at the top or the bottom of the hour. These five minutes enable everyone to have time to transition mindfully to their next meeting.

Promote Physical Movement

Although a well-trained mind can maintain focus for extensive periods of time without moving, most of us benefit from some form of physical activity during the day. Movement brings better blood circulation and thereby more oxygen and energy to the brain. Getting up, getting out, or getting moving can also provide a new perspective on work, enabling enhanced creativity.

Many organizations we work with have invested in resources to support people in being active at work. Perhaps not surprisingly, Nike is a leader in this area. The company has world-class sports facilities integrated into its major campuses. Meetings at Nike can take place on a basketball court, running track, or in the gym. And although many companies have fitness facilities, the difference at Nike is that it's a job requirement. Everyone is expected to take at least half an hour a day for exercise.

Although Nike is an outlier in its commitment, some organizations we work with are investing in other creative ways to support physical movement. A global pharmaceutical company we work with has meeting rooms where tables and chairs are replaced by treadmills, so people can walk while meeting. And for long days at the desk, employees can pick a chair with pedals, so they can cycle while working. The company has also developed extensive walking paths around the campus and encourages people to have walking meetings. In our experience, encouraging more physical activity is a simple and easy way to bring more energy and focus to an organizational culture.

Offer Healthy Food and Drinks

Most modern offices today offer snacks and drinks as comfort food for employees during the day. This is great, but many of the snacks and drinks served are not conducive to enhancing mental performance.

Take sugar. While it may instill an immediate energy boost when first consumed, research has found that after the initial boost, it causes a dive in energy and focus. And even worse, that dive leads to a craving for more sugar. The result, for many people, is an ongoing abuse of sugar throughout the day.[2]

Coffee is another good example of a misunderstood performance substance. As described in chapter 3, coffee may be experienced as a focus-enhancing drink, but what it really does is scatter our focus. However, we don't notice, because the caffeine suppresses our tiredness and makes us feel more focused and energized. Offering snacks and drinks is great to enhance a more welcoming and collaborative office culture, but surrounding people with items that detract from focus may not be the best approach.

Forward-thinking organizations are now employing nutritionists as part of their employee wellness initiatives. In addition to offering courses on healthy eating, these experts are often engaged in influencing what food should be offered in the corporate cafeteria, which snacks are the healthy choices for effective working, and how food and beverages should be managed in corporate training programs. This can be as simple as ensuring there are more fruits, vegetables, and nuts freely available to employees and encouraging people to reduce their consumption of sugar, caffeine, and alcohol.

Encourage Boundary Setting

Organizational focus and prioritization is an art in today's PAID reality. There's always more to do, an email to answer, a meeting to attend, a report to prepare, or client to contact. Having the ability and mandate to hit the pause button and say no to an incoming task—being able to separate the critical tasks from the busywork—has become a precious skill.

Creating a culture where setting boundaries and saying no is not seen as a weakness but as a strength, and where leadership publicly praises employees for pushing back, is becoming increasingly important. Without it, focus, prioritization, and well-being will suffer.

Making this shift is not as hard as it may seem. We have seen teams and organizations shift from being hopelessly distracted to being collectively focused within months through the creation of a more mindful culture. An important part of this transformation is managing organizational distractions by minimizing digital and environmental disruptions.

Manage Organizational Distractions

To create a more mindful organizational culture, it is critical to minimize unnecessary distractions. In our experience, there are some relatively simple things that can be done to reduce organizational "noise" and create a more mindful culture. The easiest places to start are technology and office layout.

Minimize Digital Distractions

The first quick wins can be found in simple changes in technology. We live and work in environments that are filled with digital distractions. Even when we have clear goals and priorities, it can be difficult to avoid becoming overwhelmed by the onslaught of emails, text messages, and updates that beep, buzz, ding, or otherwise call out for our attention. In chapter 3, we explored how important it is for leaders to create personal time to focus and manage their own digital distractions. For the same reasons examined in chapter 3, it's equally important for leaders to help set digital boundaries in their organizations

France has recently introduced a "Right to Disconnect" law that forces employers to create systems that disable email during days off, weekends, and vacations. Although this may sound extreme, it is an acknowledgment of how the boundaries between work and home have become tenuous. Too many people spend too much time tethered to work. Although for some organizations this may sound good, it's not. Research has shown that expectations of being available to answer emails after work hours—regardless of actual time spent on emails—increases emotional exhaustion and negatively impacts well-being and job performance.[3] In other words, even when we aren't using our technology, the fact that we might need to at any moment creates stress. A continuous level of stress, even low levels, over time can negatively impact our health.

But organizations shouldn't create more mental space in a digital age just for health reasons—it's also good for business. In 2011, Atos Origin, an international IT services company with more than seventy thousand employees, made it an organizational goal to decrease email. CEO Thierry Breton surveyed employees and found that too many people were spending too much time sending and receiving email—so much so, that they were feeling overwhelmed by this one technological tool. Breton noted, "We're producing data on a massive scale that is fast polluting our working environments and also encroaching into our personal lives."[4] Atos Origin, of course, is not alone in this problem. A 2012 report by McKinsey Global Institute found that on average, employees spend 28 percent of their time on email—and that number is increasing every year.[5]

For Breton, the answer was a more sophisticated use of collaboration tools that allowed employees to choose when to participate in discussions and when to have uninterrupted time. This was the same solution offered in the 2012 report by McKinsey Global Institute. The authors of the report estimated that by using collaboration and social interaction technologies—such as Google Docs, Basecamp, Teamwork Projects, and Trello—companies could raise the productivity of knowledge workers by

20 to 25 percent. As a case in point, an independent assessment of Atos Origin in 2013 showed that overall email use had been cut by 60 percent, reducing average email messages per week from one hundred per employee to fewer than forty per employee. In the same year, the company's operating margin increased from 6.5 percent to 7.5 percent, earnings per share rose by more than 50 percent, and administrative costs declined from 13 percent to 10 percent. As David Burkus, author of *Under New Management*, pointed out, although not all these improvements are directly correlated to reducing email, these are still pretty compelling results.[6]

Leveraging collaborative tools and reducing email are only a couple of options for increasing focus in our world of numerous digital distractions. To cultivate a more mindful culture, we believe it's important to consider all major sources of "mental pollution." A strategy doesn't need to be as radical as eliminating email. There are many simple first steps, such as ensuring people "turn off" when they "take off." This type of policy allows employees to enjoy evenings, weekends, and vacations without being tethered to the office. In addition, organizations can consider other simple policies, like turning off all email notifications, so that people aren't distracted by incoming messages. And many companies we work with have policies for turning off devices—or at least putting them on silent—during meetings so that people can make better use of their time.

Take a moment to consider the digital communication culture in your organization. Are there boundaries or policies in place so employees can "unplug"? Are email and other forms of digital communication polluting your work environment? If so, take a moment to consider steps you can take to help your organization create more mental space in this digital age.

Revise Office Layouts

Our environment shapes our minds and thereby our cultures. And let's be clear. Today's open office layouts are not great for focus. Open offices reduce office costs and can be beneficial for enabling communication and creativity, but the level of distractions they bring can be detrimental to people's ability to focus and be effective.

Open office spaces will not go away. And they don't have to. If you help shape a culture that respects and enables focus in the open offices, you can get much benefit from it.

The main challenge of open offices is that there is nowhere to go for doing deep focus work. That can be remedied by creating small rooms and areas that support such focused work. Google does a great job in this respect. Among their vast areas of open offices, you'll find countless small, soundproof rooms for having focused conversations or for just sitting and working in quiet. Some rooms have built in white noise machines, others music systems, so people can tailor their environment to support their focus. Some rooms are built for movement, others for sitting at a desk, and yet others for brainstorming on large whiteboard walls.

In the same way that noise distracts our focus, so can physical clutter. Our mind is like a sponge, absorbing everything it encounters. Clutter in our environment becomes clutter in our mind. Incorporate this fact into how you decorate your offices and how you instill a culture of clean, un-cluttered, minimal distraction work spaces.

In today's work realities, thinking about the mental effectiveness of work environments is not just about the office but the home as well. In a 2017 Gallup poll, 43 percent of employed Americans said they spent at least some time working remotely.[7] Working from home has and will likely continue to be a growing workplace trend, as it can have many benefits. Not only can organizations save costs on office space and offer more flexible work conditions, but the practice can help people be more focused so long as they are properly set up.

Without a good home work environment, working from home has its perils. When you work from home, your home life can interfere with your focus, because your private-life sphere surrounds you when you are at work. In our experience, organizations that invest in helping employees create good home work environments realize the most benefit. Cisco stands out as a company that provides consultation to all employees in how to set up their home office optimally.

Make Work Activities Mindful

In developing a mindful organizational culture, it's useful to examine policies and collective work rules. As part of the training programs we deliver to our clients, we support the development of new guidelines around email, meetings, and many other work activities.

These simple guidelines are powerful in getting everyone centered and focused on working toward shared objectives. In our book *One Second Ahead: Enhance Your Performance at Work with Mindfulness*, we provide strategies for introducing more mindful behaviors to a broad range of daily work life, including email, meetings, scheduling, and even commuting.[8] Here are a few examples of strategies that have been implemented successfully by hundreds of organizations.

Three-by-Two Morning Prioritization

Action addiction is a very real thing for most of us, and having many action-addicted people creates an action-addicted culture, where everybody may run fast but in fact produce very little. A simple exercise in the morning, and repeated throughout the day, can enable strong prioritization and focus.

As you get to your work space in the morning, dedicate six minutes to set yourself up for a focused day. Take two minutes to practice mindfulness and simply sit and let your mind settle into focus, calm, and clarity. Then for two minutes, consider and write down the most important priorities for your day. Finally, take two minutes to plot those priority activities into your calendar.

These three short steps enable you to schedule your priorities rather than prioritize your schedule, and they can be repeated during the day as needed. If you as a leader do this and train your people to do the same, you will tackle collective action addiction and enable stronger team focus.

No Emails First Thing in the Morning

Action addiction also shows up in our way of managing emails. Most of us check email first thing in the morning. But if we have had a good night's sleep, the morning is when we have the most creative and expansive mind. When we check our emails first thing, our creative and expansive mind is replaced by all the details and issues from yesterday's unread messages. This just adds a lot of clutter to our mind, limiting our potential for bigger thoughts.

Rather than checking emails in the morning, spend the first hour or two on more important work, like strategic planning, important conversations, or reflection. And as a leader, work on instilling a culture where being on top of morning emails is not a badge of honor but a creative liability.

Be Curious

Your curiosity is important in support of a more mindful culture. Many work processes and tools become habitual; we fail to see when they become outdated and need replacement. We see what is there rather than questioning what could be. Be curious about the underlying causes of distraction in your organization. Question why things are done the way they are. Could they be done better or more efficiently? Question your meeting and email guidelines. Question your inter-organization communication. Question the way town halls are conducted. These are all areas in most organizations that could be improved, as well as being initial pathways for creating a more mindful organization.

Creating an organizational culture where people are more focused, less distracted, and work more mindfully will bring an organization well on the path of higher engagement, satisfaction, and performance. Also, it is the foundation for developing a more selfless culture, which will be described in chapter 12.

Quick Tips and Reflections

- ✓ Reflect on the potential benefits of a more mindful organizational culture; what business challenges or opportunities could it help address?

- ✓ Write down three things that would be visible and valuable indicators of more mindfulness in your organizational culture.

- ✓ Commit to one thing you will do to move your culture toward becoming more mindful and enhancing organizational focus and awareness.

- ✓ Consider policies and procedures you could introduce to integrate mindfulness into how work is performed.

- ✓ Reflect on what mindfulness means for you and your leadership; create your "mindfulness story," and use your own experience to inspire and influence others.

12

Lead for a Selfless Organization

Ray Dalio, philanthropist and founder of Bridgewater, the largest hedge fund firm in the world, offers a great example of a leader modeling a selfless culture. He was invited by a team to join a very important meeting with a large client. After the meeting, he received an email from a junior colleague on the team, who unequivocally criticized his performance:

> Ray—you deserve a "D–" for your performance today . . . you rambled for 50 minutes . . . It was obvious to all of us that you did not prepare at all because there is no way you could have been that disorganized at the outset if you had prepared. We told you this prospect has been identified as a "must-win" . . . today was really bad . . . we can't let this happen again.[1]

Coming from a junior employee to the founder of the company, this email may seem like career suicide. But not in this case. Ray understands the value of ignoring hierarchical status and dissenting when needed. One of his philosophies is that no one has the right to hold a critical opinion without speaking up about it. This is the philosophy the junior colleague took him up on, and tested by sending the email.

How did Ray respond? He forwarded the message to the other meeting attendees, asking them to rate his performance. They concurred with the "D–" rating. And to reinforce a culture that values dissent, he shared the whole email thread with the entire organization. By doing so, he modeled his philosophy that hierarchies, status, and ego are not conducive for a healthy organizational culture.

When you enter an organization with selfless traits, certain characteristics jump out. An organization with a selfless culture likely doesn't celebrate the employee of the month. Instead, it's acknowledged that every achievement is a result of interconnected collaboration. Consequently, the team is celebrated. In a selfless culture, everybody matters. There's likely no picture of the firm's founder on the wall. In a selfless organization, the founder rarely wants to take center stage, instead preferring that the focus be on the organization and on its purpose. Because of this, there will likely be photos of collective achievements on the walls, as well as photos showing people having fun as they support the organization and the communities they serve. The message is clear: People matter. Purpose matters. Service matters.

A selfless organizational culture is not about the individual, but about the collective mission and purpose. A selfless culture does not lack ambition and drive. Rather, it has the type of healthy confidence and self-interest to drive for results and achievement as one united team.

The selflessness matrix introduced in chapter 1 presents the potential of selflessness combined with self-confidence for leaders but it can equally be potent for a culture. A selfless, self-confident culture is where everyone looks out for one another's interest, and all work for the common greater good.

Consider a challenging situation in your team you have experienced recently. Were team members focused on their own narrow interests or on the interest of the team, the challenge, and the organization? If it was the former, how would cultivating a more selfless culture be of benefit?

This chapter looks at environmental factors that can support the establishment of a selfless culture. We will also look at inequality and how it negatively impacts selflessness. Further, we will specifically explore how selflessness can be strategically applied to enable more meaningful and effective processes for managing performance.

Traits and Tips for a Selfless Culture

In a selfless culture, there are more constructive conversations and less gossip. Not because there are fewer difficulties—every office has different personalities and varied opinions—but because there's less finger pointing. Difficult conversations are intended to solve issues that support the shared purpose of the organization rather than to place blame or find fault. Similarly, a selfless culture is more willing to acknowledge mistakes. Apologizing can be hard, but if people aren't too attached to their egos, they won't fear looking weak or compromised when they make a mistake. Specific traits of a selfless culture that are easy to cultivate include an abundance of gratitude, a reduction in symbols of status, and a visible incorporation of wise selflessness.

Show Gratitude

A selfless culture is rich in gratitude. As described in chapter 8, gratitude is the natural response to understanding how interconnected we all are, how much we rely on others' skills and contributions for our own success. With this understanding, we are bound to have greater humility, and as a result, gratitude flows naturally. Gratitude in organizations has proven to improve productivity, well-being, mental strength, and job satisfaction.[2] Furthermore, gratitude is contagious. When leaders show appreciation and gratitude, there's likely to be a ripple effect. Showing gratitude toward someone is likely to inspire that person to thank other people.[3]

In traditional company cultures, the people with the best sales numbers are rewarded and get the bonus. But with the wisdom of selflessness and interconnectedness, this approach seems shortsighted. It is rarely just one person who makes great sales happen. A selfless culture makes a point of identifying and showing gratitude to all those people who make the invisible contributions to the shared success.

A client of ours, a global pharmaceutical company, created a system where everyone was prompted daily to acknowledge others' work contributions that had affected their own work and day. Not surprisingly, it was not the best-performing salespeople who were awarded most often but rather the administrative assistants and other office staff. As a result, these normally slightly invisible contributions became clear to everyone. As a result, a greater cultural sense of interconnectedness and equality was established.

Reduce Status Symbols

A company with a selfless culture likely has no big corner offices. Corner offices were invented during the industrial revolution, symbolizing the status and power of the CEO and senior leaders. Jakob Meding, former CEO of HP in Denmark, raised eyebrows throughout the organization when, on his first day, he left his corner office and sat at one of the communal workstations with the rest of the employees. He made this change because he wanted to minimize the risk of ending up in the CEO bubble described in chapter 4. He shared how the move drastically impacted how people viewed him and how they engaged with him. Suddenly, he was just like everyone else, and people talked to him and shared important ideas and suggestions. This was valuable information he would never have obtained if he were sequestered in his corner office.

In a selfless culture, there is a spirit of interconnectedness. Each individual is only successful because of the shared efforts of everybody. Think of King Arthur's round table—a symbolic and tangible mechanism to create a culture where all voices can be heard and everyone matters.

Take a moment to stroll through your office environment. Look for visible indicators of status and hierarchy versus team work and collaboration. Consider simple ways you can shift the environment toward promoting greater equality and interconnectedness.

Employ Selfless Wisdom

A selfless culture also has the space for wisdom. When Antoine Raymond, CEO of ARaymond, a global manufacturer of fasteners and connectors, and his leadership team learned that their biggest competitor was close to bankruptcy, they called an emergency meeting—not to celebrate and or to strategize how they could leverage the situation. Instead, they discussed how they could best support the competitor to keep it from going out of business. They recognized how their company was interconnected with its competitor in many ways. As Antoine explained to us: "Our industry, like any industry, is an ecosystem of clients, providers, and partnerships. We knew that if our biggest competitor left that ecosystem, it would destabilize the market. Beyond the obvious pain it would cause their employees, it would also hurt us." Antoine picked up the phone, called the CEO of the competitor, and offered him financial support.

Marshall Goldsmith, world-renowned executive coach and author of several bestselling books on leadership, shared some insights with us. He has observed that one of the main problems for ego-driven organizations is the constant desire to win. According to Marshall, if we're constantly driven by the desire for victory, we lose the ability to think in terms of "win-win" solutions. We lose the wisdom of seeing the bigger picture: we lose the holistic awareness of the interconnected ecosystems we all operate in. This is what the leadership team of ARaymond had in mind when they supported their struggling competitor. But few leadership teams behave this way. Understandably, many would have popped a bottle of champagne and celebrated a victory. And while that may be appropriate in some situations, there's a risk when it's done out of an obsession with winning and a thirst for dominance.

If you truly value all employees and believe that everyone matters, a great mechanism for cultivating a more selfless organization is in how performance is managed.

Redefine Performance Management

Feedback on performance is one of the most important conversations between people at work. To improve work performance and collaboration, people need feedback that helps guide them and reinforces particular behaviors. In many organizations, this occurs through a formal performance management process that very few employees actually find valuable. A 2013 Mercer Global Performance Management Survey discovered that only 3 percent of companies reported that their performance management system delivered significant value.[4] Given numbers like this, many organizations are redefining how they manage, rank, rate, and discuss performance. Companies like Accenture, Deloitte, Adobe, Juniper Systems, Dell, Microsoft, and IBM have replaced annual reviews with more engaging and interconnected ways of supporting people's performance.

There's much we can learn about how to effectively support people's performance. One of the most important lessons is that leaders must have ongoing, present, and personal conversations with their employees. To truly engage people, to give them a sense of real human connection, leaders must have frequent and informal conversations with employees. Leaders must understand what employees find meaningful, what engages them, and how they want to contribute. These topics and questions address foundational human motivations. To get to this level of personal connection, leaders must apply selflessness by letting go of outdated and distancing power hierarchies. According to the Mercer survey, the main reason for the failure of traditional performance reviews is the leader's inability to effectively engage the employee.[5]

In today's overly busy, complex, and often geographically dispersed work settings, personal human connections often get lost. In many cases, leaders don't have the time or the skills to effectively engage people in meaningful conversations. And even if they do, their minds are racing so fast that they're not truly present during the conversation. So although there's merit in getting rid of performance reviews and replacing them with regular, informal check-ins, leaders must be equipped to do so in an effective way. Learning to be present—to be solely focused on the current situation—during the conversations is a great starting point. But skillful performance conversations require more than presence. It requires understanding how the mind responds to feedback and how feedback can be more effectively delivered.

Researchers have found that the phrase, "I would like to give you some feedback" activates the same pain response in our brains as someone holding up a stick to strike us.[6] How is this possible? As social animals, one of our greatest fears is being kicked out of the tribe—of being isolated, which for our early ancestors would mean death. Today, feedback has become synonymous with criticism. And criticism is a strong indication of possible isolation. In this way, the word *feedback* signifies an evolutionary threat, a possibility that we'll be excluded from the tribe.

And what makes matters worse is that most people do not like giving other people feedback because they don't like inflicting pain. As a result, too often organizations end up in situations where really important conversations about how people can enhance their performance go terribly wrong or don't happen at all.

If instead we embrace the premise that we all have an intrinsic desire to have meaning and purpose in our life and that work, for many of us, is a big part of life, it makes sense that we would all want guidance and support on how we can add more value. This can best occur in a culture where everyone is valued and constructive feedback is viewed as a means toward collective improvement. A truly selfless approach to performance management requires a culture where giving and receiving feedback is valued as a mechanism for greater collaboration and collective development. Feedback should be something that everyone welcomes and receives, including all employees and in all directions.

As noted in chapter 10, one of the best things a leader can do is model desired behavior. When a leader is willing to receive criticism publicly, it sends a powerful message to the rest of the organization that ego should not get in the way of collective success. Ray Dalio demonstrated this behavior when he shared his "D–" rating with the entire organization. But modeling selflessness is only the first step. Organizations that want to support a more progressive approach to performance management by creating a more selfless, "not about me," culture need to implement systems and structures to support it.

In our conversation with Debi Daviau, president of the Professional Institute of the Public Service of Canada, representing more than fifty-five thousand workers in the public sector, she spoke about the importance of creating a culture of constructive feedback: "The success of the organization cannot be about me. It has to be about 'the whole,' which is why people, including myself, need to know when we are doing well and where we have opportunities for improvement." She believes it is essential that recognition and feedback go hand in hand. "If people do not feel recognized and appreciated for what they contribute, they will not respond well to hearing about things they didn't do very well."

In our experience, making an organizational norm of giving and receiving feedback is key to enhancing performance. Making time at the end of each meeting or formally at the end of each week to reflect on team and individual performance, including discussions on how we can improve, makes having these conversations much easier. In addition, creating a value around "sharing feedback" as core to organizational success and performance is key. And reinforcing this through guidelines on "right speech," which say that I shouldn't be talking about another person unless it is in their best interest and unless I am willing to say it to them directly in support of our collective success.

Take a moment to consider the performance reviews you have with your people. What results do you think these conversations yield? Are you creating authentic human connections? Are you engaging your employees' or team members' basic desire for happiness? For meaning and purpose? When developing a selfless culture, another important question to ask is how equal or unequal your culture is.

Selflessness and Equality

Selflessness goes hand in hand with equality. Imagine you have two monkeys in front of you. You teach them that every time they give you a pebble, you give them a piece of cucumber. After a few rounds of giving both of them their reward of cucumber slices, you suddenly give one of them a grape—their favorite fruit. What happens? The one getting the grape is thrilled. The other, however, is deeply offended. It throws the piece of cucumber at you, and demands a grape. This is exactly what happened in a study directed by Emory University professors Frans de Waal and Sarah Brosnan. Monkeys have a strong sense of fairness and resist conditions of inequality.[7]

Humans are very much the same.

In many organizations today, there are significant differences in how people are treated. This inequality has deep, far-reaching consequences. Keith Payne, professor of psychology at the University of North Carolina and author of *The Broken Ladder: How Inequality Affects the Way We Think, Live, and Die*, has researched the effect of inequality on society and found that monkeys aren't the only primates with an instinctive reaction to inequality. Inequality kills social connectedness, makes people unhappy, erodes trust, and kills engagement. Unless we're the ones on the better side of the inequality spectrum.

The following is an example many of us can relate to. We board a plane, entering at the front. Our first sight is the beautiful, spacious seats in first class. With wide armrests and ample leg room, they look like luxury cocoons. Maybe a glass or two of champagne has been served, and a few seated passengers glance through the menu, deciding on steak, fish, or chicken. But we keep plodding toward the back until we reach our own seat in economy class; crowded, cramped, and vaguely stale. Our mood sours. Interestingly, studies have found that air rage and fights on airplanes happen four times more often if the plane has a first-class cabin. In fact, having a first-class cabin on a plane increases the risk of serious conflict as much as nine-hour delays do.[8]

From a performance point of view, research has found that in baseball—an occupation with wide income disparities—equality in incentives and pay created better social cohesion and team performance. A study showed that with more equality, not only did the lesser-paid players perform better, but so did the best-paid players.[9] The final report of the World Health Organization Commission on the Social Determinants of Health found that societies with higher levels of inequality have worse health issues, more crime, and more social problems.[10]

In organizations, the same patterns apply. Organizations with higher inequality have been shown to have higher resentment among employees, which adversely affects the company through decreased effort, a lack of cooperation, and even outright sabotage. Companies with extreme pay inequality are riskier, perform worse, and experience greater shareholder dissent.[11] Studies have also shown that inequality harms performance-related outcomes such as product quality, leads to feelings of unfairness, and increases employee turnover.[12] This is just about everything that can afflict a poorly performing company, which speaks to the destructive force of inequality.

We intuitively know the benefits of equality. In a study across forty countries, people were asked how much more CEOs should be paid compared to unskilled workers. Although there were significant differences across countries, when compared with what CEOs actually make, the conclusion of the research was that universally, the pay gap is too big.[13] According to a 2015 report by the Economic Policy Institute, the top US CEOs make more than three hundred times the salary of the average worker.[14] That's a dramatic gap. Between 1978 and 2014, inflation-adjusted CEO pay has increased 1,000 percent, while the typical US worker's salary has only increased 10 percent.[15] There may be some valid arguments for why a CEO deserves so much more, but our focus is on how this difference impacts perceptions of fairness and creates a culture of entitlement, hierarchy, self-importance, greed, and selfishness.

The current levels of inequality are not compatible with selfless leadership behavior, a selfless culture, or a people-centered organization. We recommend that leaders who truly want to create a more selfless culture start by reviewing the compensation levels throughout their organizations. Is there a sense of equity? Do you think that people are valued appropriately for their contribution? If compensation packages were visible to everyone, do you think it would enhance engagement? Or would it detract from performance?

Although we know money doesn't provide genuine happiness, we also know that inequality fosters the opposite: dissatisfaction, dissension, and division. Because of this, a people-centered, performance-oriented organization must attempt to avoid inequality wherever and whenever possible. This is also a great step toward creating a more compassionate culture, where everyone truly cares about one another's performance and well-being.

Quick Tips and Reflections

- ✓ Reflect on the degree of selflessness in your organization and how this enhances or detracts from creating a collective sense of engagement, meaning, and purpose.

- ✓ Consider how people are recognized and rewarded; commit to one thing you can do to enhance appreciation and gratitude in and across teams, departments, and levels.

- ✓ Consider how you currently manage and measure performance; is there anything you can do to make it a more engaging, meaningful, and impactful process?

- ✓ Identify five people who make significantly less money than you do; invite them for coffee to find out who they are, what they do, and reflect on their value to the organization.

- ✓ Reflect on the level of equity in your organization and commit to at least one thing you will do toward enhancing it.

13

Lead for a Compassionate Organization

Nancy Green, CEO of Athleta, a Gap Inc. brand, experienced compassion early in her career. When she joined Gap, she was twenty-five and soon after she became pregnant with her first child. "I didn't think I could do the job because I didn't see other women that were doing the job as mothers." But there was one exception. Another woman on the team pushed her to come back or else she'd never know what was possible. It worked. Nancy continued to grow at the company, leading to successive leadership appointments all the way to the C-suite—while raising four children.

The experience of being shown compassion made Nancy commit to always strive to cultivate a compassionate culture in her teams. In our interview with her, she said, "By showing compassion for the people we work with, by genuinely connecting with them human to human, and by recognizing their whole person and life, we will have far stronger professional relationships and results."

Nancy's approach to leadership is to be compassionate by constantly balancing power with softness: "I can be very demanding, and I have extremely high standards, but I understand that people are human. I try to balance being powerful and soft at the same time." In this way, Nancy balances the two aspects of the matrix of wise compassion—the intention to be of benefit to others—on the one hand, and wise discernment—considering business objectives—on the other.

In a compassionate organizational culture, people support one another in being successful and happy. The culture supports positive intentions toward others, and at the same time instills the wisdom and professionalism in everyone to make tough choices. This includes sometimes doing things that are difficult but will benefit the culture and the organization in the long term. If your organization cares for employees and their well-being, those employees will be happier and more productive. And if your employees are more productive, the organizational bottom line will benefit.

As explained in chapter 9, organizations with more compassionate leaders have stronger connections between people, increased collaboration, higher levels of trust, enhanced loyalty, and lower turnover. Compassion makes employees feel more valued and have more pride in their work. For these reasons, compassion is a cornerstone of people-centered organizations. In this chapter, we'll take a closer look at the attributes of a compassionate organization, the relationship between compassion and trust, and the power of social cohesion.

Attributes of the Compassionate Organization

When you walk into the offices of a compassionate organization, you can feel it: from the way you're greeted by the receptionist to how people engage with one another. In a compassionate organization, the lowest-level employees are respected as equals and encouraged to take an active part in organizational success. US accounting firm Moss Adams has many compassionate traits in its culture—and it shows. When you enter the reception area of its headquarters in Seattle, you're greeted with a genuine smile from the receptionist. If you have been there before, chances are he'll remember your name and quite likely, he'll also remember your preferred drink. He isn't trained to do this. It comes naturally, because he's part of a culture that values true interest in others. This is one of the hallmarks of a compassionate organization.

Compassionate organizations focus on caring for the whole person, not just the working person. Health, family, and private lives matter. When Cisco started planning for its global mindfulness and resiliency program, the leadership team knew it would benefit the business, but that was not the main objective. The main objective was for people to be taken care of as whole beings. Therefore, they considered how the program could be offered to employees and their family members. In creating the program, Cisco understood that compassion and caring doesn't stop at the office door or parking lot, but extends to employees' lives beyond corporate walls.

In a compassionate organization, people are seen as human beings before they're seen as a job title. This means that lower-level employees are equally recognized as an integral part of the team. Meeting with lower-level employees is a good litmus test for organizational compassion. If the receptionist, clerical workers, or the cleaning crew are hidden away, avoid eye contact, or don't greet you, it is a good indicator of how valued they feel and the level of caring and compassion in the organizational culture.

Bob Chapman, chairman and CEO of manufacturing company Barry-Wehmiller, tells a story in his book *Everybody Matters* about the power of listening to your people. Encouraged by Chapman, a factory worker shared his experience of the organization's culture: "I walk in the same door with engineers, accountants, and other people who work in the office. Why is it that when they go to the office and I go into the plant, we're treated completely differently? You trust them to decide when to get a cup of coffee or call home, but you don't trust me." The next day, Chapman and his leadership team removed the time clocks and break bells and issued the following statement: "No matter what door people walk in, everyone is treated the same—with the trust and respect they deserve."[1] Barry-Wehmiller is a great example of an organization that incorporates compassion as an intrinsic part of its culture. And not just as words or slogans, but where it truly matters—as part of its policies and procedures.

We have observed that compassion in organizations is gaining traction around the globe. Leaders are starting to see the benefits compassion brings to their culture, their people, and their clients. But it's still new territory for most organizations. And, unfortunately, many of those organizations are still stuck in the old paradigm of treating people as tools for maximizing shareholder wealth. Many leaders still believe that a compassionate, people-centered culture and a healthy, shareholder-focused bottom-line focus are mutually exclusive. The result? Corporate cultures that put inhuman pressure on their people.

To be clear: pressure is not a problem—if administered with care. A global bank we worked with provided a troubling example of the mismanaged application of pressure. During a training session, we noticed a high level of tension emanating from one of the participants, a forty-something-year-old man. He had a hard time sitting still. Constantly fidgeting, he seemed uncomfortable in his own skin. When one of us asked him if he was all right, he exploded. With tears welling in his eyes, he shouted that he had no time to sit around for a session. He'd just worked sixteen hours nonstop on a project that was far from done and he was only participating in this training to meet his manager's expectations.

In a compassionate organization, there's space and encouragement for self-compassion—certainly not the case in this example. Compassionate organizations do their best to help their people take care of themselves. This starts with the right to draw lines and set boundaries, as discussed in chapter 11, especially when the pressure starts to build.

The problem when pressure gets too high is that it can become habitual, and working long hours and not getting enough sleep becomes the norm. When we are under pressure, we tend to just try to push through. We get stuck in action mode until we collapse. So the skill of self-compassion must be trained and ingrained in the culture before the going gets tough. An important step in this process is to create a physical environment that allows and encourages self-compassion and care.

When it designed its new headquarters in Sweden, IKEA designed it for self-care. The building includes several rooms for power napping, mindfulness practice, and physical movement. But unlike most companies with similar initiatives, these rooms are not hidden away in the basement or in some fixed-up storage room. IKEA places these rooms close to the entrance, so you can't avoid seeing them as you enter the building. Self-compassion is placed at the front door.

The mental environment is equally important for self-compassion, and the legitimacy of setting boundaries and saying "no." Ted Kezios, global head of benefits for Cisco, shared with us how they have created a culture where it is fully accepted to withdraw if one feels personally overwhelmed. He got to experience this firsthand when one day, in the midst of finalizing a large project, he received a call about a serious family issue. While his first impulse was to stay with the team and push through, his team members saw that he was not well, and insisted on him going home. "It was so touching and heartwarming," he shared. "Everyone got together around me, with genuine love and concern. While I didn't want to abandon them, they assured me they had my back and urged me to go home. I was deeply touched by feeling their genuine concern and support, despite the work pressure they also had."

Creating a compassionate culture is about having people who are willing and able to bring compassion to work. Building compassion into recruitment helps create this type of culture. When LinkedIn CEO Jeff Weiner interviews job candidates, he likes to ask, "What would you do if you were about to step into a meeting with a very important client to close a deal and you get a call that a valued colleague has been rushed to hospital?" There's no correct answer to this question, but the reflection helps in getting a sense of how the applicant prioritizes compassion.

A global professional services firm we work with uses community service as a way of creating a compassionate culture. We were invited to facilitate a workshop as part of a three-day offsite with their ASEAN (Association of Southeast Asian Nations) offices and take part in their community work. The event took place in Cambodia, which had just been subjected to serious flooding that resulted in lack of food and clean water for many people. For the first full day, all partners, consultants, and staff were packing and distributing food, helping rebuild schools, and doing other humanitarian work. Everyone, from secretaries to managing partners, were working shoulder to shoulder to alleviate the suffering of other human beings. At the end of the day, back at the offsite venue, the regional managing partner took the stage and exclaimed: "This is what we are. This is why we are here. To be of service." The atmosphere in the room was palpable. Compassion could be seen in the eyes of everyone.

Take a moment to reflect on how compassionate your organizational culture is. Imagine for a moment that your employees are actually your family—your parents, your husband or wife, your children, your siblings. How would you like them to feel if they worked in your organization? How would you want them to feel every day as they arrived at the office? Every day as they left the office? Does your current culture align with how you would want your family to feel about your organization? If not, what could you change that would increase compassion in your organizational culture?

Compassion and Trust

In a compassionate organization, people know their colleagues have their backs. Employees feel trusted, and they have trust in others. Trust and compassion go hand in hand. When you know your leader has genuine concern for you, you'll have natural trust. And when he or she knows you genuinely care about the work, the team and the organization, again trust will follow. In chapter 7, we showed that trust provides employees with a sense of safety, instills in them a sense of meaning, and significantly contributes to their overall sense of happiness. It's an equally significant contributor to an employee's sense of purpose, engagement, and performance. Trust speeds up processes and makes organizational culture more efficient and more productive. As professor, consultant, and author Warren Bennis wrote, "Trust is the lubricant that makes it possible for organizations to work."[2]

Trust is a relational quality between people, but it's also a cultural characteristic. Some cultures have a strong sense of trust; others don't. Organizational cultures with high levels of trust have a real advantage over those with a low level of trust.

A great example of how trust enables the speed of business is a company that was founded on speed: FedEx. FedEx has been consistently included on *Fortune* magazine's lists of "World's Most Admired Companies" and "100 Best Companies to Work for in America." One of the reasons for this consistent admiration is FedEx's trust in and commitment to its people. CEO and founder Fred Smith believes that employees should be empowered to make decisions in support of the goal of 100 percent customer satisfaction 100 percent of the time. The extent of this empowerment includes employees being able to charter flights to meet customer delivery requirements without having to seek approval, and FedEx truck drivers being able to define their own routes based on their assessment of how to best meet customer needs. These kinds of policies instill a strong sense of empowerment—and responsibility—in each employee. They also help develop a mutual sense of trust, which speeds up the processes and interactions and enhances performance.

The efficacy of trust can also be observed by comparing processes and policies of a company in different countries. In our work, we engage in contracting with organizations for our services around the globe. Some years ago, we started working with the Danish office of a global consulting firm. Our contracting process was simple. Once we agreed on the scope of work with the business leader, we sent an email confirming the details, price, and start date and were good to go.

A year later, we began working with the same firm in an office in the United States. After an agreement was reached with the business leader, we were instructed to connect with the procurement department. We were asked to submit various forms and then provided with a lengthy contract for review. When we asked to have a meeting to review the contract, we were told by the procurement department that they would only meet with us if our lawyer was present. We then spent several months going back and forth on details and experienced multiple delays for various required reviews. Once the contract was signed, it still took a couple of months before the actual work could commence and a few more months after starting before a purchase order was created so we could send an invoice. All in all, the process from "let's work together" to working today took eight months and many resources in the United States, as opposed to a couple of days between two people in Denmark.

The difference between the two experiences is stark and can be partly explained by the cultural level of trust in the two countries. Denmark, according to OECD research, scores at the top in terms of trust, while the United States scores much lower.[3] The level of national trust levels spill over into how companies operate in the country.

In cultures, whether national or organizational, where there's a low level of trust, we build control mechanisms, policies, and bureaucracy. These levels of bureaucracy and control hamper efficiency. More importantly, such control neurologically impacts us in ways that shape our minds, our behavior, and ultimately the culture we work in.

The research of Paul J. Zak, director of the Center for Neuroeconomics at Claremont Graduate University, has found that the culture we work in directly impacts our behavior and thereby, how we contribute to that culture.[4] In our discussion with him, he shared his findings on how leaders who exhibit compassionate behavior enhance the oxytocin levels in the people they lead. Oxytocin enables higher levels of trust, fosters kindness, and increases generosity. Paul's research also found that trust can lead people—and the cultures they help shape—into a virtuous cycle. When you show trust in someone, oxytocin is released in their brain, impacting their behavior, which in turn impacts the release of oxytocin in your brain. In this sense, trust is contagious. And the more that it's induced in the culture, the more efficiently the organization will operate. In much the same way, distrust is contagious. Distrust your people, and their oxytocin levels will literally dry up, making them less trusting—and in turn will cause the same to happen to you.

Even with all of these benefits, trust is fragile. It can be shattered in a moment. Dr. Ritu Anand, deputy CHRO of Tata Consultancy Services, one of the world's largest IT services companies, has observed that when there's a gap between what a leader says and does, trust vanishes. "Keep commitments, be accountable, behave ethically; that's how you keep trust," she revealed to us. "Do the right thing rather than the expedient thing—always." She went on to explain, "You maintain a culture of trust by telling the truth, even when it's hard. People ultimately remember you for what you do. Be trustworthy, rather than just talking about it, and you can create an outstanding culture." The golden rule for creating a trusting culture is for leaders to put their words into action, to model the behaviors that they extol. Consistency and authenticity between what's said and what's done creates trust for the long run.

Trust matters. It impacts you, your people, your culture, and your organization. As a leader, you represent the strongest influence on the creation of your organization's culture.

Take a moment to consider how you can show more trust in your people. How can you catalyze and perpetuate the virtuous cycle of trust? These are important questions to consider, especially since trust is critical to maintaining social cohesion.

Compassion and the Power of Social Cohesion

Social cohesion is the invisible glue that connects us as human beings in cultures. It's the bond that makes us stick together, collaborate, and collectively contribute to a shared purpose. Compassion and trust create social cohesion, and social cohesion can make the difference between a good company and a great company.

To better understand this relationship, consider Southwest Airlines. Southwest is the most profitable airline in the world and one of the fastest-growing companies since it was established in 1976. The company made headlines throughout the airline industry when it achieved record-setting gate turnaround times. Turnaround time may not sound exciting, but in the airline industry, turnaround time is money. As Southwest cofounder and former CEO Herb Kelleher said, "Planes make money in the air, not sitting on the ground."[5] When planes are parked, they're a direct cost to the company. So when Southwest cracked the turnaround time code, it was big news throughout the airline industry. Of course, in a short time, every other airline copied Southwest's turnaround procedures.

But there was a problem. Nothing changed for the other airlines when they copied Southwest's actions.

Even using Southwest's procedures, other airlines couldn't cut their turnaround times. Why? Because other airlines lacked Southwest's social cohesion. Southwest had established a strong culture of compassion in its teams, which led to a stronger sense of social cohesion—the bond for collaboration. To get a plane turned around requires up to twelve different teams to collaborate efficiently and willingly. Pilots, ticketing agents, baggage handlers, maintenance teams, and tarmac crews all need to work together to more quickly get a plane in the air. In most airlines, these functions aren't particularly keen to collaborate because of distinct power hierarchies and cross-team disputes. The culture instilled in Southwest Airlines, however, is one of genuine respect and concern. Pilots aren't seen as superior, and maintenance crew members aren't seen as expendable. They're all part of the same organism, with the same purpose of getting their passengers in the air as quickly as possible—and accomplishing this while experiencing joy and kindness toward one another.

Much to the chagrin of other airlines, operational procedures are not the cause of quick turnaround times—compassion and social cohesion are.

Every organization needs social cohesion. Every organization has different teams with different roles and functions that must coordinate efforts seamlessly to be successful. But without a compassionate and trusting culture, this coordination can be challenging. How often have you experienced friction and active, but hidden, resistance between functions like marketing and finance or operations and sales?

Today, social cohesion is eroding because of inequality, financial pressure, technology, and globalization. Inequality makes the lowest-paid employee resent the highest paid. Unreasonable financial pressure from shareholders makes leaders single-mindedly focus on short term results. Technology separates us, making it harder and harder to treat one another as human beings. And globalization removes the sense of belonging to a tribe. But cultivating social cohesion in your organization is both a competitive advantage and a tremendous gift to your employees. It improves performance. It builds trust. It enables purpose. It engenders happiness. And it creates the foundation on which a compassionate culture is built.

Consider the benefits of a more compassionate organizational culture. How could it enhance performance and engender a stronger sense of cohesion and connectedness? Consider how being a more compassionate organization could be part of your strategy. And if you are willing, why not get started today?

Quick Tips and Reflections

- ✓ Consider ways to introduce wise compassion into your organization: What resources could you share? What programs could you offer? What space could you provide for people to practice?

- ✓ Commit to at least one thing you will do to focus more on the "whole person" at work—to see people equally and inspire greater care and kindness.

- ✓ Identify ten people at various levels and from different areas of your organization and invite them to describe the culture; ask whether they feel cared for and how much they feel trusted.

- ✓ Ask each of the ten people you have identified to point out one policy and procedure that they find negatively impacts their performance and engagement; commit to acting on at least one of their suggestions.

- ✓ Consider ways to enhance social cohesion at work, including how people are engaged, how teams are recognized, how people are treated, how caring and kindness are brought into everyday work.

Afterword

Leadership for a Hard Future

When asked about the importance of his legacy, Heineken CEO Jean-François van Boxmeer commented, "That's a strange thing to ask and think about. I am just a short chapter in a long book. There have been many good CEOs before me and many will follow. My role is merely to prepare the organization for the next generations." As leaders, as mighty and important as our roles may feel, we are just short chapters in a much bigger tale. But while we play this role, we have significant impact and power.

With the power of our leadership comes responsibility. Responsibility to the people and the societies we serve. They are the lives we have the power to influence, for better or worse. And ultimately, we can never blame our boss or shareholders. We carry the burden of the choices we make.

Leadership must be about serving for the greater good. We are all children of this planet. We all want to be happy. No one wants to suffer. Our most honorable responsibility as leaders is to help increase happiness and kindness and decrease unnecessary suffering. And to serve our societies in a way that they become a little better by means of our actions.

In this light, we as leaders must think and lead for the long term. We must have the courage to face the facts of the challenges lying ahead of us and be ready to make unpopular decisions when needed. And such decisions are much needed today.

In the book *No Ordinary Disruption*, the authors—directors of the McKinsey Global Institute—lay out findings from years of research and analysis on the changes taking place on our planet.[1] Global economic power balances will shift dramatically, among other things making Africa a key player and leaving the United States behind. Technology will change in ways we currently can't comprehend, escalating disruptive changes in business, geopolitics, international law, warfare, economics, and much more. The global population will grow and age, resulting in an unprecedented burden on the planet and working population. The way countries and companies are run will change foundationally. And finally, due to overpopulation and climate changes, we will see troubling scarcities of water, food, and other foundational resources for life. If just half of what McKinsey predicts happens, we are facing a hard future.

The same worrying messages come from researchers and organizations like the United Nations, OECD, and Intergovernmental Panel on Climate Change. The biggest and most dramatic challenge is undoubtedly climate change, which forever will impact our life on this precious planet. The seas will rise. The weather will become unpredictable. Some regions will dry out. Others will wash away. The natural balance of nature is being disturbed far beyond our reach of understanding and influence. Why are we not reacting?

Because our brains don't perceive it.

Imagine this: You are standing on the highway and a truck is coming toward you at full speed. What do you do? Do you start contemplating whether the truck is real and how much it will hurt you to be hit? Or do you do everything you can to get out of the way?

Our brain is designed to help us survive by being tuned to immediate changes, such as an oncoming storm, or the roar of a truck coming full speed toward us. But the brain doesn't sense the thinning of the ozone layer; the increased carbon dioxide levels in the air and oceans; and the very slow changes in climate, temperature, and rising seas. We have no neurological alarm system for slow change. When it comes to slow change, the normal fight-or-flight reaction of the amygdala draws a blank.

If the brain could react to slow change like it does to a fast-approaching truck, we would all be dogmatic about decreasing our individual environmental footprints and would take to the streets to make companies and governments do the same. But it doesn't. And we are all blind to the fact that we may be killing the planet as a habitat for our children. We are indeed facing a hard future, and we don't really see it coming.

As leaders today, we have a responsibility to face the hard challenges of the future. Even if the brains of the people we lead are not alarmed by the slow threats we face, we can't neglect them. We have to stand up to face the future with clear minds. Because when the challenges hit, as slowly as they will, if we don't stand together—clear minded, with selflessness and compassion—we will do what humans have always done: stick with our tribe and fight the others.

We can't change the tsunami of challenges coming our way, but we can prepare ourselves. Prepare to stand together, rather than fight one another. We can start now by building more mindfulness, selflessness, and compassion in our organizations and societies, so that trust and social cohesion is in place when things become more challenging. That is the responsibility we all have, and especially those in positions of power. And it starts with our own minds.

Any conflict or war, at any time in history, has always originated in a mind or in a collection of minds. Conflicts do not come out of nowhere, and wars are not made of weapons but of minds that hold anger, attachment, or ignorance. In a rapidly changing world, with hard challenges coming our way, we need leaders with stable minds who can respond mindfully, with selfless confidence and wise compassion. It gives us great hope to see that leaders across the world and across industries and cultures are embracing these qualities and creating more social cohesion in their organizations. Thank you for your interest.

Appendix A

The Mind of the Leader App

To support you in engaging in the mind training practices introduced in this book, we have created a Mind of the Leader app. The app follows the practices in the order they have been presented in this book and also provides suggestions on training plans to support you in your journey toward cultivating greater mindfulness, selflessness, and compassion. For information on how to access the app, please go to http://www.themindoftheleaderbook.com.

Appendix B

Practices for Training Compassion

In addition to the compassion practices introduced in this book, there are some additional practices we would like to share. (*Note:* These practices are also included in the Mind of the Leader app.)

Each of the following practices focuses on one of the four qualities of compassion examined in chapter 9: wishing others happiness, wishing to alleviate suffering, enjoying others' success, and seeing others equally.

We recommend beginning each practice with a few moments of mindfulness practice to settle and prepare the mind. Then pick whichever of the four practices you deem most useful.

Start the practice by simply focusing on one or two people you care for. When you are successful with that, you can gradually expand your training until you can practice it even for people you find difficult to deal with or don't like. Then extend it to your community and your country until you can develop universal compassion. As you do this, it changes your way of perceiving the world, your way of engaging with others, and your way of leading.

Wishing Others Happiness

1. Set a timer for three minutes.

2. Take three deep breaths and allow your mind to quiet down.

3. Consider for a moment that all beings wish to be happy and avoid suffering, and that you have the power to impact anyone you meet.

4. Bring to mind a person you love—your child, partner, parent, or a friend. Imagine yourself giving the person a big hug, and allow yourself to be filled with the love you have for this person. Remain in this experience of love without thinking about it or analyzing it.

5. Now bring to mind a person who is neutral to you. Remember, this person wants to be happy just like you. Connect with the love of the previous exercise and extend it to this person. Be with the experience without thinking about it.

6. Finally, bring to mind a person whom you find challenging. Recall that he or she wants to be happy too. If you can, extend love or the wish that he or she may be happy.

7. End this exercise by saying these words: "May all who come into my presence be a little happier by means of my kindness."

Wishing to Alleviate Suffering

1. Set a timer for three minutes.

2. Take three deep breaths and allow your mind to quiet down.

3. Consider for a moment that all beings wish to be happy and avoid suffering, and that you have the power to impact anyone you meet. This includes alleviating their suffering a little.

4. Recall a person you truly care for who is facing serious difficulties at the moment. Recall the expression on this person's face

as she or he is suffering. Connect with the suffering she or he is experiencing.

5. Let the experience of the person's pain transform into a deep-felt desire that she or he may be free of it. If useful, visualize embracing the person and bringing comfort.

6. Now recall a person who is neutral to you who is experiencing difficulties. Remember that this person, just like everybody else, wants to be happy and not suffer. Connect with the person's pain and let it transform into a desire that she or he may be free of it.

7. Finally, recall a person whom you find challenging and who is suffering. Recall that she or he wants to be happy too. Connect with the person's pain and, if you can, allow the desire to free the person from pain to arise.

8. End the exercise by saying these words: "May all who come into my presence experience a little less suffering by means of my presence."

Enjoying Others' Success

1. Set a timer for three minutes.

2. Take three deep breaths and allow your mind to quiet down.

3. Consider for a moment that all beings wish to be happy and have success in all aspects of life.

4. Now recall a person close to you who has recently had great success. Recall the person's expressions and his or her joy in that success.

5. Allow a spontaneous sense of joy in the person's success to arise for you. For a few moments, simply sit with the joy of celebrating another person's good fortune.

6. Now repeat the exercise, visualizing a person who is neutral to you.

7. Do the same with a person whom you find challenging.

8. End this exercise by saying these words: "May everybody I know be successful, and may I do my best to contribute to that."

Seeing Others Equally

1. Set a timer for three minutes.

2. Take three deep breaths and allow your mind to quiet down.

3. Imagine the people you love the most sitting around you. For a moment, simply acknowledge their desire to be happy and avoid suffering.

4. Now imagine people who are neutral to you sitting around you and your loved ones. For a moment, acknowledge that they also want to be happy and avoid suffering.

5. Finally, imagine people you find challenging sitting around the others. Acknowledge their wish for happiness, too.

6. Consider how all beings are equal in wanting happiness and wanting to avoid problems. And despite role, gender, status, or likes and dislikes, they all benefit from your respect and kindness.

7. End this exercise by saying these words: "May I see everybody I meet as equal in wanting to be happy, and may I be a source of their happiness and success."

Notes

Introduction

1. Unless otherwise noted, quotations in this book are from our interviews conducted between September 2016 and June 2017.

2. M. Bazigos and E. Caruso, "Why Frontline Workers Are Disengaged," *McKinsey Quarterly*, March 2016, http://www.mckinsey.com/business-functions/organization/our-insights/why -frontline-workers-are-disengaged.

3. B. Rigoni and B. Nelson, "Do Employees Really Know What's Expected of Them?" *Business Journal*, September 27, 2016, http://www.gallup.com/businessjournal/195803/employees -really-know-expected.aspx?g_source=EMPLOYEE_ENGAGEMENT&g_medium=topic&g _campaign=tiles.

4. B. Carroll, R. Singaraju, and E. Park, *Corporate Learning Factbook 2015: Benchmarks, Trends, and Analysis of the U.S. Training Market*, Bersin by Deloitte, August 8, 2015, https://www.bersin .com/Login.aspx?p=http://bersinone.bersin.com/resources/research/?docid=19202&h=1.

5. J. C. Magee et al., "Leadership and the Psychology of Power," in *The Psychology of Leadership: New Perspectives and Research*, ed. D. M. Messick and R. M. Kramer (Mahwah, NJ: Lawrence Erlbaum Associates, 2005).

6. P. Drucker, "Managing Oneself," in *The Drucker Lectures: Essential Lessons on Management, Society and Economy*, ed. R. Wartzman (New York: McGraw-Hill, 2010).

Chapter 1

1. For results on physiology, see R. J. Davidson et al., "Alterations in Brain and Immune Function Produced by Mindfulness Meditation," *Psychosomatic Medicine* 65 (2003): 564–570; for psychology, see D. M. Davis and J. A. Hayes, "What Are the Benefits of Mindfulness? A Practice Review of Psychotherapy-Related Research," *Psychotherapy* 48 (2011): 198–208; for work performance, see U. R. Hülsheger et al., "Benefits of Mindfulness at Work: The Role of Mindfulness in Emotion Regulation, Emotional Exhaustion, and Job Satisfaction," *Journal of Applied Psychology* 98 (2013): 310–325.

2. For results on the immune system and blood pressure, see S. Rosenzweig et al., "Mindfulness-Based Stress Reduction Is Associated with Improved Glycemic Control in Type 2 Diabetes Mellitus: A Pilot Study," *Alternative Therapies in Health and Medicine* 13 (2007): 36–37; for results on heart rate, see F. Zeidan et al., "Effects of Brief and Sham Mindfulness Meditation on Mood and Cardiovascular Variables," *Journal of Alternative and Complementary Medicine* 16 (2010): 867–873.

3. For results on sleep patterns, see L. E. Carlson and S. N. Garland, "Impact of Mindfulness-Based Stress Reduction (MBSR) on Sleep, Mood, Stress and Fatigue Symptoms in Cancer Outpatients," *International Journal of Behavioral Medicine* 12 (2005): 278–285; for stress, see A. Chiesa

and A. Serretti, "Mindfulness-Based Stress Reduction for Stress Management in Healthy People: A Review and Meta-Analysis," *Journal of Alternative and Complementary Medicine* 15 (2009): 593–600.

4. B. K. Hölzel et al., "Mindfulness Practice Leads to Increases in Regional Brain Gray Matter Density," *Psychiatry Research: Neuroimaging* 191 (2011): 36–43.

5. For memory, see M. D. Mrazek et al., "Mindfulness Training Improves Working Memory Capacity and GRE Performance While Reducing Mind Wandering," *Psychological Science* 24 (2013): 776–781; for concentration, see K. A. MacLean et al., "Intensive Meditation Training Improves Perceptual Discrimination and Sustained Attention," *Psychological Science* 21 (2010): 829–839; for enhanced cognitive flexibility, see J. Greenberg, K. Reiner, and N. Meiran, "'Mind the Trap': Mindfulness Practice Reduces Cognitive Rigidity," *PloS ONE* 7 (2012): e36206; for improved reaction times, see F. Zeidan et al., "Mindfulness Meditation Improves Cognition: Evidence of Brief Mental Training," *Consciousness and Cognition* 19 (2010): 597–605.

6. P. Grossman et al., "MS Quality of Life, Depression, and Fatigue Improve after Mindfulness Training: A Randomized Trial," *Neurology* 75 (2010): 1141–1149.

7. Based on research by Professor Jochen Reb of Singapore Management University on Potential Project Corporate Based Mindfulness Training Programs at Carlsberg and If Insurance. At time of writing, these results have been presented at conferences but not yet published.

8. N. E. Ruedy and M. E. Schweitzer, "In the Moment: The Effect of Mindfulness on Ethical Decision Making," *Journal of Business Ethics* 95 (2010): 73–87.

9. A. Chiesa, A. Serretti, and J. C. Jakobsen, "Mindfulness: Top-Down or Bottom-Up Emotion Regulation Strategy?" *Clinical Psychology Review* 33 (2013): 82–96; F. Zeidan, "The Neurobiology of Mindfulness Meditation," in *Handbook of Mindfulness: Theory, Research & Practice*, ed. K. W. Brown, J. D. Creswell, and R. M. Ryan (New York: Guilford Press, 2015), 171–190.

10. Y. Y. Tang et al., "Improving Executive Function and Its Neurobiological Mechanisms through a Mindfulness Based Intervention: Advances within the Field of Developmental Neuroscience," *Child Development Perspectives* 6 (2012): 361–366.

11. M. A. Killingsworth and D. T. Gilbert, "A Wandering Mind Is an Unhappy Mind," *Science* 330 (2010): 932.

12. J. Collins, *Good to Great: Why Some Companies Make the Leap—and Others Don't* (New York: HarperBusiness, 2001).

13. D. Keltner, "Don't Let Power Corrupt You," *Harvard Business Review*, October 2016, https://hbr.org/2016/10/dont-let-power-corrupt-you.

14. M. H. Davis, *Empathy: A Social Psychological Approach* (Madison, WI: Westview Press, 1994).

15. J. Weiner, "Managing Compassionately," *LinkedIn Pulse*, October 15, 2012. https://www.linkedin.com/pulse/20121015034012-22330283-managing-compassionately/.

16. O. M. Klimecki et al., "Differential Pattern of Functional Brain Plasticity after Compassion and Empathy Training," *Social Cognitive and Affective Neuroscience* 9 (2013): 873–879.

17. S. Melwani, J. S. Mueller, and J. R. Overbeck, "Looking Down: The Influence of Contempt and Compassion on Emergent Leadership Categorizations," *Journal of Applied Psychology* 97 (2012): 1171–1185.

18. For stronger connections, see P. Frost et al., "Narratives of Compassion in Organizations," in *Emotion in Organizations*, ed. S. Fineman (London: Sage, 2000); and E. H. Powley, "Reclaiming Resilience and Safety: Resilience Activation in the Critical Period of Crisis," *Human Relations* 62 (2009): 1289–1326; for improved collaboration and better trust, see J. Dutton, J. Lilius, and J. Kanov, "The Transformative Potential of Compassion at Work," in *Handbook of Transformative Cooperation: New Designs and Dynamics*, ed. S. K. Piderit, R. E. Fry, and D. L. Cooperrider (Stanford, CA: Stanford Business Books, 2007); and A. M. Grant, J. E. Dutton, and B. D. Rosso, "Giving Commitment: Employee Support Programs and the Prosocial Sensemaking Process," *Academy of Management Journal* 51 (2008): 898–918. For stronger commitment, see ibid; for lower turnover, see ibid. and J. M. Lilius et al., "The Contours and Consequences of Compassion at Work," *Journal of Organizational Behavior*, 29 (2008): 193–218.

19. M. Worline and J. E. Dutton, *Awakening Compassion at Work: The Quiet Power That Elevates People and Organizations* (Oakland, CA: Berrett-Koehler, 2017).

20. J. Weiner, "Managing Compassionately," *LinkedIn Pulse*, October 15, 2012, https://www.linkedin.com/pulse/20121015034012-22330283-managing-compassionately/.

Part 1

1. T. D. Wilson et al., "Just Think: The Challenges of the Disengaged Mind," *Science* 345 (2014): 75–77.

Chapter 2

1. B. George (with P. Sims), *True North: Discover Your Authentic Leadership* (San Francisco: Jossey-Bass, 2007).

2. R. C. J. Dahl, A. Lutz, and R. J. Davidson, "Reconstructing and Deconstructing the Self: Cognitive Mechanisms in Meditation Practice," *Trends in Cognitive Sciences* 19, no. 9 (2015): 515–523.

3. H. Schachter, "Do MBA's Make the Best CEOs?" *Globe and Mail*, March 31, 2017. http://www .theglobeandmail.com/report-on-business/careers/management/studies-show-ceos-with-mbas -more-likely-to-fail/article34504662/?utm_source=Shared+Article+Sent+to+User&utm _medium=E-mail:+Newsletters+/+E-Blasts+/+etc.&utm_campaign=Shared+Web +Article+Links.

4. D. Miller and X. Xu, "MBA CEOs, Short-Term Management and Performance," *Journal of Business Ethics* (2017): 1–16.

5. M. A. Killingsworth, and D. T. Gilbert, "A Wandering Mind Is an Unhappy Mind," *Science* 330 (2010): 932.

6. K. Takemura, "Influence of Elaboration on the Framing of Decision," *Journal of Psychology* 128 (1994): 33–39.

7. C. Y. Olivola and A. Todorov, "Fooled by First Impressions? Reexamining the Diagnostic Value of Appearance-Based Inferences," *Journal of Experimental Social Psychology* 46 (2010): 315–324; F. J. Adam and J. K. Maner, "Warmth, Spatial Proximity, and Social Attachment: The Embodied Perception of a Social Metaphor," *Journal of Experimental Social Psychology* 48 (2012): 1369–1372; J. Willis and A. Todorov, "First Impressions: Making Up Your Mind after a 100-ms Exposure to a Face," *Psychological Science* 17 (2006): 592–598.

8. M. F. Mason et al., "Wandering Minds: The Default Network and Stimulus-Independent Thought," *Science* 315 (2007): 393–395.

9. D. Drachman, "Do We Have Brain to Spare?" *Neurology* 64 (2005): 2004–2005.

10. S. Begley, *Train Your Mind, Change Your Brain: How a New Science Reveals Our Extraordinary Potential to Transform Ourselves* (New York: Ballantine Books, 2007).

11. A. Lutz et al., "Attention Regulation and Monitoring in Meditation," *Trends in Cognitive Sciences* 12 (2008): 163–169.

12. K. Ganguly and M. M. Poo, "Activity-Dependent Neural Plasticity from Bench to Bedside," *Neuron* 80 (2013): 729–741.

13. R. Hougaard, J. Carter, and G. Coutts, *One Second Ahead: Enhance Your Performance at Work with Mindfulness* (Houndmills, Basingstoke, Hampshire, UK/New York: Palgrave Macmillan, 2016).

14. W. Wood, J. M. Quinn, and D. A. Kashy, "Habits in Everyday Life: Thought, Emotion, and Action," *Journal of Personality and Social Psychology* 83 (2002): 1281–1297.

15. Ethics Resource Center, *National Business Ethics Survey of the U.S. Workforce* (Arlington, VA: Ethics Resource Center, 2014), https://www.ibe.org.uk/userassets/surveys/nbes2013.pdf.

16. F. Warneken and M. Tomasello, "Altruistic Helping in Human Infants and Young Chimpanzees," *Science* 311 (2006): 1301–1303.

17. L. B. Aknin et al., "Prosocial Spending and Well-Being: Cross-Cultural Evidence for a Psychological Universal," *Journal of Personality and Social Psychology* 104 (2013): 635.

18. M. Ricard, *Altruism: The Power of Compassion to Change Yourself and the World* (London: Atlantic Books, 2015).

19. N. E. Ruedy and M. E. Schweitzer, "In the Moment: The Effect of Mindfulness on Ethical Decision Making," *Journal of Business Ethics* 95 (2010): 73–87.

20. United Nations, *World Happiness Report 2017* (New York: United Nations, 2017), http:// worldhappiness.report/ed/2017/.

21. L. Richard, *Happiness: Lessons from a New Science* (London: Allen Lane, 2005).

22. S. J. Solnick, and D. Hemenway, "Is More Always Better? A Survey on Positional Concerns," *Journal of Economic Behavior & Organization* 37 (1998): 373–383.

23. W. Schultz, "Potential Vulnerabilities of Neuronal Reward, Risk, and Decision Mechanisms to Addictive Drugs," *Neuron* 69 (2011): 603–617.

Chapter 3

1. M. A. Killingsworth and D. T. Gilbert, "A Wandering Mind Is an Unhappy Mind," *Science* 330 (2010): 932.

2. For more information on our survey results, visit www.themindoftheleaderbook.com.

3. E. Hallowell, "Overloaded Circuits: Why Smart People Underperform," *Harvard Business Review*, January 2005, https://hbr.org/2005/01/overloaded-circuits-why-smart-people-underperform.

4. T. Davenport, *Attention Economy: Understanding the New Currency of Business* (Boston: Harvard Business School Press, 2001).

5. P. Drucker, *The Effective Executive: The Definitive Guide to Getting the Right Things Done* (New York: HarperBusiness, 2006).

6. D. H. Weissman, L. M. Warner, and M. G. Woldorff, "The Neural Mechanisms for Minimizing Cross-Modal Distraction," *Journal of Neuroscience* 24 (2004): 10941–10949.

7. W. Hasenkamp et al., "Mind Wandering and Attention during Focused Meditation: A Fine-Grained Temporal Analysis of Fluctuating Cognitive States," *Neuroimage* 59, no. 1 (2012): 750–760.

8. Ibid.

9. G. A. Miller, "The Magical Number Seven, Plus or Minus Two: Some Limits on Our Capacity for Processing Information," *Psychological Review* 63 (1956): 81–97.

10. K. K. Loh and R. Kanai, "Higher Media Multi-Tasking Activity Is Associated with Smaller Gray-Matter Density in the Anterior Cingulate Cortex," *PLoS ONE* 9 (2014): e106698.

11. B. K. Hölzel et al., "Mindfulness Practice Leads to Increases in Regional Brain Gray Matter Density," *Psychiatry Research: Neuroimaging* 191, no. 1 (2011): 36–43.

12. S. Danziger, J. Levav, and L. Avnaim-Pesso, "Extraneous Factors in Judicial Decisions," *Proceedings of the National Academy of Sciences of the United States of America* 108 (2011): 6889–6892.

13. P. Ekman, *Emotions Revealed: Recognizing Faces and Feelings to Improve Communication and Emotional Life* (New York: St. Martin's Press, 2007).

14. B. L. Fredrickson, "Positive Emotions Broaden and Build," in *Advances in Experimental Social Psychology*, ed. P. Devine and A. Plant, vol. 47 (Burlington, VT: Academic Press, 2013).

15. P. J. Rogers et al., "Faster but Not Smarter: Effects of Caffeine and Caffeine Withdrawal on Alertness and Performance," *Psychopharmacology* 226 (2013): 229–240; A. G. Parker et al., "The Effects of Alpha-Glycerylphosphorylcholine, Caffeine or Placebo on Markers of Mood, Cognitive Function, Power, Speed, and Agility," *Journal of the International Society of Sports Nutrition* 12 (2015): P41.

16. E. Ophir, C. Nass, and A. D. Wagner, "Cognitive Control in Media Multitaskers," *Proceedings of the National Academy of Sciences* 106 (2009): 15583–15587.

17. D. Bawden and L. Robinson, "The Dark Side of Information: Overload, Anxiety and Other Paradoxes and Pathologies," *Journal of Information Science* 25, no. 2 (2009): 180–191.

18. T. M. Amabile, C. N. Hadley, and S. J. Kramer, "Time Pressure and Creativity in Organizations—A Longitudinal Field Study," Harvard Business School Working Paper 02–073, Cambridge, MA, 2002.

19. H. Bruch and S. Ghosal, "Beware the Busy Manager," *Harvard Business Review*, February 2002, https://hbr.org/2002/02/beware-the-busy-manager.

20. K. Kogon, L. Merrill, and L. Rinne, *The 5 Choices: The Path to Extraordinary Productivity* (New York: Simon & Shuster, 2015).

21. Bureau of Labor Statistics, US Department of Labor, *American Time Use Survey*, 2012, www.bls.gov/tus/home.htm#data.

22. D. J. Good et al., "Contemplating Mindfulness at Work: An Integrative Review," *Journal of Management* 42 (2016): 114–142.

23. C. Newport, *Deep Work: Rules for Focused Success in a Distracted World* (New York: Grand Central Publishing, 2016).

Chapter 4

1. B. Hood, *The Self Illusion: How the Social Brain Creates Identity* (Oxford: Oxford University Press, 2012).

2. C. J. Dahl, A. Lutz, and R. J. Davidson, "Reconstructing and Deconstructing the Self: Cognitive Mechanisms in Meditation Practice," *Trends in Cognitive Sciences* 19, no. 9 (2015): 515–523.

3. L. Scherwitz, L. E. Graham, and D. Ornish, "Self-Involvement and the Risk Factors for Coronary Heart Disease," *Advances* 2 (1985): 6–18.

4. S. Rude, E. M. Gortner, and J. Pennebaker, "Language Use of Depressed and Depression-Vulnerable College Students," *Cognition & Emotion* 18 (2004): 1121–1133.

5. S. W. Stirman and J. W. Pennebaker, "Word Use in the Poetry of Suicidal and Nonsuicidal Poets," *Psychosomatic Medicine* 63 (2001): 517–522.

6. R. S. Campbell and J. W. Pennebaker, "The Secret Life of Pronouns: Flexibility in Writing Style and Physical Health," *Psychological Science* 14 (2003): 60–65.

7. E. Kacewicz et al., "Pronoun Use Reflects Standings in Social Hierarchies," *Journal of Language and Social Psychology* 33 (2014): 125–143.

8. N. K. Steffens and S. A. Haslam, "Power through 'Us': Leaders' Use of We-Referencing Language Predicts Election Victory," *PloS ONE* 8 (2013): e77952.

9. M. Goldsmith, *What Got You Here Won't Get You There: How Successful People Become Even More Successful* (New York: Hyperion, 2007).

10. B. F. Skinner, *Science and Human Behavior* (New York: Macmillan, 1953).

11. D. Keltner, "Don't Let Power Corrupt You," *Harvard Business Review*, October 2016, https://hbr.org/2016/10/dont-let-power-corrupt-you.

12. Ibid.

13. H. Gregersen, "Bursting the CEO Bubble," *Harvard Business Review*, March–April 2017, https://hbr.org/2017/03/bursting-the-ceo-bubble.

14. J. A. Frimer et al., "The Integration of Agency and Communion in Moral Personality: Evidence of Enlightened Self-Interest," *Journal of Personality and Social Psychology*, 101 (2011): 149–163.

Chapter 5

1. www.sleepfoundation.org.

2. F. P. Cappuccio et al., "Sleep Duration and All-Cause Mortality: A Systematic Review and Meta-Analysis of Prospective Studies," *Sleep* 33, no. 5 (2010): 5850593; S. Banks and D. F. Dinges, "Behavioral and Physiological Consequences of Sleep Restriction," *Journal of Clinical Sleep Medicine* 3 (2007): 519–528.

3. P. Alhola and P. Polo-Kantola, "Sleep Deprivation: Impact on Cognitive Performance," *Neuropsychiatric Disease and Treatment* 3, no. 5 (2007): 553.

4. D. Dawson and K. Reid, "Fatigue, Alcohol and Performance Impairment," *Nature* 388 (1997): 235.

5. A. P. Spira, L. P. Chen-Edinboro, M. N. Wu and K. Yaffe, "Impact of Sleep on the Risk of Cognitive Decline and Dementia," *Current Opinion in Psychiatry* 27, no. 6 (2014): 478.

6. J. C. Gillin, "How Long Can Humans Stay Awake?" *Scientific American*, March 25, 2002, https://www.scientificamerican.com/article/how-long-can-humans-stay/.

7. B. Wood et al., "Light Level and Duration of Exposure Determine the Impact of Self-Luminous Tablets on Melatonin Suppression," *Applied Ergonomics* 44, no. 2 (2013): 237–240.

8. A. Altun and B. Ugur-Altun, "Melatonin: Therapeutic and Clinical Utilization," *International Journal of Clinical Practice* 61 (2007): 835–845.

9. M. G. Figueiro et al., "The Impact of Light from Computer Monitors on Melatonin Levels in College Students, *Neuroendocrinology Letters* 32, no. 2 (2011): 158–163.

10. G. C. Brainard et al., "Action Spectrum for Melatonin Regulation in Humans: Evidence for a Novel Circadian Photoreceptor," *Journal of Neuroscience* 21 (2001): 6405–6412.

11. L. A. Irish et al., "The Role of Sleep Hygiene in Promoting Public Health: A Review of Empirical Evidence," *Sleep Medicine Reviews* 22 (2015): 23–36.

12. P. Hauri, "Sleep/Wake Lifestyle Modifications: Sleep Hygiene," in *Therapy in Sleep Medicine*, ed. T. R. Barkoukis et al. (Philadelphia: Elsevier Saunders, 2011), 151–160.

13. Deloitte, *2016 Global Mobile Consumer Survey: US Edition. The Market-Creating Power of Mobile*, https://www2.deloitte.com/us/en/pages/technology-media-and-telecommunications/articles/global-mobile-consumer-survey-us-edition.html.

14. S. Turkle, *Alone Together: Why We Expect More from Technology and Less from Each Other* (New York: Basic Books, 2011).

15. L. A. Perlow, *Sleeping with Your Smartphone: How to Break the 24/7 Habit and Change the Way You Work* (Boston: Harvard Business Review Press, 2012).

16. D. Goleman, "To Strengthen Your Attention Span, Stop Overtaxing It," *Harvard Business Review*, November 2013.

17. D. Seo, C. J. Patrick, and P. J. Kennealy, "Role of Serotonin and Dopamine System Interactions in the Neurobiology of Impulsive Aggression and Its Comorbidity with Other Clinical Disorders," *Aggression and Violent Behavior* 13 (2008): 383–395.

18. W. Hofmann, K. D. Vohs, and R. F. Baumeister, "What People Desire, Feel Conflicted About, and Try to Resist in Everyday Life," *Psychological Science* 23, no. 6 (2012): 582–588.

19. D. A. Sbarra, H. L. Smith, and M. R. Mehl, "When Leaving Your Ex, Love Yourself," *Psychological Science*, 23, no. 3 (2012). http://journals.sagepub.com/doi/abs/10.1177/0956797611429466

20. O. S. Curry, L. Rowland, S. Zlotowitz, J. McAlaney and H. Whitehouse, "Happy to Help? A Systematic Review and Meta-Analysis of the Effects of Performing Acts of Kindness on the Well-Being of the Actor," *Open Science Framework* (October 2017), osf.io/ytj5s.

21. S. K. Nelson et al., "Do unto Others or Treat Yourself? The Effects of Prosocial and Self-Focused Behavior on Psychological Flourishing," *Emotion* 16, No. 6 (2016): 850–861.

22. E. S. Kim, V. J. Strecher, and C. D. Ryff, "Purpose in Life and Use of Preventive Health Care Services," *Proceedings of the National Academy of Sciences* 111 (2014): 16331–16336.

Chapter 6

1. M. Bertrand and S. Mullainathan, "Are Emily and Greg More Employable Than Lakisha and Jamal?" *American Economic Review* 94 (2004): 991–1013.

2. C. Summerfield et al., "Neural Repetition Suppression Reflects Fulfilled Perceptual Expectations," *Nature Neuroscience* 11 (2008): 1004–1006.

3. V. Ottati et al., "When Self-Perceptions of Expertise Increase Closed-Minded Cognition: The Earned Dogmatism Effect," *Journal of Experimental Social Psychology* 61 (2015): 131–138.

4. J. Greenberg, K. Reiner, and N. Meiran, "'Mind the Trap': Mindfulness Practice Reduces Cognitive Rigidity," *PLoS ONE* 7 (2012): 1–8.

5. X. M. Bezuijen et al., "Pygmalion and Employee Learning: The Role of Leader Behaviors," *Journal of Management* 35 (2009): 1248–1267.

6. B. A. Olshausen, C. H. Anderson, and D. C. van Essen, "A Neurobiological Model of Visual Attention and Invariant Pattern Recognition Based on Dynamic Routing of Information," *Journal of Neuroscience* 13 (1993): 4700–4719.

7. B. R. Newell and D. R. Shanks, "Unconscious Influences on Decision Making: A Critical Review," *Behavioral and Brain Sciences* 37, no. 1 (2014): 1–19.

8. D. Hirshleifer and T. Shumway, "Good Day Sunshine: Stock Returns and the Weather," *Journal of Finance* 58 (2003): 1009–1032.

9. P. Ekman, *The Atlas of Emotions*, available online: http://atlasofemotions.org/.

10. P. Ekman, *Emotions Revealed: Recognizing Faces and Feelings to Improve Communication and Emotional Life* (New York: St. Martin's Press, 2007); P. Ekman, *Telling Lies: Clues to Deceit in the Marketplace, Politics, and Marriage* (New York: W. W. Norton & Company, 2009).

11. C. A. Bartel and R. Saavedra, "The Collective Construction of Work Group Moods," *Administrative Science Quarterly* 45 (2000): 197–231.

12. M. Jabbi, M. Swart, and C. Keysers, "Empathy for Positive and Negative Emotions in the Gustatory Cortex," *Neuroimage* 34, no. 4 (2007): 1744–1753.

13. D. Goleman, R. Boyatzis, and A. McKee, *Primal Leadership: Unleashing the Power of Emotional Intelligence* (Boston: Harvard Business Review Press, 2013).

14. D. Goleman, R. Boyatzis, and A. McKee, "Primal Leadership: The Hidden Driver of Great Performance," *Harvard Business Review*, December 2001.

15. T. L. Spinrad et al., "Relation of Emotion-Related Regulation to Children's Social Competence: A Longitudinal Study," *Emotion* 6 (2006): 498–510; J. D. Mayer, D. R. Caruso, and P. Salovey, "Selecting a Measure of Emotional Intelligence: The Case for Ability Scales," in *The Handbook of Emotional Intelligence*, ed. R. Bar-On and J. D. A. Parker (New York: Jossey-Bass, 2000); D. R. Richardson et al., "Empathy as a Cognitive Inhibitor of Interpersonal Aggression," *Aggressive Behavior* 20 (1994): 275–289.

16. M. H. Davis, "Measuring Individual Differences in Empathy: Evidence for a Multidimensional Approach," *Journal of Personality and Social Psychology* 44 (1983): 113–126; D. Grühn et al., "Empathy across the Adult Lifespan: Longitudinal and Experience-Sampling Findings," *Emotion* 8 (2008): 753–765; S. Konrath, M. H. Ho, and S. Zarins, "The Strategic Helper: Narcissism and Prosocial Motives and Behaviors," *Current Psychology* 35 (2016): 182–194.

17. N. Eisenberg et al., "Consistency and Development of Prosocial Dispositions: A Longitudinal Study," *Child Development* 70 (1999): 1360–1372; Grühn et al. "Empathy across the Adult Lifespan."

18. R. Castillo et al., "Effects of an emotional intelligence intervention on aggression and empathy among adolescents," *Journal of Adolescence* 36 (2013): 883–892. S. Konrath et al., "Can Text Messages Increase Empathy and Prosocial Behavior? The Development and Initial Validation of Text to Connect," *PLoS ONE* 10 (2015): e0137585.

19. P. Bloom, *Against Empathy: The Case for Rational Compassion* (Cambridge, MA: Random House, 2017).

20. P. Bloom, "Empathy and Its Discontents," *Trends in Cognitive Sciences* 21, no.1 (2017): 24–31.

21. J. S. Felton, "Burnout as a Clinical Entity—Its Importance in Health Care Workers," *Occupational Medicine* 48 (1998): 237–250.

22. Bloom, *Against Empathy*.

23. M. H. Davis, *Empathy: A Social Psychological Approach* (Madison, WI: Westview Press, 1994).

Chapter 7

1. M. A. Killingsworth and D. T. Gilbert, "A Wandering Mind Is an Unhappy Mind," *Science* 330 (2010): 932; K. W. Brown and R. M. Ryan, "The Benefits of Being Present: Mindfulness and Its Role in Psychological Well-Being," *Journal of Personality and Social Psychology* 84 (2003): 822–848.

2. C. Zook and J. Allen, *The Founder's Mentality: How to Overcome the Predictable Crises of Growth* (Boston: Harvard Business Review Press, 2016).

3. J. Reb, J. Narayanan, and S. Chaturvedi, "Leading Mindfully: Two Studies on the Influence of Supervisor Trait Mindfulness on Employee Well-Being and Performance," *Mindfulness* 5 (2014): 36–45.

4. D. R. Carney, A. J. C. Cuddy, and A. J. Yap, "Review and Summary of Research on the Embodied Effects of Expansive (vs. Contractive) Nonverbal Displays," *Psychological Science* 26, no. 5 (2015): 657–663.

5. D. R. Carney, A. J. C. Cuddy, and A. J. Yap, "Power Posing: Brief Nonverbal Displays Affect Neuroendocrine Levels and Risk Tolerance," *Psychological Science* 21, no. 10 (2010): 1363–1368.

6. P. J. Zak, *Trust Factor: The Science of Creating High-Performance Companies* (New York: AMACOM, 2017).

7. S. M. R. Covey and D. R. Conant, "The Connection between Employee Trust and Financial Performance," *Harvard Business Review*, July 2016, https://hbr.org/2016/07/the-connection -between-employee-trust-and-financial-performance.

8. PwC, *20th CEO Survey*, 2017, http://www.pwc.com/gx/en/ceo-survey/2017/pwc-ceo-20th -survey-report-2017.pdf.

9. Edelman, *2017 Edelman Trust Barometer: Global Report*, http://www.edelman.com/trust2017/.

10. Ernst & Young, *Trust in the Workplace: Global Study*, http://www.ey.com/gl/en/about-us /our-people-and-culture/ey-global-study-trust-in-the-workplace.

11. A. Morrone, N. Tontoranelli, and G. Ranuzzi, "How Good Is Trust? Measuring Trust and Its Role for the Progress of Societies," OECD Statistics Working Paper (Paris: OECD, 2009).

12. C. Duhigg, "What Google Is Learning from Its Quest to Build the Perfect Team," *New York Times Magazine*, February 25, 2016, https://www.nytimes.com/2016/02/28/magazine /what-google-learned-from-its-quest-to-build-the-perfect-team.html?smid=pl-share&_r=2.

Chapter 8

1. Lao Tzu, *Tao Te Ching*, trans. Tom Butler-Bowden (Hoboken, NJ: Capstone, 2012).

2. R. K. Greenleaf, *Servant Leadership: A Journey into the Nature of Legitimate Power and Greatness* (New York: Paulist Press, 1977).

3. E. D. Gould and A. Hijzen, "In Equality We Trust," *Finance & Development* 54 (2017): 37–39.

4. J. Prime and E. R. Salib, *Inclusive Leadership: The View from Six Countries*, Catalyst, 2014, http://www.catalyst.org/system/files/inclusive_leadership_the_view_from_six_countries_0.pdf.

5. From Indra Nooyi's LinkedIn post: https://www.linkedin.com/pulse/leave-crown-garage -what-ive-learned-from-decade-being-indra-nooyi.

Chapter 9

1. J. C. Magee et al., "Leadership and the Psychology of Power," in *The Psychology of Leadership: New Perspectives and Research*, ed. D. M. Messick and R. M. Kramer (Mahwah, NJ: Lawrence Erlbaum Associates, 2005), 287–306.

2. J. Hogeveen, M. Inzlicht, and S. S. Obhi, "Power Changes How the Brain Responds to Others," *Journal of Experimental Psychology: General* 143, no. 2 (2014): 755–762.

3. Ibid.

4. D. Owen and J. Davidson, "Hubris Syndrome: An Acquired Personality Disorder? A Study of US Presidents and UK Prime Ministers over the Last 100 Years," *Brain* 132 (2009): 1396–1406, doi:10.1093/brain/awp008.

5. S. Melwani, J. S. Mueller, and J. R. Overbeck, "Looking Down: The Influence of Contempt and Compassion on Emergent Leadership Categorizations," *Journal of Applied Psychology* 97 (2012): 1171–1185.

6. For stronger connections, see P. Frost et al., "Narratives of Compassion in Organizations," in *Emotion in Organizations*, ed. S. Fineman (London: Sage, 2000); and E. H. Powley, "Reclaiming Resilience and Safety: Resilience Activation in the Critical Period of Crisis," *Human Relations* 62 (2009): 1289–1326; for better collaboration, see J. Dutton, J. Lilius, and J. Kanov, "The Transformative Potential of Compassion at Work," in *Handbook of Transformative Cooperation: New Designs and Dynamics*, ed. S. K. Piderit, R. E. Fry, and D. L. Cooperrider (Stanford, CA: Stanford Business Books, 2007); for trust, stronger commitment, and lower turnover, see ibid.; A. M. Grant, J. E. Dutton, and B. D. Rosso, "Giving Commitment: Employee Support Programs and the Prosocial Sensemaking Process," *Academy of Management Journal* 51 (2008): 898–918; and J. M. Lilius et al., "The Contours and Consequences of Compassion at Work," *Journal of Organizational Behavior* 29 (2008): 193–218.

7. C. Sandi and J. Haller, "Stress and the Social Brain: Behavioural Effects and Neurobiological Mechanisms," *Nature Reviews Neuroscience* 16 (2015): 290–304.

8. M. Mongrain, J. M. Chin, and L. B. Shapira, "Practicing Compassion Increases Happiness and Self-Esteem," *Journal of Happiness Studies* 12 (2011): 963–981.

9. J. Vahtera et al., "Hostility and Ill Health: Role of Psychosocial Resources in Two Contexts of Working Life," *Journal of Psychosomatic Research* 48 (2000): 89–98; H. S. Friedman, *Hostility, Coping, & Health* (Washington, DC: American Psychological Association, 1992); C. Peterson, N. Park, and M. E. P. Seligman, "Orientations to Happiness and Life Satisfaction: The Full Life versus the Empty Life," *Journal of Happiness Studies* 6 (2005): 25–41; G. Rein, M. Atkinson, and R. McCraty, "The Physiological and Psychological Effects of Compassion and Anger," *Journal of Advancement in Medicine* 8 (1995): 87–105.

10. P. Ekman, *Emotions Revealed: Recognizing Faces and Feelings to Improve Communication and Emotional Life* (New York: St. Martin's Press, 2007).

11. B. L. Fredrickson et al., "Open Hearts Build Lives: Positive Emotions, Induced through Loving-Kindness Meditation, Build Consequential Personal Resources," *Journal of Personality and*

Social Psychology 95 (2008): 1045–1062. S. G. Hofmann, P. Grossman, and D. E. Hinton, "Loving-Kindness and Compassion Meditation: Potential for Psychological Interventions," *Clinical Psychology Review* 31 (2011): 1126–1132.

12. O. M. Klimecki et al., "Functional Neural Plasticity and Associated Changes in Positive Affect after Compassion Training," *Cerebral Cortex* 23 (2012): 1552–1561.

Chapter 10

1. N. Boaz and E. A. Fox, "Change Leader, Change Thyself," *McKinsey Quarterly* (March 2014), http://www.mckinsey.com/.

2. S. T. Fiske and S. E. Taylor, *Social Cognition: From Brains to Culture* (Thousand Oaks, CA: Sage, 2013).

3. D. C. Park and C. M. Huang, "Culture Wires the Brain: A Cognitive Neuroscience Perspective," *Perspectives on Psychological Science* 5 (2010): 391–400.

4. D. Kumaran, H. L. Melo, and E. Duzel, "The Emergence and Representation of Knowledge About Social and Nonsocial Hierarchies," *Neuron* 76, no. 3 (2012): 653–666.

5. D. Goleman, R. Boyatzis, and A. McKee, "Primal Leadership: The Hidden Driver of Great Performance," *Harvard Business Review*, December 2001.

6. E. H. Schein, *Organizational Culture and Leadership*, vol. 2 (Hoboken, NJ: John Wiley & Sons, 2010).

7. J. Archer, "20 Words You Can Drop from Your Core Values Right Now," *Inc.*, January 22, 2014, https://www.inc.com/james-archer/20-words-you-can-drop-from-your-core-values-right-now.html.

8. M. C. Jensen and W. H. Meckling, "Theory of the Firm: Managerial Behavior, Agency Costs and Ownership Structure," *Journal of Financial Economics* 3, no. 4 (1976): 305–360.

9. J. L. Bower and L. S. Paine, "The Error at the Heart of Corporate Leadership," *Harvard Business Review*, May–June 2017.

10. J. L. Bower, H. B. Leonard, and L. S. Paine, *Capitalism at Risk: Rethinking the Role of Business* (Boston: Harvard Business Press, 2011).

11. B. Chapman and R. Sisodia, *Everybody Matters: The Extraordinary Power of Caring for Your People Like Family* (New York: Portfolio/Penguin, 2015).

Chapter 11

1. R. Williams, "How to Bring Mindfulness into Meetings—10 Tips," *Psychology Today* blog, October 12, 2015, https://www.psychologytoday.com/blog/wired-success/201510/how-bring-mindfulness-meetings-10-tips.

2. R. E. Thayer, "Energy, Tiredness, and Tension Effects of a Sugar Snack versus Moderate Exercise," *Journal of Personality and Social Psychology* 52 (1987): 119–125.

3. L. Belkin, W. Becker, and S. Conroy, "After-Hours Email, Work-Family Balance and Identification," *Academy of Management Proceedings* (January 2016), http://proceedings.aom.org/content/2016/1/10353.short.

4. D. Burkas, "Why Atos Origin Is Striving to Be a Zero-Email Company," *Forbes*, July 12, 2016.

5. McKinsey Global Institute, *Minding Your Digital Business: McKinsey Global Survey Results*, May 2012, http://www.mckinsey.com/business-functions/digital-mckinsey/our-insights/minding-your-digital-business-mckinsey-global-survey-results.

6. D. Burkus, "Some Companies Are Banning Email and Getting More Done," *Harvard Business Review*, June 2016, https://hbr.org/2016/06/some-companies-are-banning-email-and-getting-more-done.

7. A. Mann and A. Adkins, "America's Coming Workplace: Home Alone," *Gallup News Business Journal*, March 15, 2017.

8. R. Hougaard, J. Carter, and G. Coutts, *One Second Ahead: Enhance Your Performance at Work with Mindfulness* (Houndmills, Basingstoke, Hampshire, UK/New York: Palgrave Macmillan, 2016).

Chapter 12

1. A. Grant, "Billionaire Ray Dalio Had an Amazing Reaction to an Employee Calling Him Out on a Mistake," *Business Insider*, February 2, 2016, http://www.businessinsider.com/ray-dalio-management-strategy-bridgewater-2016-1?IR=T

2. R. A. Emmons and M. E. McCullough, "Counting Blessings versus Burdens: An Experimental Investigation of Gratitude and Subjective Well-Being in Daily Life," *Journal of Personality and Social Psychology* 84 (2003): 377–389; L. Waters, "Predicting Job Satisfaction: Contributions of Individual Gratitude and Institutionalized Gratitude," *Psychology* 3 (2012): 1174–1176.

3. J. H. Fowler and N. A. Christakis, "Cooperative Behavior Cascades in Human Social Networks," *Proceedings of the National Academy of Sciences* 107 (2010): 5334–5338.

4. Mercer, *2013 Global Performance Management Survey Report*, https://www.mercer.ca/content/dam/mercer/attachments/global/Talent/Assess-BrochurePerfMgmt.pdf.

5. Ibid.

6. N. I. Eisenberger, M. D. Lieberman, and K. D. Williams, "Does Rejection Hurt? An Fmri Study of Social Exclusion," *Science* 302 (2003): 290–292.

7. S. F. Brosnan and F. B. de Waal, "Monkeys Reject Unequal Pay," *Nature* 425 (2003): 297–299.

8. K. Payne, *The Broken Ladder: How Inequality Affects the Way We Think, Live, and Die* (New York: Viking, 2017).

9. D. H. Rivers and T. D. Deschriver, "Star Players, Payroll Distribution, and Major League Baseball Attendance," *Sport Marketing Quarterly* 11, no. 3 (2002): 164–173.

10. M. Marmot and R. Bell, "Fair Society, Healthy Lives," *Public Health* 126 (2012): S4–S10.

11. S. Crawford, K. K. Nelson, and B. Rountree, "The CEO-Employee Pay Ratio," *SSRN* (November 21, 2014), https://papers.ssrn.com/sol3/Papers.cfm?abstract_id=2529112.

12. G. A. Akerlof and J. L. Yellen, "Fairness and Unemployment," *American Economic Review* 78 (1988): 44–49; G. A. Akerlof and J. L. Yellen, "The Fair Wage–Effort Hypothesis and Unemployment," *Quarterly Journal of Economics* 105 (1990): 255–283; E. P. Lazear, "Pay Equality and Industrial Politics," *Journal of Political Economy* 97 (1989): 561–580.

13. S. Kiatpongsan and M. Norton, "How Much (More) Should CEOs Make? A Universal Desire for More Equal Pay," *Perspectives on Psychological Science* 9, no. 6 (2014): 587–593.

14. E. Sommeiller, M. Price, and E. Wazeter, *Income Inequality in the U.S. by State, Metropolitan Area, and County* (Washington, DC: Economic Policy Institute, 2016), http://www.epi.org/publication/income-inequality-in-the-us/.

15. Ibid.

Chapter 13

1. B. Chapman and R. Sisodia, *Everybody Matters: The Extraordinary Power of Caring for Your People Like Family* (New York: Portfolio/Penguin, 2015).

2. https://www.brainyquote.com/quotes/quotes/w/warrenbenn384360.html.

3. Organisation for Economic Co-operation and Development, *Trust in Society at a Glance 2011: OECD Social Indicators* (Paris: OECD, 2011), http://www.oecd-ilibrary.org/sites/soc_glance-2011-en/08/01/index.html?itemId=/content/chapter/soc_glance-2011-26-en.

4. Paul J. Zak, *Trust Factor: The Science of Creating High-Performance Companies* (New York: AMACOM, 2017).

5. K. Dell, "Airline Maverick," *Time*, September 21, 2007, http://content.time.com/time/specials/2007/article/0,28804,1663316_1684619,00.html.

Afterword

1. R. Dobbs, J. Manyika, and J. Woetzel, *No Ordinary Disruption: The Four Global Forces Breaking All the Trends* (New York: Public Affairs, 2015).

Index

Acknowledgments

Most of what is in this book has been generously offered by others. As authors, we just brought it all together. We stand on the shoulders of giants in mind training, science, and business.

This book is dedicated to the masters who have role-modeled and taught the practices of mindfulness, selflessness, and compassion for decades, including the Dalai Lama, Lama Zopa Rinpoche, Lama Yeshe, Lakha Lama, Yangsi Rinpoche, Alan Wallace, Matthieu Ricard, Venerable Antonio Satta, Stephan Pende, Nyingje Chichester, Venerable Charles, Glen Svensson, and Sangye Khadro.

The book has gained its scientific rigor and validity through the work and support of great scientists, including Richard Davidson, Judson Brewer, Paul J. Zak, Dan Siegel, Hans Melo, and Paul Ekman.

Extraordinarily kind and wise business leaders have generously shared their insights and experiences and time. There are far too many to list them all, but a few must be named, including Dominic Barton, Michael Rennie, Arne Sorenson, Chris Schmidt, Nate Boaz, Rahul Varma, and Loren Shuster.

As nonprofessional writers, we have been blessed by incredible editorial support by Jeff Leeson of Benson Collister. Jeff's commitment to clarity and simplicity has helped distill complex matter into clear insights. Our agent Jim Levine, of Levine Greenberg Rostan Literary Agency, is passionate about bringing the practices of this book into leadership. Jim's dedication has been a great driving force in the process. Our editor Tim Sullivan from Harvard Business Press has had our back throughout. His firmness and clarity have provided great guidance and direction.

Completing a manuscript is one thing; bringing it to the world is another. We want to thank Laurie Harting, our freelance editor and writer, for her passion for our work, strategic content review, and postproduction project management. We are also grateful to work once again with Mark Fortier and Pamela Peterson of Fortier Public Relations. Mark and Pamela are great at what they do and wonderful partners in marketing and media engagement. We also want to acknowledge the amazing team at HBR Press. In particular, we would like to thank Julie Devoll, Keith Pfeffer, Sally Ashworth, Kenzie Travers, and Monica Jainschigg.

Finally, this book is dedicated to our families, who supported and inspired us throughout the entire process: Mark, Ben, Nick, and Cam and Caroline, Florien, Emil, and Joris.

About the Authors

Rasmus Hougaard is the founder and Managing Director of Potential Project, the global leading provider of leadership and organizational effectiveness solutions based on training the mind. Rasmus has practiced and taught mindfulness for more than two decades and is recognized as a leading international authority on training the mind to be more focused, effective, and clear in an organizational context. His first book, *One Second Ahead: Enhance Your Performance with Mindfulness*, was published by Palgrave Macmillan in 2015. He is a regular contributor to *Harvard Business Review* as well as a sought-after speaker for his thought leadership. Before founding Potential Project, Rasmus worked at the Sony Corporation and as a researcher in organizational development.

Jacqueline Carter is an International Partner and North American Director for Potential Project. She has over twenty years of experience working with organizations around the globe to enhance effectiveness and improve performance. Jacqueline is a coauthor of *One Second Ahead: Enhance Your Performance at Work with Mindfulness*. She is a regular contributor to business publications including *Harvard Business Review*, and is a sought-after speaker for her thought leadership, knowledge, and engaging facilitation skills. She holds a master's degree in organizational behavior and undergraduate degrees in labor management relations and mathematics. Before joining Potential Project, Jacqueline held a number of senior leadership roles and worked with Deloitte Consulting's Change Leadership practice.

About Potential Project

Potential Project is a global leadership and corporate training organization. For over a decade, it has provided corporate mindfulness training to enhance performance, well-being, and innovation in *Fortune* 500 companies such as Accenture, Cisco, Google, Microsoft, Nike, KPMG, Microsoft, Ernst & Young, IKEA, Amex, the LEGO Group, and more across North America, Europe, Asia, and Australia. Potential Project has operations in twenty-eight countries and over two hundred highly skilled facilitators and consultants. For more information, go to www. themindoftheleaderbook.com.

Potential Project facilitates a global network of leaders interested in the practices of mindfulness, selflessness, and compassion. Members are invited to webinars, learning circles, practice retreats, and other activities. If you are a leader and interested in joining the network, please go to www.themindoftheleaderbook.com to learn how to join.

This book has come to life through our work and conversations with thousands of leaders around the world. If you have comments, questions, or experiences to share about the practices in this book and your leadership journey, please email us at rasmus.hougaard@potentialproject.com or jacqueline.carter@potentialproject.com. While we may not be able to respond to all messages, we would love to hear from you.